Doctor Leeds' Selection Of Popular Epic Recitations

For Minstrel And Stage Use

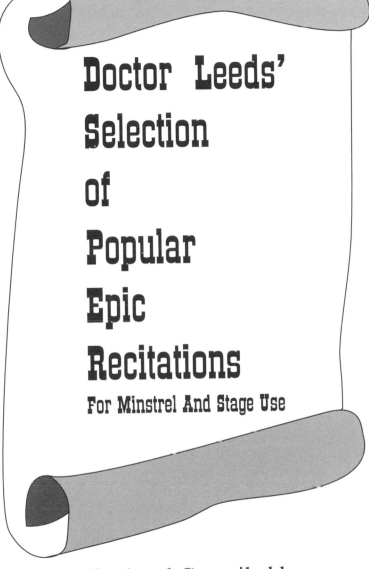

Doctor Leeds' Selection of Popular Epic Recitations

For Minstrel And Stage Use

Edited and Compiled by

Robert X. Leeds

Epic Publishing Company

Las Vegas, Nevada USA

ISBN 0-9674025-0-6
Library Of Congress Catalog Card Number 94-12045

Cover Design by Maryanna Zeidler
Scope Design Company
Lake Zurich, Illinois USA
and
Evan Hill Design, Inc.
Buffalo Grove, Illinois USA

Printed by Cushing-Malloy, Inc.
Ann Arbor, Michigan

This book may be ordered from all major bookstores.
In the event you are unable to obtain additional copies
from your bookstore, copies may be ordered
directly from the publisher:
Epic Publishing Company
8814 Big Bluff Avenue
Las Vegas NV 89148-1418

POEMS

Robert X. Leeds

(With all due respect to Joyce Kilmer)

I think that I shall never own
A tree as lovely as a poem.
A poem whose flowing mouth in zest
Evokes the shadows within our breast.
A poem that stirs the quiet soul,
Summons the future and long ago.
A poem that sponsors laughter and tears,
Honored deeds of bygone years.
Upon whose bosom, years may lie
Until some editor happens by.
Trees are planted by fools like me,
But only a poet can make every verse rhyme.

DEDICATION

More than anything else in the pursuit of writing or compiling a manuscript is the faith of your family, friends, and agent and the total absence of trivial interruptions. These two considerations, more than anything else, supports an authors aspirations and achievements.

By this criteria I make the following acknowledgements:

I am not dedicating this book to my darling wife, Peggy, who inquired daily why I didn't quit wasting my time compiling a book of poetry and instead write my autobiography. Another consideration was her interruption of my efforts at least once a month with a threat to move our garbage into my office if I didn't help her take it outside for collection.

I am not dedicating this book to my children, Leslie, Michael, Marc, Myong Ok, and Gail, who kept asking me, "Who reads poetry?"

I am not dedicating this book to my grandchildren, Damian, Marcus, and Heather, who chastised me constantly for not including their favorite poems from Dr. Seuss! (I hope I made the right decision.)

I am not dedicating this book to my Agent who said, "You're writing what? Nobody publishes poetry! There's no money in poetry!" Her parting words were, "Please don't even submit it to me!"

Most of all, I certainly am not dedicating this book to my Jack Russell Terrier, Bingo, who was trained to do everything except not to interrupt me. She was the most flagrant violator of my no-interruption edict. At least a thousand times a day she would enter my office, place her front paws up on my lap, stare into my eyes and say, "If you don't take me outside right now, I will not be responsible for any discolorations in your new white carpeting!"

There is one person whose help I do wish to acknowledge; Susan Schwartz, my editing assistant. Her proof-reading and editorial assistance made the completion of this first volume possible. (Come to think of it, Susan has yet to comment on this work so I think I might add that this acknowledgement is tentative and may be retracted at any time!)

TABLE OF CONTENTS

TABLE OF CONTENTS

TABLE OF CONTENTS

TABLE OF CONTENTS

TABLE OF CONTENTS

INTRODUCTION

Prepare!

You are going on a long journey, a journey into the past.

Long before radio, movie theaters, television, or the opulent opera house in America, it was the local tavern and later the burlesque house that provided the stage where entertainment came to the American public. Actors, singers, dancers, and jugglers journeyed from one end of this country to the other plying their talent in the quest for fame and fortune on the rough frontier stages of America. Few succeeded.

Among these troopers were a number of actors whose repertoire consisted of emotionally charged poems. If one was fortunate, he might even have seen the famous English actress, Lilly Langtree, parade back and forth across the stage in the latest full-length French evening gown while she recited Rudyard Kipling's Gunga Din.

A spectator would have been equally fortunate to have witnessed the recitals by such frontier poets and performers as Herbert H. Taylor, John Mason, Nina Farrington, George Thatcher, William Devere, De Wolf Hopper, Jennie O'Neill Potter, Mrs. James Brown Potter, Col. John Hay and a host of others. Ah! What emotions their passionate renditions stirred!

Regrettably, these performers have passed from the scene. Unfortunately, so has most of their poetry. However, every once in a while someone comes across a copy of their recitations either in an ancient Captain Billy Whizbang publication or one compiled by Herbert H. Taylor, a prolific producer of homespun American poetry in the 1800's.

Here is the genesis of this book.

Poetry was not my favorite subject in high school. I was not too good in any other subject, but eleventh grade English and poetry gave me the most trouble. I didn't like English and I didn't understand the poetry that I was assigned to read.(It was perfect match. My English teacher didn't like my English and didn't understand me.) A parting of the ways came when I was asked to recite, and explain to the class, the classic poem, Cuckoo Song:

"Sumer is icumen in,
Lhude sing cuccu;
Groweth sed and bloweth med
And springth the wude nu.
Sing cuccu!
Awe bleteth after lomb,
Lhouth after calve cu;
Bulluc stereth, bucke vereth;
Murie sing cuccu. Cuccu, cuccu, etc., ect.".

As I recall, in my explanation I think I inferred that the writer of this masterpiece was "cuccu". Whatever I said, everyone thought I was very funny. Everyone except Miss. Hildigard. As a consequence of my critique, I was banished from her English class for the balance of the semester. As a consequence of being banished, I dropped out of school and went to sea. I sure taught her a lesson!

It was during the lonely four-hour shifts in the ships' engine rooms that I discovered a "different" kind of poetry: poetry that made me laugh and cry, poetry that taught me humility and compassion, poetry whose meanings did not elude me and whose words did not intimidate me. I did not have to refer to reference books or study the text of a poem for days to understand what the author was trying to say. This is the poetry I came to love.

On my very first trip to the South Pacific, I was blessed to be teamed with two engineers who possessed an unbelievable talent for rendering dirty jokes and epic poetry in a continuous stream, all from memory, for the entire three month trip. It was during this trip that I was introduced to many of the "gutsy" poems included in this anthology. I became enamored with the works of Robert Service and Rudyard Kipling. These were not the poems my teachers had us read in the classroom. These were poems of the common man, about everyday people and everyday life. They were frontier sermons, and I got religion. I wonder how many more students would have learned and enjoyed poetry had these two engineers taught school.

It was usually on the quiet 4:00 a.m. to 8:00 a.m. shift that the show went on, and under the threat of air raids and submarine attacks, it was a welcome diversion. There were no curtains or stage lights, but we needed none. I was a great audience and with pencil in hand I struggled to copy each line so I might memorize it at a later time. Many of these poems are included in this volume.

When WW II ended, I set out to spend seven years traveling around the world. It was during these travels that I discovered, contrary to public perception, poetry and song were common talents of the common class. It was not always with benefit of proper documentation that I found myself in some of these countries, so on several occasions I became a guest of the State. In detention barracks, jails, and prisons I spent my time reading and listening to poetry of bygone years. It made no difference where I was: Europe, Africa, China, the Middle East; it was a rare occasion when I did not find myself exchanging verses with a fellow traveler.

My greatest regret is that I lacked the foresight and means with which to record all of those sessions. What a great volume that would have been! Instead, I have been able to bring you only a sampling of these works. Still, I have also been able to include poems by several contemporary poets who write in the style of the "frontier poets".

It was not my intent to include a disproportionate number of poems about dogs. However, of all the subjects covered, these occurred most frequently and met our criteria. It may tell you something of the regard and affection men and women have for their four legged companions.

These are not poems to be dissected and analyzed in a classroom. They were written to share some heartfelt emotion or to just entertain, not for critical acclaim. In them you will relive your childhood days. You will engage in the rough existence of the Wild West and the frozen Northlands. You will share the trauma of war, shipwreck, and prison. Lost loves and lost friends will rise up to renew old acquaintances. There are lessons to learn, morals to be reminded of. Humor, pathos, love, and loathing will move you as we travel through this time warp. These are not the poems you studied in school. The Miss Hildigards may tell us what poems we ought to read, but these are the poems you will want to read.

So, join me as we begin our journey back into the days of the traveling minstrel. Light the stage lanterns. Draw back the curtain. Let your emotions soar.

THE VOLUNTEER ORGANIST

S. W. Foss

The great big church wuz crowded
      Full uv broadcloth an' uv silk,
An' satins rich as cream that grows
      On ol' brindle's milk;
Shined boots, biled shirts, stiff dickeys
      An' stove-pipe hats were there,
An' doods 'ith troousrloons so tight
      They cou'dn't kneel down in prayer.

The elder in his poolpit high,
      Said, as he slowly riz:
"Our organist is kep' to hum,
      Laid up 'ith roomatiz.
An as we have no substitoot,
      As brother Moore ain't here,
Will some'un in the congregation
      Be so kin's to volunteer?

An' then a red-nosed, drunken tramp,
      Of low-toned, rowdy style,
Give an interductory hiccup,
      An' then staggered up the aisle.
Then thro' thet holy atmosphere
      There crep' a sense er sin,
An thro' thet air of sanctity
      The odor uv ol' gin.

Then Deacon Purington he yelled,
      His teeth all sot on edge:
"This man purfanes the house er God!
      W'y this is sacrilege!"
The tramp didn't hear a word he said,
But slouched 'ith stumblin feet,
An' sprawled an' staggered up the steps,
      An' gained the organ seat.

He then went pawrin' thro' the keys,
      An' soon there rose a strain,
Thet seemed to jest bulge out the heart,
      An' lectrify the brain

An' then he slapped down on the thing
        'Ith hands an' head an' knees,
He slam dashed his hull body down
        Kerflop upon the keys.

The organ roared, the music flood
        Went sweepin' high an' dry.
It swelled into the rafters
        And bulged out into the sky.
The ol' church shook an' staggered
        An' seemed to reel an' sway
An' the elder shouted,
        "Glory!" an' I yelled out "Hooray!"

An' then he tried a tender strain
        That melted in our ears,
That brought up blessed memories
        And drenched 'em down 'ith tears.
An' we dreamed uv ol' time kitchens,
        'Ith Tabby on the mat,
Uv home, an' luv, an' baby-days,
        An' mother, an' all that!

An' then he struck a streak uv hope—
        A song from souls forgiven—
Thet burst from prison bars, uv sin,
        An' stormed the gates uv Heaven.
The morning stars they sung together —
        No soul was left alone,
We felt the universe was safe
        An' God wuz on His throne!

An' then a wail uv deep despair
        An' darkness come again,
An' a long, black crape hung on the doors
        Uv all the homes uv men;
No luv, no light, no joy, no hope,
        No songs of glad delight.
An' then—the tramp, he staggered down
        And reeled into the night!

But we knew he'd tol' his story,
     Tho' he never spoke a word,
An' it wuz the saddest story that
     Our ears had ever heard.
He hed tol' his own life history,
     An' no eye was dry thet day,
W'en the elder rose an' simply said:
     "My brethren, let us pray."

BREATHES THERE THE MAN
WITH SOUL SO DEAD

Sir Walter Scott

Breathes there the man with soul so dead,
    Who never to himself hath said,
    This is my own, my native land!
Whose heart hath ne'er within him burn'd,
As home his footsteps he hath turn'd
    From wandering on a foreign strand!
If such there breathe, go, mark him well;
For him no Minstrel raptures swell;
High though his titles, proud his name,
Boundless his wealth as wish can claim;
Despite those titles, power, and pelf,
The wretch, concentred all in self,
Living, shall forfeit fair renown,
And, doubly dying, shall go down
To the vile dust, from whence he sprung,
Unwept, unhonour'd, and unsung.

THE FACE ON THE BAR-ROOM FLOOR

H. Antoine D'Arcy

'Twas a balmy summer evening
    And a goodly crowd was there,
Which well nigh filled Joe's barroom,
    On the corner of the square;
And as songs and witty stories
    Echoed through the open door,
A vagabond crept slowly in
    And poised upon the floor.

"Where did it come from?" someone said.
    "The wind must have blown it in."
'What does it want?" another cried,
    "Some whiskey, rum, or gin?"
"Here, Toby, seek him,
    If your stomach's equal to the work—
I wouldn't touch him with a fork,
    He's as filthy as a Turk."

This badinage the poor wretch took
    With stoical good grace;
In fact, he smiled as tho' he thought
    He'd struck the proper place.
"Come boys, I know there's kindly hearts
    Among so good a crowd—
To be in such good company
    Would make a deacon proud.

Give me a drink—that's what I want—
    I'm out of funds you know;
When I had cash to treat the gang,
    This hand was never slow.
What? You laugh as if you thought
    This pocket never held a sou;
I once was fixed as well, my boys,
    As any one of you.

4

There, thanks, that braced me nicely;
    God bless you one and all.
Next time I pass this good saloon,
    I'll make another call.
Give you a song? No, I can't do that,
    My singing days are past;
My voice is cracked, my throat's worn out,
    And my lungs are going fast.

Say! Give me another whiskey,
    And I"ll tell you what I'll do—
I'll tell you a funny story,
    And a fact I promise, too.
That I was ever a decent man,
    Not one of you would think;
But I was some four or five years back.
    Say, give us another drink.

Fill her up, Joe, I want to put
    Some life into my frame—
Such little drinks, to a bum like me,
    Are miserably short, and tame.
Five fingers—there, that's the scheme—
    And corking whiskey, too,
Well, here's luck, boys, and landlord,
    My best regards to you.

You've treated me pretty kindly,
    And I'd like to tell you how
I came to be the dirty sot
    You see before you now.
As I told you, once I was a man
    With muscle, frame, and health,
And, but for a blunder,
Ought to have made considerable wealth.

I was a painter—
Not one who daubed on bricks and wood,
But an artist, and, for my age,
    Was rated pretty good;

I worked hard at my canvas,
And was bidding fair to rise,
For gradually I saw the star
Of fame before my eyes.

I made a picture perhaps you've seen,
'Tis called the 'Chase of Fame'
It brought me fifteen hundred pounds,
And added to my name.
And then I met a woman –
Now comes the funny part—
With eyes that petrified my brain
And sunk into my heart.

Why don't you laugh?
'Tis funny that the vagabond you see
Could ever love a woman
And expect her love for me;
But 'twas so, and for a month or two
Her smiles were freely given,
And when her loving lips touched mine,
It carried me to heaven.

Boys, did you ever see a woman
For whom your soul you'd give,
With a form like Milo Venus,
Too beautiful to live;
With eyes that would beat the Koh-I-noor,
And a wealth of chestnut hair?
If so 'twas she, for there never could be
Another half so fair.

I was working on a portrait,
One afternoon in May,
Of a fair haired boy, a friend of mine,
Who lived across the way;
And Madeline admired it,
And much to my surprise,
Said she'd like to know the man
That had such dreamy eyes.

It didn't take long to know him,
And before the month had flown,
My friend had stole my darling
And I was left alone;
And ere a year of misery
Had passed above my head,
The jewel that I had treasured so
Was tarnished and was dead.

That's why I took to drink, boys.
Why I never saw you smile,
I thought that you would be amused
And laughing all the while.
Why! What's the matter, friend?
There's a teardrop in your eye,
Come, laugh like me, 'tis only babes
And women that should cry.

Say, boys, if you give me
Just another whiskey, I'll be glad
And I'll draw, right here, a picture
Of the face that drove me mad.
Here, friend, give me the chalk
With which you mark the baseball score—
You shall see the lovely Madeline
Upon the bar-room floor."

Another drink, and chalk in hand,
The vagabond began
To sketch the face that well might buy
The soul of any man.
Then, as he placed another lock
Upon the shapely head,
With fearful shriek he leaped and fell
Across the picture, dead.

THE VAGABOND AND HIS DOG

Robert X. Leed

It was another Christmas day
And **God** looked out to see
What scriptured promise came to pass,
What promise would not be.
And turning aside, **HE** turned his eyes
To those who'd dwell inside,
To those who'd warm by Heaven's hearth
And those who'd be denied.

And **HE** saw a man at St. Peter's gate,
A mongrel dog at his feet,
And a line that reached to the dark of night
As far as the eye could see.
And St. Peter looked at the disheveled two
And challenged the wretch to say,
What deeds he'd done, what praise he'd won
To walk in Heaven's way.

And the vagrant stood in his shabby robe
And not one word he spoke,
As though he heard not a single word
This man in the tattered cloak.
"What deeds have you done to think you've won
The grace of Heaven's line?
What honors earned? What evils spurned?
Pray help me be inclined."

But the wretched soul and his shepherd hound
Stayed on without a sound
As though no deed could come to mind,
As though no reason found.
"Can you not find one deed so fine,
To merit entrance here?
Can none attest some honored quest,
A challenge still unclear?"

And still he stood and but held the leash
That stayed the mongrel hound.
Until he knelt to feel the ground
And kiss the furry crown.

As love was cast in skin and bone,
He held the dog around,
And Heaven watched and Heaven judged
This vagabond and his hound.

"What seeds were sowed that a flower'd grow
When you'd depart the scene?
A single tree? One slave made free?
One clean and shining sea?
Was not one life made free of strife
Along the path you strolled?
Was not one child encouraged to smile?
No good that can be told?"

And all looked on at the vagabond
Who held the unkempt dog.
But not one voice to sway the choice,
Came from the mist and fog.
And when at last, his patience past,
St. Peter bid unkind
And motioned on to the dark beyond,
"No reason you can find?"

"Not one but simple virtue be
That all of us may see?
Not one redeeming act of faith
Did bring you here to me?
In all your time can you not find
One voice for yours to plea?
In all your time can you not find
One voice to vouch for thee?"

And now at last his time though past,
The vagabond turned to speak;
And his eyes were filled with tears that spilled
And coursed his craggy cheeks.
And from his heart the speech did start
To argue not his sake,
But to plead the cause of the mongrel dog,
That lay in Heaven's wake.

"Perhaps it ain't for me to see
The paradise within.
I was a simple soul on earth
This hound my only kin.

But if the children's smiles count,
His cup's filled to the brim.
Oh, I can vouch for this hound, your grace.
I can vouch for him.

You should'a seen the children laugh and run
When he was all their game.
You should'a seen the love he gave
And never once complain.
And when the tide of time arose
And naught was there to eat,
He shared the taste of an empty plate
And stayed at these failing feet.

It ain't for me," he whispered soft,
"It ain't for me I ask.
But don't deprive this poor old hound
For what his master lacks.
If caring and sharing and loyalty
Are virtues of your size,
Consider one who lacks of none,
Let Heaven be his prize.

It matters not what comes of me,
Or what may come about.
But it just ain't fair. It wouldn't be fair
To keep my poor hound out.
No friend has ever been so true.
No man has walked a line,
Who never strayed, but not this dog,
This hound that I call mine."

His fingers stroked the shaggy coat
And the dog licked back the hand;
And as much was said in the silence there,
Than since God's quest began.
And then abrupt, the hound looked up
And labored with its head
To lick this face of human grace,
This man of tattered thread.

And suddenly a calm would be
That tethered every sound.
And a warm breeze blew that embraced the two,
This vagabond and his hound.

And St. Peter turned to the mist beyond
And paused with uplifted head.
To heed the voice of Almighty God
And to do as HE has said.

"I've set the task and I have asked
For virtues held and shared.
To dwell in a world of every kind
And for every kind have cared.
And now I've seen dimensions dreamed
That seldom I've seen before,
A simple man and his faithful hound,
Denied at my own door?"

With pen in hand, St. Peter began
To enter on his list,
The names of those whom God had chose
To dwell in Heaven's bliss.
And one belonged to a vagabond
And the other he called his kin;
The vagabond who vouched for an old hound dog
And the hound dog who vouched for him.

A CHIP ON HIS SHOULDER

Author Unknown

He always has something to grumble about,
Has the man with a chip on his shoulder.
The world to the dogs is going, no doubt,
To the man with a chip on his shoulder.
The clouds are too dark. The Sun is too bright.
No matter what happens it is never right.
When peace is prevailing he is spoiling to fight,
The man with a chip on his shoulder.

A DOG WAS BORN

Author Unknown

Ages ago a heartfelt prayer
Arose from a man in deep despair.
"Oh God," he pleaded, "hear my cry,
A weak and selfish sinner am I.

Deserted alike by friend and foe,
No way to turn, no place to go.
Though I deserve such misery,
Oh God, restore some hope to me."

The Father heard, "His need is great,
For such poor mortals I'll create
A loyal friend, who'll stay close by,
To love, to share, to live and die.

His willing slave, who'll ask no more,
Than just to worship and adore,
A friend who'll never criticize,
Will never question or advise.

"Who cannot speak or lift a hand
To help – but will just understand."
And so it came to pass, at morn,
An answered prayer
A dog was born!

ALWAYS FINISH

Author Unknown

If a task is once begun
Never leave it till it's done.
Be the labor great or small,
Do it well or not at all.

WANTED – A MINISTER'S WIFE

Author Unknown

At length we have settled a pastor—
I am sure I cannot tell why
The people should grow so restless
Or candidates grow so shy.
But after two years' searching
For the "smartest" man in the land,
In a fit of desperation
We took the nearest at hand.

And really he answers nicely
To "fill the gap," you know,
To "run the machine" and "bring up the rear,"
And make things generally go.
He has a few little failings,
His sermons are commonplace quite,
But his manner is very charming,
And his teeth are pearly white.

And, so, of all the "dear people,"
Not one in a hundred complains,
For beauty and grace of manner
Are so much better than brains;
But the parish have all concluded
He needs a partner for life,
To shine, a gem, in the parlor:
"Wanted – a minister's wife!"

Wanted – a perfect lady,
Delicate, gentle, refined,
With every beauty of person,
And every endowment of mind,
Fitted by early culture
To move in fashionable life—
Please notice our advertisement:
"Wanted — a minister's wife!"

Wanted – a thoroughbred worker,
Who well to her household looks,
(Shall we see our money wasted
By extravagant Irish cooks?"

13

Who cuts the daily expenses
With economy sharp as a knife
And washes and scrubs in the kitchen—
"Wanted – a minister's wife."

A "very domestic person,"
To callers she must not be "out";
It has such a bad appearance
For her to be gadding about—
Only to visit the parish
Every year of her life,
And attend the funerals and weddings—
"Wanted – a minister's wife."

To conduct the "ladies meetings,"
The "sewing circle" attend,
And when we have work for the soldiers
Her ready assistance to lend:
To clothe the destitute children,
Where sorrow and want are rife;
To hunt up Sunday-school scholars-
"Wanted – a minister's wife!"

Careful to entertain strangers,
Traveling agents and "such,"
Of this kind of "angels' " visits
The deacons have had so much
As to prove a perfect nuisance,
And hope these "plagues of their life"
Can soon be sent to the parson's –
"Wanted – a minister's wife!"

A perfect pattern of prudence
To all others, spending less,
But never disgracing the parish
By looking shabby in dress.

Playing the organ on Sunday
Would aid our laudable strife
To save the society's money—
"Wanted – a minister's wife."

And when we have found the person;
We hope, by working the two,
To lift our debt and build a new church—
Then we shall know what to do;

For they will be worn and weary,
Needing a change of life,
And so we'll advertise,
"Wanted. A minister and his wife!"

A FAREWELL

Author Unknown

The time has come and we must part;
The tear drop dims mine eye;
How oft I've clasped thee to my heart
With joy in days gone by!

When first I saw thee I was sure
Thou camest to me to stay.
But nothing earthly doth endure—
All things must pass away.

How oft in days forever past,
My form thou hast embraced;
Another takes thy place at last
And clasps me round the waist.

But such is life—we meet to part,
In midst of change we dwell;
I clasp another to my breast—
Old corset, fare thee well!

A GIFT AND A PRESENT

Linda Robertson

A present is something practical,
A gift can be extravagant.
A present could be a can opener;
A gift could be an elephant.

A present serves a purpose;
A gift will serve a cause.
A present you give for reasons;
A gift is "just because".

A present is given with a smile,
And a smile is then returned.
A gift is given with lots of love,
And the quality of love is earned.

So when you're choosing what to give,
This is how to start:
A present is a purchase –
A gift is of the heart.

BYGONES

AuthorUnknown
(From A Prison Wall)

Let's let bygones be bygones
And start all over again.
Let us forget we parted
And be the same as we started.
Remember, the sunshine
Must always follow the rain.
So, let's let bygones be bygones
And start all over again.

A LITTLE ANGEL

Linda Robertson

A little angel wandered
Past St. Peter at the gate.
She scurried past the entry guard
Because she had a date.

A date to open her beautiful eyes,
A date without any harm,
A date to find a mom and dad
Whose love would keep her warm.

She looked through clouds beneath her feet,
To all the homes below.
She selected one from all the rest,
A home where she wanted to go.

She planned her wanderings very well
To arrive at her journey's end.
She picked a home where love could grow
A place to find a friend.

You have been blessed with a beautiful child,
Someone who needs your love.
So share your laughter, time, and care
With your angel from Heaven above.

A SMILE

Author Unknown

Let others cheer the winning man,
There's one I hold worth while;
'Tis he who does the best he can
Then loses with a smile.
Beaten he is, but not to stay
Down with the rank and file.
That man will win some other day,
Who loses with a smile.

A MATTER OF BUSINESS

Author Unknown

"Working" is a simple term—
By common sense defined.
As "hustle," "get there," "shake a leg"—
In language unrefined.
We're working something all the time—
No matter what we do,
But watch the other fellow, for—
He may be working you.

For instance, there are business schemes
In which you would invest,
Your friend decides to let you in—
Because he loves you best.
He doesn't want to make a cent,
Perhaps it may be true,
But keep your eye upon your friend—
He may be working you.

Now, you, of course, would not abuse
The friendship of a man,
But when you see a dollar
You will seize it if you can.
You would not work a friend—oh, no—
For friends are very few,
But look out for your warmest friend—
He may be working you.

You may have a friend in business
Who would sell you goods at cost,
He does so just to please you
And no matter what he's lost,
He bows and scrapes and thanks you
Just as other people do,
But never for a moment
Would he think of working you.

You work a snap yourself sometimes,
And in a quiet way,
Invite your friends to join the dance
And then the fiddler pay;
They don't know what you're driving at
Because the scheme is new,
But while you're working all your friends—
Perhaps they're working you.

Today your bank accounts run short,
You simply borrow ten,
And pay it back tomorrow
With profoundest thanks—and then,
Your friend returns the compliment
And multiplied by two,
You thought that you were working him—
While he was working you.

The moral of the thing is this—
We've all an axe to grind;
Wait until your turn comes round,
You may be left behind.
Just take your chance at the wheel
As all of us must do,
And work the other fellow, while
He thinks he's working you!

I'LL RETURN

Author Unknown
(From a prison wall)

When these prison gates are open,
When I'm a free man once again,
And the lovelight in your eyes more brightly shines,
Just remember when you're lonely,
Just remember darling only
When these prison gates are open, I'll return.

A METAPHYSICAL DILEMMA

Author Unknown

A learned professor, once making a speech
To a bevy of youngsters, attempted to teach
  This nice point of mystical lore:
How a thing can be mended and mended again
Until of its primitive parts none remain,
  And still be the same thing as before.

Then one of his hopeful disciples arose
And said: "By your leave, sir, I rise to propose
  A question for once in my life.
I bought me a jackknife; it had but one blade;
The blade was soon lost, but another was made;
  Pray tell, was it still the same knife?"

The professor declared his assent, and the youth,
With the air of an amateur seeking the truth,
  And now holding a knife up to view,
Resumed: "Next the handle was lost, but ere long
I had it replaced by another as strong;
  Pray is this the old knife, or a new?"

"It is still the same weapon; the truth is quite clear,"
Quoth the doctor; but young Academicus here
  Another like weapon disclosed.
"It is made of the old blade and handle," quoth he;
"Pray tell us, Professor, what knife this may be?"
  It is plain the professor was posed!

A RUSTIC CONVERT

Author Unknown

"You karn't ketch nothin' with them thar things,
With yarn fer bodies an' feathers for wings.
You must think trout is terrible fools
Ter be ketched with such outlandish tools.
An' look at that pole – why that won't do!
A good, big trout would bust it in two
An' never think nothin' ov what he did
As quick as lightnin' away he slid.
Well, I'll be durn, you can shoot me dead
Ef here ain't a windlass filled with thread;
An' the littlest sort ov thread at that—
Why, man, that wouldn't hold a gnat!
You'll find a good place over here,
Under the rapids, deep an' clear.
You'd better take worms an' er hick'ry pole,
Or you won't ketch nothin', 'pon my soul!"

Sixteen beauties, speckled bright,
The baskets bore ere the fall of night;
He counted them o'er on the bank of fern,
And all that he said was, "Wa'al – I'll be durn!"

ON BUYING A DOG

Edgar Klauber

"I wish to buy a dog," she said,
"A dog you're sure is quite well bred,
In fact, I'd like some guarantee,
He's favored with a pedigree."
"My charming friend," the pet man said,
"I have a dog that's so well bred,
If he could talk, I'll guarantee,
He'd never speak to you or me."

A STORY OF ST. PETER

Author Unknown

St. Peter stood guard at the golden gate,
With a solemn mien and an air sedate,
When up to the top of the golden stair
A man and a woman ascended there;
Applied for admission, there came and stood
Before St. Peter, so great and good—
In hopes the City of Peace to win—
Asked St. Peter to let them in.

The woman was little and lank and lean,
With a scraggly beardlet on her chin;
The man was short and thick and stout,
And his stomach was built so it rounded out.
His face was pleasant and all the while
He wore an honest, genial smile.
The choir in the distance the echoes awoke
And the man kept still while the woman spoke.

"Oh, the grandest, the Golden Gate," said she,
"We two come hither beseeching Thee
To let us enter the heavenly land
And play our harps with the angel band.
Of me, St. Peter, there is not a doubt
There is nothing in Heaven to bar me out;
I've been to the meetings three times a week
And almost always I rise and speak.

I've told the sinners about the day
When they would repent of their evil ways;
I've told my neighbors—I've told them all
About Adam and Eve in the Primal fall;
I've marked their faith in duty clear,
Laid out their plans for their whole career;
So, good St. Peter, you'll plainly see
That the gate of heaven is open to me.

But my old man, I regret to say,
Hasn't walked exactly in the narrow way.
He smokes and he swears and grave faults he's got,
And I don't know whether he'll pass or not.
He never would pray with an honest vim,
Or go to revivals, or join in a hymn,
So I had to leave him in sorrow there
While I with the chosen united in prayer.

He ate what the pantry chose to afford,
While I, in my purity, sang to the Lord;
And then if cucumbers were all he got
There's a chance if he merited them or not.
But, Oh! St. Peter, I love him so,
To the pleasures of Heaven please let him go.
I've been enough of the saint I've been,
Now won't that atone—can't you let him in?

By my grim gospel! I know this is so—
That the unrepentant must fry below,
But isn't there some way you can see
To let him in who is dear to me?
'Tis a narrow gospel by which I pray,
But the chosen expect to find some way
Of coaxing, or bribing, or fooling you,
So their relations can amble through.

And say, St. Peter my sight is dimmed;
I don't like the way your whiskers are trimmed.
They are cut too narrow and outward tossed—
They would look far better cut straight across.
Well, we must be going, our crowns to win,
So open, St. Peter, and we'll pass in."
St. Peter stood still and stroked his staff,
And in spite of his office he had to laugh.

Then said, with the fire agleam in his eye,
"Who's tending this gate, you or I?"
And thus arose in his stature tall
And pressed the button upon the wall,
And said, to the imp that answered the bell,
"Escort this woman down into Hell."
The man stood still as a piece of stone,
And stood sadly, gloomily there alone.

23

A lifelong, settled idea he had
That his wife was good and he was bad.
If she had to go to the regions dim
There wasn't the ghost of a show for him.
Slowly he turned, by habit bent,
To follow that woman wherever she went.
St. Peter, standing on duty there,
Observed that the top of his head was bare.

And calling the gentleman back he said,
"Say, friend, how long have you been wed?"
"Thirty years," with a weary sigh,
And then he thoughtfully added, "Why?"
St. Peter first looked up, then down,
Then raised his hand and scratched his crown;
Then, seeming a different thought to take,
Slowly half to himself he spake.

"Thirty years with that woman there;
No wonder the man hasn't any hair.
Swearing is wicked and smoking is not good.
He smoked and he swore, I should say he would.
Thirty years with a tongue so sharp.
Say, Angel Gabriel, bring him a harp—
A jeweled harp, with golden strings,
Good sir, pass in when the angel sings."

Gabriel gave him a seat alone—
One with a cushion up near the throne.
"See that on the finest aroma he feeds;
He has had about all the hell he needs.
It isn't just the right thing to do
To roast him on earth and the future, too."
They gave him a robe and glittering wings
And a jeweled harp with golden strings.

And he said as he entered the realm of day,
"Well, this beats cucumbers, anyway."
And the scripture was read from that time past,
"That the last shall be first and the first shall be last."

A YALLER DOG'S LOVE FOR A NEGRO

Author Unknown

(Recited by George Thatcher)

Dar's a grave on de oder side of de creek
    Dat knows no Decoration Day,
For him as lef' dar all alone to sleep
    Is only a negro, dey say.

He died an ole vagunt, entirely unknown,
    An' lef' not a soul to be sad,
Dey gave him his freedom, but took away his home,
    And an ole yaller dog was all dat he had.

Dey dug a rude hole and dey laid him away,
    Dis poor citizen slave;
Not a prayer for his res' did anyone say,
    And de ole yaller dog laid down on his grave.

And still you may see him dar, day after day,
    At mornings, noons and eves,
For dar's no inducements can call him away,
    From his place 'side the grave where he grieves.

Dar's a mighty fine monument standin' right nigh,
    But finer, dis poor mound seems so,
For dar's a monument money can't buy –
    A yaller dog's love for dat negro.

A TALE OF CONSCIOUS VIRTUE

Author Unknown

A man there was who thought himself
    (And many such there be)
Especially endowed with talent
    And profundity;
Whether poet, seer or statesman
    Was a question he had brooded,
But just what sort of genius suited best
    He had not yet concluded;
Yet confident he was that
    He should arsenate the nation,
And only waited 'round
    For smiling Fate and Inspiration.

Now all his friends (he had a few)
    Were driven to admit
He had some very clever parts,
    And more or less of wit;
Of learning and perception
    He was surely well possessed,
But lacked practicability
    Most sadly, all confessed.
Meanwhile, to earn a living,
    In an absent-minded way,
At a patent-lawyer's office
    He had scribbled every day.

It happened that he noticed,
    While at his daily grind,
A circumstance of quite
    A most extraordinary kind;
A little push and cleverness
    In proper combination,
Would get there with the rest of them—
    He called it inspiration.
With this in mind he made a name
    And fortune in a day,
Though just precisely in what line
    I'm sure I couldn't say.

Now all his friends (he's got some more)
        Unanimously bray,
"He's found practicability,"
        And let him have his way.
He calls it inspiration still,
        And I'm not sure he's wrong,
Particularly since it serves
        His purpose right along.
But what was most astonishing
        About this fellow's gall,
Was that he bragged he'd do great things
        And went and did them all.

ALL OF ONE SIZE

Author Unknown

There's many a coat that is tattered and torn
        That beneath lies a true, honest heart.
But because he's not dressed like his neighbors in style,
        Why, "Society" keeps them apart.
For on one, fortune smiles, while the other one fails,
        Yes, no matter what venture he tries;
But time calls them both to the grave in the end
        And six feet of earth makes us all of one size.

Then when you once see a poor fellow that tries
        To baffle the world and its frown,
Let us help him along and perchance he'll succeed—
        Don't crush him because he is down.
For a cup of cold water, in charity given,
        Is remembered with joy in the skies;
We are all but human. We have all got to die
        And six feet of earth makes us all of one size.

A THANKFUL PARSON

Author Unknown

A pious parson, good and true,
    Was crossing o'er the seas,
When suddenly there fiercely blew
    A wild and sweeping breeze.
He feared the storm the ship would wreck,
    His heart was sore afraid,
He sought the captain on the deck
    And found him undismayed.

The captain saw his awful fear
    And led him up to where
The servant of the Lord could hear
    The sailors loudly swear.
"You clearly see," the captain said,
    "If danger hovered nigh,
They'd all be on their knees instead
    And asking grace to die."

The parson felt his words were true,
    And when the skies grew fair,
He marveled how the sailors knew
    Just when to pray or swear.
But when the seas which wildly flowed
    Had ceased to plunge and spout,
Unto himself he said, "It showed
    They know what they're about."

But later on another storm
    Came fiercer than before,
The parson heard with wild alarm
    The ocean's angry roar.
He sought the deck in awful dread
    To near the sailors get,
He listened—then he bowed his head—
    "Thank God, they're swearing yet."

AN ELEGY ON THE DEATH OF A MAD DOG

Oliver Goldsmith

Good people all, of every sort,
  Give ear unto my song;
And if you find it wond'rous short
  It cannot hold you long.

In Islington there was a man,
  Of whom the world might say,
That still a godly race he ran,
  Whene'er he went to pray.

A kind and gentle heart he had,
  To comfort friends and foes;
The naked every day he clad,
  When he put on his clothes.

And in that town a dog was found,
  As many dogs there be,
Both mongrel, puppy, whelp, and hound,
  And curs of low degree.

This dog and man at first were friends;
  But when a pique began,
The dog, to gain some private ends,
  Went mad and bit the man.

Around from all the neighboring streets
  The wond'ring neighbors ran,
And swore the dog had lost its wits,
  To bite so good a man.

The wound it seem'd both sore and sad
  To every Christian eye;
And while they swore the dog was mad,
  They swore the man would die.

But soon a wonder came to light,
  That showed the rogues they lied:
The man recover'd of the bite,
  The dog it was that died.

ABDULLAH BULBUL AMIR

OR

IVAN PETROFSKY SKOVAR

Author Unknown

The sons of the Prophet are valiant and bold,
And quite unaccustomed to fear;
And the bravest of all was a man, so I'm told
Called Abdullah Bulbul Amir.

When they wanted a man to encourage the van,
Or harass the foe from the rear,
Storm fort or redoubt, they were sure to call out
For Abdullah Bulbul Amir.

There are heroes in plenty, and well known to fame,
In the legions that fight for the Czar;
But none of such fame as the man by the name
Of Ivan Petrofsky Skovar.

He could imitate Irving, tell fortunes by cards,
And play on the Spanish guitar;
In fact, quite the cream of the Muscovite guards,
Was Ivan Petrofsky Skovar.

One day this bold Muscovite shouldered his gun,
Put on his most cynical sneer,
And was walking downtown when he happened to run
Into Abdullah Bulbul Amir.

"Young man," said Bulbul, "is existence so dull
That you're anxious to end your career?
Then, infidel, know you have trod on the toe
Of Abdullah Bulbul Amir.

So take your last look at the sea, sky and brook,
Make your latest report to the war;
For I mean to imply that you are going to die
O Ivan Petrofsky Skovar."

So this fierce man took his trusty chibouk,
And murmuring, "Allah Aklar!:"
With murder intent he most savagely went
For Ivan Petrofsky Skovar.

The Sultan rose up, the disturbance to quell,
Likewise, give the victor a cheer
He arrived just in time to bid hasty farewell
To Abdullah Bulbul Amir

A loud sounding splash from the Danube was heard
Resounding o'er meadow afar;
It came from the sack fitting close to the back
Of Ivan Petrofsky Skovar.

There lieth a stone where the Danube doth roll,
And on it in characters queer
Are "Stranger when passing by, pray for the soul
Of Abdullah Bulbul Amir."

A Muscovite maiden her vigil doth keep
By the light of the pale northern star,
And the name she repeats every night in her sleep
Is Ivan Petrofsky Skovar.

HORSE SENSE

Author Unknown

A horse can't pull while kicking.
This fact I merely mention.
And he can't kick while pulling,
Which is my chief contention.

Let's imitate the good old horse
And lead a life that's fitting.
Just pull an honest load and then
There'll be no time for kicking.

AN OLD SWEETHEART OF MINE

James Whitcomb Riley
(Recited by John Mason)

As one who cons at evening o'er an album all alone,
And muses on the faces of the friends that he has known,
So I turn the leaves of fancy till in shadowy design
I find the smiling features of an old sweetheart of mine.

The lamplight seems to glimmer with a flicker of surprise
As I turn it low to rest me of the dazzle in my eyes,
And light my pipe in silence, save a sigh that seems to yoke
Its fate with my tobacco and to vanish in the smoke.

'Tis a fragrant retrospection, for the loving thoughts that start
Into being are like perfumes from the blossoms of the heart;
And to dream the old dreams over is a luxury divine,
When my truant fancy wanders with that old sweetheart of mine.

Though I hear, beneath my study, like a fluttering of wings,
The voices of my children and the mother as she sings,
I feel no twinge of conscience to deny me any theme
When care has cast her anchor in the harbor of a dream.

In fact, to speak in earnest, I believe it adds a charm
To spice the good a trifle with a little dust of harm;
For I find an extra flavor in memory's mellow wine
That makes me drink the deeper to that old sweetheart of mine.

A face of lily beauty and a form of airy grace
Floats out of my tobacco as the genie from the vase;
And I thrill beneath the glances of a pair of azure eyes
As glowing as the summer and as tender as the skies.

I can see the pink sunbonnet and the little checkered dress
She wore when I first kissed her, and she answered the caress
With the written declaration that "As surely as the vine
Grew around the stump," she loved me—
That old sweetheart of mine.

And again I feel the pressure of her slender little hand.
As we used to talk together of the future we had planned;
When I should be a poet, and with nothing else to do
But to write the tender verses that she set the music to.

When we should live together in a cozy little cot
Hid in a nest of roses, with a tiny garden spot.
Where the vines were ever fruitful and the weather ever fine,
And the birds were ever singing for that old sweetheart of mine.

When I should be her lover forever and a day,
And she my faithful sweetheart till the golden hair was gray;
And we should be so happy that when either's lips were dumb
They would not smile in heaven till the other's kiss had come.

But, ah, my dream is broken by a step upon the stair
And the door is softly opened, and my wife is standing there;
Yet with eagerness and rapture all my visions I resign
To meet the living presence of that old sweetheart of mine.

AN OUTCAST EVEN IN HELL

Harry S. Grannatt

During a lull in the Stygian flames,
    A group of shades were exchanging names
And telling of places they had been
    With bits of gossip and tales of sin.

A lonely shade who was standing by
    Approached to speak; but without reply
Each wrapped himself in his ghostly shawl –
    Robbers, knaves and blackguards all—
With a whispered word and averted stare
    Vanished and left him standing there.

"Who was he?" I asked as they turned and fled.
"He poisoned his neighbor's dog," they said.

33

ANNABEL LEE

Edgar Allen Poe

It was many and many a year ago,
In a kingdom by the sea,
That a maiden there lived whom you may know
By the name of Annabel Lee;
And this maiden she lived with no other thought
Than to love and be loved by me.

She was a child and I was a child,
In this kingdom by the sea,
But we loved with a love that was more than love—
I and my Annabel Lee—
With a love that the winged seraphs of Heaven
Coveted her and me.

And this was the reason that, long ago,
In this kingdom by the sea,
A wind blew out of a cloud chilling
My beautiful Annabel Lee;
So that her high-born kinsmen came
And bore her away from me,
To shut her up in a sepulchuer
In this kingdom by the sea.

The angels, not half so happy in Heaven,
Went envying her and me:—
Yes! That was the reason (as all men know,
In that kingdom by the sea)
That the wind came out of the cloud chilling
And killing my Annabel Lee.

But our love it was stronger by far than the love
Of those who were older than we—
Of many far wiser than we—
And neither the angels in Heaven above,
Nor the demons down under the sea,
Can ever dissever my soul from the soul
Of the beautiful Annabel Lee:

For the moon never beams without bringing me dreams
Of the beautiful Annabel Lee,
And the stars never rise but I feel the bright eyes
Of the beautiful Annabel Lee:
And so all the night-tide, I lie down by the side
Of my darling, my darling, my life and my bride
In her sepulchre there by the sea,
In her tomb by the side of the sea.

AS MY UNCLE USED TO SAY

James Whitcomb Riley

I've thought a power on men and things,
As my uncle ust to say,
And ef folks don't work as they pray, I jings!
W'y they ain't no use to pray!
Ef you want somepin', and jes dead-set
A-pleadin' for it with both eyes wet,
And tears won't bring it, w'y, you try sweat,
As my uncle ust to say.

They's some don't know their A. B. C.'s,
As my uncle ust to say,
And yit don't waste no candle grease,
Ner whistle their lives away;
But ef they can't write no book, ner rhyme
No ringin' song fer to last all time,
They can blaze the way fer the march sublime,
As my uncle ust to say.

Whoever's Foreman of all things here,
As my uncle ust to say,
He knows each job 'at we're best fit fer,
And our round-up, night and day;
And a-sizin' His work, east and west,
And north and south, and worst and best,
I ain't got nothin' to suggest,

ARE YA REALLY A GENUINE MEMBER?

Author Unknown
(Adapted by Robert X. Leeds)

Are ya one o' them inactive members,
An' ya figure ya won't be missed?
Do ya walk around just contented
That your name is on the list?

Do ya make each weekly meeting
And mingle with the crowd?
Or do ya figger to stay a' home
An' crab both long and loud?

Do ya make that extra effort
When there's rain or snow so slick?
Or do ya leave that for the same ol' few
Then talk about the clique?

There's quite a program scheduled
An' a world a good deeds ta do,
'Cause someone's gotta do somethin'
An' that someone is me an' you.

Like the teeth on a gear that goes aroun' an' 'roun'
An' makes the engine run,
Success depends on your being there,
It depends on everyone!

So, Member, think this over,
Am I right or am I wrong?
Are ya really a genuine member?
Or do ya just kinda belong?

BOHEMIA

Author Unknown
(Recited by John Mason)

I long for the glow of a kindly heart
And the clasp of a friendly hand;
And I'd rather live in Bohemia
Than in any other land.

There are no titles inherited there,
No hoard or hope for the brainless heir;
No gilded dullard native born
To stare at his fellow with leaden scorn.

Bohemia has none but adopted sons,
Its limits where Fancy's bright stream runs;
Its honors not garnered for thrift or trade,
But for beauty and truth men's souls have made.

To the empty heart in a jeweled breast
There is value, maybe, in a purchased crest;
But the thirsty of soul soon learn to know
The moistureless froth of the social show.

The vulgar sham of the pompous feast,
Where the heaviest purse is the highest priest;
The organized charity scrimped and iced,
In the name of a cautious, statistical Christ.

The smile restrained, the respectable cant,
When a friend in need is a friend in want;
Where the only aim is to keep afloat,
And a brother might drown with a cry in his throat.

Oh! I long for the glow of a kindly heart,
And the clasp of a friendly hand;
And I'd rather live in Bohemia
Than in any other land.

BALLAD OF CHRISTMAS PRESENT

Jerry Betts

(An annual event reported by a Chicago newspaper.)

Christmas is a happy time, with children all aglow,
Thinking of toys and holiday joys, Santa and mistletoe,
The girls of dolls and clothes and such, boys of trucks and horns,
They know will be beneath the tree on early Christmas morn.
Yet there are children in the land who do not know it so,
Whose Christmas fare is sparse and spare, whose Christmas hopes are low.

It is a Christmas in Chicago, in a small department store,
In a neighborhood where all that are, are desperate and poor.
A very little girl comes in, her clothes are ragged and worn;
She shivers with cold in a coat that is old. Old and tattered and torn.
She clutches the hand of a smaller boy, while craning her neck to see,
With him behind, trying to find where all the toys might be.

They see the shelves of countless toys. Each heaves a glad little sigh;
All it seems, in their wildest dreams, are here before their eyes.
And as they move along the aisles, in utter awe they bask.
Bright eyes glow, and grow and grow. . . Is it too much to ask?
But in their hearts they sadly know that it can never be.
Oh, but then, just to pretend. . . Such wondrous things to see.

A man is watching the children, as he has in years before;
Every year he watches here, in this same department store.
He comes with his holiday bonus and a heart that reaches out
So in his way, he can say, what Christmas is about.
He makes a sign to the salesgirl, a little wave of the hand;
Well she knows, and quickly goes, to where the children stand.

"Well, Well," she says to the children, "Whatever have we here?"
They clutch tight, in sudden fright, pretending not to hear.
Dropping the toys in their places, they look around to fly,
But she with a grin, glancing at him, standing in the shadow nearby,
Picks up the space commando and the doll with the golden hair,
And blinking her eye, so not to cry, gives them to the urchin pair.

"Santa Claus was here today," Said she with a choke in her voice,
"And told me then, to make sure when you two had made a choice,
To give these toys to you to have, before you went away,
So they could be beneath your tree on early Christmas day."
They took the toys with trembling hands, eyes so wide and bright,
And all four knew the spirit true, that filled their hearts that night.

He paid the bill without a word, emotion holding sway,
On modest means, he lived his dreams, waiting for this day.
For so he spent his Christmas, each and every year,
With simple joys for girls and boys, replacing bitter tears.
True Christmas came to four that day and four hearts touched each other,
And way up high above the sky, 'twas noted by another.

BUYING LOYALTY

Anne Campbell

You can't buy loyalty, they say.
I bought it, though, this very day!
You can't buy friendship, firm and true.
I bought sincerest friendship, too.

And truth and kindness, I got,
And happiness, oh, such a lot!
So many joyous hours-to-be
Were sold with this commodity!

I bought a life of simple faith
And love that will be mine till death.
And two brown eyes that I could see
Would not be long in knowing me.

I bought protection. I've a guard
Right now and ever afterward.
Buy human friendship? Maybe not!
You see, it was a dog I bought.

BARBARA FRIETCHIE

John Greenleaf Whittier

Up from the meadows rich with corn,
Clear in the cool September morn,
The clustered spires of Frederick stand
Green-walled by the hills of Maryland.

Round about them orchards sweep,
Apple and peach tree fruited deep,
Fair as the garden of the Lord
To the eyes of the famished rebel horde,

On that pleasant morn of the early fall
When Lee marched over the mountain-wall;
Over the mountains winding down,
Horse and foot, into Frederick town.

Forty flags with their silver stars,
Forty flags with their crimson bars,
Flapped in the morning wind; the sun
Of noon looked down, and saw not one.

Up rose old Barbara Frietchie then,
Bowed with her fourscore years and ten;
Bravest of all in Frederick town,
She took up the flag the men hauled down;

In her attic window the staff she set,
To show that one heart was loyal yet.
Up the street came the rebel tread,
Stonewall Jackson riding ahead.

Under his slouched hat left and right
He glanced; the old flag met his sight.
"Halt!" — the dust-brown ranks stood fast,
"Fire!" –out blazed the rifle-blast.

It shivered the window, pane and sash;
It rent the banner with seam and gash.
Quick, as it fell, from the broken staff
Dame Barbara snatched the silken scarf.

40

She leaned far out on the window-sill
And shook it forth with a royal will.
"Shoot, if you must, this old gray head,
But spare your country's flag," she said.

A shade of sadness, a blush of shame,
Over the face of the leader came;
The nobler nature within him stirred
To life at the woman's deed and word;

"Who touches a hair of yon gray head
Dies like a dog! March on!" he said.
All day long through Frederick street
Sounded the tread of marching feet:

 All day long that free flag tossed
Over the heads of the rebel host.
Ever it torn folds rose and fell
On the loyal winds that loved it well;

And through the hill-gaps sunset light
Shone over it with a warm good-night.
Barbara Frietchie's work is o'er,
And the Rebel rides on his raids no more.

Honor to her! And let a tear
Fall, for her sake, on Stonewall's bier.
Over Barbara Frietchie's grave,
Flag of Freedom and Union wave!

Peace and order and beauty draw
Round thy symbol of light and law;
And ever the stars above look down
On thy stars below in Frederick town!

BUM

Author Unknown

He's a little dog, with a stubby tail
And a moth-eaten coat of tan,
And his legs are short of the wobbly sort;
I doubt if they ever ran.

And he howls at night, while in broad daylight
He sleeps like a blooming log;
And he likes the feed of the gutter breed.
He's a most irregular dog.

I call him Bum, and in total sum
He's all that his name implies,
For he's just a tramp with a highway stamp
That culture cannot disguise.

And his friends, I've found, in the streets abound,
Be they urchins or dogs or men;
Yet he sticks to me with a fiendish glee,
It is truly beyond my ken.

I talk to him when I'm lonesome like,
And I'm sure that he understands
When he looks at me so attentively
And gently licks my hand.

Then he rubs his nose on my tailored clothes,
But I never say aught thereat
For the Good Lord knows I can buy more clothes,
But never a friend like that!

So my good old pal, my irregular dog,
My flea-bitten stub-tailed friend,
Has become a part of my very heart
To be cherished till lifetimes end.

And on Judgement day, if I take the way
That leads where the righteous meet,
If my dog is barred by the Heavenly guard
—We'll both of us brave the heat!

COLLEGE REVISITED

Author Unknown

He was a guileless college youth,
    That mirrored modesty and truth;
And sometimes at his musty room
    His sister called to chase the gloom.
One afternoon, when she was there,
    Arranging things with kindly care,
As often she had done before,
    There came a knock upon the door.
Our student, sensitive to fears
    Of thoughtless comrades' laughing jeers,
Had only time to make deposit
    Of his dear sister in a closet.
Then haste the door to open wide,
    His guest unbidden stepped inside.

He was a cheery-faced old man,
    And with apologies began
For calling, and then let him know
    That more than fifty years ago
When he was in his youthful bloom,
    He'd occupied that very room;
So thought he'd take the chance, he said,
    To see the changes time had made.

"The same old window, same old view—
    Ha! Ha! The same old pictures, too!"
And then he tapped them with his cane,
    And laughed his merry laugh again.
"The same old sofa, I declare!
    Dear me! It must be worse for wear.
The same old shelves!" And then he came
    And spied the closet door. "The same—"
Oh, my! A woman's dress peeped through.
    Quick as he could he closed it too.
He shook his head. "Ah! Ah! the same
    Old game, young man, the same old game!"

"Would you my reputation slur!"
    The youth gasped; "That's my sister, Sir!"
"Ah!" said the old man, with a sigh,
    "The same old story—The same old lie!"

CASEY AT THE BAT

Ernest Lawrence Thayer
(Recited by De Wolf Hopper)

It looked extremely rocky for the Mudville nine that day;
The score stood two to four, with but an inning left to play.
So, when Cooney died at second, and Burrows did the same,
A pallor wreathed the features of the patrons of the game.

A straggling few got up to go, leaving there the rest,
With that hope which springs eternal within the human breast.
For they thought: "If only Casey could get a whack at that,"
They'd put even money now, with Casey at the Bat.

But Flynn preceded Casey, and likewise so did Blake,
And the former was a pudd'n, and the latter was a fake.
So on that stricken multitude a deathlike silence sat;
For there seemed but little chance of Casey's getting to the bat.

But Flynn let drive a "single," to the wonderment of all.
And the much-despised Blakey "tore the cover off the ball."
And when the dust had lifted, and they saw what had occurred,
There was Blakey safe at second, and Flynn a-huggin' third.

Then from the gladdened multitude when up a joyous yell-
It rumbled in the mountaintops, it rattled in the dell;
It struck upon the hillside and rebounded on the flat;
For Casey, mighty Casey, was advancing to the bat.

There was ease in Casey's manner as he stepped into his place,
There was pride in Casey's bearing and a smile on Casey's face;
And when responding to the cheers he lightly doffed his hat,
No stranger in the crowd could doubt; 'twas Casey at the bat.

Ten thousand eyes were on him as he rubbed his hands with dirt,
Five thousand tongues applauded when he wiped them on his shirt;
Then when the writhing pitcher ground the ball into his hip,
Defiance glanced in Casey's eye, a sneer curled Casey's lip.

And now the leather-covered sphere came hurtling through the air,
And Casey stood a-watching it in haughty grandeur there.
Close by the sturdy batsman the ball unheeded sped;
"That ain't my style," said Casey. "Strike one," the umpire said.

From the benches, black with people, there went up a muffled roar,
Like the beating of the storm waves on the stern and distant shore.
"Kill him! Kill the umpire!" shouted someone on the stand;
And it's likely they'd have killed him had not Casey raised his hand.

With a smile of Christian charity great Casey's visage shone;
He stilled the rising tumult, he made the game go on;
He signaled to the pitcher, and once more the Spheroid flew;
But Casey still ignored it, and the umpire said, "Strike two."

"Fraud!" cried the maddened thousands, and the echo answered "Fraud!"
But one scornful look from Casey and the audience was awed;
They saw his face grow stern and cold, they saw his muscles strain,
And they knew that Casey wouldn't let the ball go by again.

The sneer is gone from Casey's lips, his teeth are clenched in hate,
He pounds with cruel vengeance his bat upon the plate;
And now the pitcher holds the ball, and now he lets it go,
And now the air is shattered by the force of Casey's blow.

Oh, somewhere in this favored land the sun is shining bright,
The band is playing somewhere, and somewhere hearts are light;
And somewhere men are laughing, and somewhere children shout,
But there is no joy in Mudville; Mighty Casey has struck out.

CASEY'S REVENGE

James Wilson

(A Sequel To "Casey At The Bat")

There were saddened hearts in Mudville for a week or even more;
There were muttered oaths and curses-every fan in town was sore.
"Just think," said one, "how soft it looked with Casey at the bat!"
And then to think he'd go and spring a bush-league trick like that."

All his past fame was forgotten; he was now a hopeless "shine,"
They called him "Strike-our Casey" from the mayor down the line,
And as he came to bat each day his bosom heaved a sigh,
While a look of hopeless fury shone in mighty Casey's eye.

The lane is long, someone has said, that never turns again,
And Fate, though fickle, often gives another chance to men.
And Casey smiled-his rugged face no longer wore a frown;
The pitcher who had started all the trouble came to town.

All Mudville had assembled; ten thousand fans had come
To see the twirler who had put big Casey on the bum;
And when he stepped into the box the multitude went wild.
He doffed his cap in proud disdain-but Casey only smiled.

"Play ball!" the umpire's voice rang out, and then the game began;
But in that throng of thousands there was not a single fan
Who thought that Mudville had a chance; and with the setting sun
Their hopes sank low-the rival team was leading "four to one".

The last half of the ninth came round, with no change in the score;
But when the first man up hit safe the crowd began to roar.
The din increased, the echo of ten thousand shouts was heard
When the pitcher hit the second and gave "four balls" to the third.

Three men on base-nobody out-three runs to tie the game!
A triple meant the highest niche in Mudville's hall of fame;
But here the rally ended and the gloom was deep as night
When the fourth one "fouled to catcher" and the fifth "flew out to right."

A dismal groan in chorus came — a scowl was on each face
When Casey walked up, bat in hand, and slowly took his place;
His bloodshot eyes in fury gleamed; his teeth were clinched in hate;
He gave his cap a vicious hook and pounded on the plate.

But fame is fleeting as the wind, and glory fades away;
There were no wild and woolly cheers, no glad acclaim this day.
They hissed and groaned and hooted as they clamored, "Strike him out!"
But Casey gave no outward sign that he had heard this shout.

The pitcher smiled and cut one loose; across the plate it spread;
Another hiss, another groan. "Strike one!" the umpire said.
Zip! Like a shot, the second curve broke just below his knee-
"Strike two!" the umpire roared aloud; but Casey made no plea.

No roasting for the umpire now — his was an easy lot;
But here the pitcher whirled again—was that a rifle shot?
A whack! A crack! And out through space the leather pellet flew,
A blot against the distant sky, a speck against the blue.

Above the fence in center field, in rapid whirling flight,
The sphere sailed on; the blot grew dim and then was lost to sight.
Ten thousand hats were thrown in air, then thousand threw a fit;
But no one ever found the ball that mighty Casey hit!

Oh, somewhere in this favored land dark clouds may hide the sun,
And somewhere bands no longer play and children have no fun;
And somewhere over blighted lives there hangs a heavy pall;
But Mudville hearts are happy now — for Casey hit the ball!

CASEY-TWENTY YEARS LATER

S. P. McDonald

(A Sequel To Casey's Revenge)

The bugville team was surely up against a rocky game;
The chances were they'd win defeat and undying fame;
Three men were hurt and two were benched; The score stood six to four.
They had to make three hard — earned runs in just two innings more.

"It can't be done," the captain said, a pallor on his face;
"I've got two pitchers in the field, a mutt on second base;
And should another man get spiked or crippled in some way,
The team would sure be down and out, with eight men left to play.

"We're up against it anyhow as far as I can see;
My boys ain't hitting like they should and that's what worries me;
The luck is with the other side, no pennant will we win;
It's mighty tough, but we must take our medicine and grin."

The eighth round opened; one, two, three; The enemy went down;
The Bugville boys went out the same, the captain wore a frown;
The first half of the ninth came round, two men had been called out,
When Bugville's catcher broke a thumb and could not go that route.

A deathly silence settled o'er the crowd assembled there.
Defeat would be allotted them; they felt it in the air;
With only eight men in the field 'twould be a gruesome fray,-
Small wonder that the captain cursed the day he learned to play.

"Lend me a man to finish with," he begged the other team;
"Lend you a man?" the foe replied; "My boy, you're in a dream;
We want to win the pennant, too — that's what we're doing here.
There's only one thing you can do — call for a volunteer."

The captain stood and pondered in a listless sort of way;
He never was a quitter and would not be today!
"Is there within the grandstand here" — His voice rang loud and clear—
" A man who has the sporting blood to be a volunteer ?"

48

Again that awful silence settled o'er the multitude;
Was there a man among them with such recklessness imbued?
The captain stood with cap in hand, while hopeless was his glance,
And then a short and stocky man cried out, "I'll take a chance."

Into the field he bounded with a step both firm and light;
"Give me the mask and mitt," he said; "let's finish up the fight.
The game is now beyond recall; I'll last at least a round;
Although I'm ancient you will find me muscular and sound."

His hair was sprinkled here and there with little streaks of gray;
Around his eyes and on his brow a bunch of wrinkles lay.
The captain smiled despairingly and slowly turned away .
"Why, he's all right," one rooter yelled. Another, "Let him play."

"All right, go on," the captain sighed; the stranger turned around,
Took off his coat and collar, too, and threw them on the ground.
The humor of the situation seemed to hit them all,
And as he donned the mask and mitt, the umpire called, "Play Ball!"

Three balls the pitcher hurled, three balls of lightning speed;
The stranger caught them all with ease and did not seem to heed.
Each ball had been pronounced a strike, the side had been put out.
And as he walked in towards the bench, he heard the rooters shout.

One Bugvbille boy went out on strikes, and one was killed at first;
The captain saw his awkward pose and gnashed his teeth and cursed.
The third man smashed a double and the fourth man swatted clear,
Then, in a thunder of applause, up came the volunteer.

His feet were planted in the earth, he swung a warlike club;
The captain saw his awkward pose and softly whispered, "Dub!"
The pitcher looked at him and grinned, then heaved a might ball;
The echo of that fearful swat still lingers with us all.

High, fast and far that spheroid flew; it sailed and sailed away;
It ne'er was found, so it's supposed it still floats on today.
Three runs came in, the pennant would be Bugville's for a year;
The fans and players gathered round to cheer the volunteer.

"What is your name," the captain asked? "Tell us your name," cried all,
As down his cheeks great tears were seen to run and fall.
For one brief moment he was still, then murmured soft and low:
"I'm mighty Casey who struck out just twenty years ago."

CASEY'S TABLE D'HOTE

Eugene Field

Oh, them days on Red Hoss Mountain,
  When the skies was fair 'nd blue,
When the money flowed like likker
  'Nd the folks wuz brave 'nd true;
When the nights wuz crisp and balmy,
  'Nd the camp wuz all astir,
With the joints all throwed wide open,
  'Nd no sheriff to demur.

Oh, them times on Red Hoss Mountain
  In the Rookies fur away—
There's no sich place nor times like them
  As I can find today.
What though the camp hez busted!
  I seem to see it still,
A lying, like it loved it,
  On that big 'nd warty hill;

And I feel a sort of yearnin'
  'Nd a chokin in my throat,
When I think of Red Hoss Mountain
  'Nd of Casey's tabble dote.
This Casey was an Irishman—
  You'd know it by his name,
And by the facial features
  Appertainin' to the same;

He'd lived in many places
  'Nd had done a thousand things,
From the noble art of actin'
  To the work of dealin' kings.
But, somehow, hadn't caught on—
  So, drifting' with the rest,
He drifted for a fortune
  To the undeveloped West;

And he came to Red Hoss Mountain
  When the little camp was new,
When the money flowed like likker
  'Nd the folks wuz brave 'nd true;

And, havin' been a steward
      On a Mississippi boat,
He opened up a caffy,
      'Nd he run a tabble dote.

The bar wuz long 'nd rangey,
      With a mirror on the shelf,
"Nd a pistol so that Casey,
      When required, could help himself;
Down underneath there wuz a row
      Of bottled beer an' wine,
'Nd a kag of Bourbon whiskey
      Of the run of '59.

Upon the walls wuz pictures
      Of hosses 'nd of girls—
Not much on dress, perhaps,
      But strong on records 'nd on curls;
Them which had been identified
      With Casey in the past—
The hosses 'nd the girls, I mean—
      And both wuz mighty fast;

But all these fine attractions
      Wuz of precious little note,
By the side of what wuz offered
      At Casey's tabble dote.
A tabble dote is different
      From orderin' aller cart,
In one case you get all there is—
      In t'other only part;

And Casey's tabble dote
      Began in French—as all begin—
And Casey's ended with the same,
      Which is to say with "vin."
But in between wuz every kind
      Of reptile, bird 'nd beast,
The same like you can git
      In high-tone restaurants down East'

'Nd windin' up wuz cake or pie,
        With coffee demy tas
Or sometimes, floatin Ireland
        In a soothin' kind of sass.
That left a sort of pleasant ticklin'
        In a fellar's parched, dry throat
'Nd make him hanker after more
        Of Casey's tabble dote.

The very recollection of them puddin's
        'Nd them pies
Brings a yearnin' to my buzzom
        'Nd the water to my eyes;
'Nd seems like cookin' nowadays
        Ain't what it used to be
In camp on Red Hoss Mountain
        In that year of '63

But, maybe, it is better
        'Nd maybe I'm to blame—
I'd like to be a-livin'
        In the mountains just the same—
I'd like to live that life again
        When skies wuz fair 'nd blue
When things wuz run wide open
        'Nd men was brave and true;

When brawny arms the flinty ribs
        Of red Hoss Mountain smote,
For wherewithal to pay the price
        Of Casey's tabble dote.

DOG

Nick Kenny

A faithful dog will play with you,
And laugh with you, — or cry.
He'll gladly starve to stay with you,
Nor ever reason why.

And when you're feeling out of sorts,
Somehow he'll understand.
He'll watch you with his shining eyes,
And try to lick your hand.

His blind, implicit faith in you
Is matched by his great love,
The kind of faith that we should have
In Our Master, up above!

When everything is said and done,
I guess it isn't odd,
For when you spell "dog" backwards,
You will get the name of God.

THE PARTICULAR PIG

Author Unknown
(From A Prison Wall)

Oh, so well I do remember
"Twas a day in late September
As I staggered down the street
With drunken pride,

Oh, my feet were all a flutter
As I lay down in the gutter
And a pig came up
And lay down by my side.

Now my heart was all a flutter
As I lay there in the gutter
And a lady passing by was heard to say,
"You can tell a man who boozes,
By the company he chooses,"
And the gosh darned pig got up and walked away!

53

COURTING IN KENTUCKY

Author Unknown

When Mary Ann Dollinger got the skule
    Daown thar on Injun Bay
I was glad, fer I like ter see
    A gal makin' her honest way.
I heerd some talk in the village
    Abaout her flyin' high,
Tew high fer busy farmer folks
    With chores ter dew ter fly;

But I paid no sorter attention
    Ter all the talk ontell
She come in her reg-lar boardin' raound
    Ter visit with us a spell.
My Jake an' her had been cronies
    Ever since they could walk
An' it tuk me aback ter hear her
    Kerrectin' him in his talk.

Jake ain't no hand at grammar,
    Though he haint his best for work;
But I sez ter myself, "Look out, my gal,
    Yer a-foolin' with a Turk!"
Jake bore it wonderful patient,
    An' said in a mournful way,
He p'sumed he was behindhand
    With the doin's at Injun Bay.

I remember once he was askin'
    For some o' my Injun buns.
An' she said he should allus say,
    "Them air," stid o' "them is" the ones.
Wal, Mary Ann kep' hem stiddy
    Mornin' an' evenin' long,
Tell he dassent open his mouth
    For fear o' talking' wrong.

One day I was pickin' currants
       Daown by the old quince tree,
When I heerd Jake's voice a-sayin',
       "Be ye willin' ter marry me?"
An' Mary Ann kerrectin',
       "Air ye willin',' yeou sh'd say."
Our Jake he put his foot daown
       In a plum, decided way.

"No wimmen-folks is a-going
       Ter be rearrangin' me,
Herafter I says 'craps,' 'the is,'
       'I calk'late,' an' 'I be.'
Ef folks don't like my talk
       They needn't hark ter what I say!
But I ain't a-goin' to take no sass
       From folks from Injun Bay.

"I ask you free an' final,
       'Be ye goin' to marry me?"
An' Mary Ann sez, tremblin',
       Yet anxious-like, "I be."

EPITAPH TO A DOG

Lord Byron
*(Found inscribed on a monument
Newstead Abbey.)*

**Near this spot
Are deposited the Remains
Of one
Who possessed Beauty
Without Vanity,
Strength without Insolence,
Courage without Ferocity,
And all the virtues of Man
Without his Vices.
This Praise, which would be unmeaning flattery
If inscribed over Human Ashes,
Is but a just tribute to the Memory of
"Boatswain," a Dog
Who was born at Newfoundland,
May, 1803
And died at Newstead Abbey
Nov. 18, 1808**

When some proud son of man returns to earth,
Unknown to glory, but upheld by birth,
The sculptur'd art exhausts the art of woe,
And stoned urns record who rests below;
When all is done, upon the tomb is seen,
Not what he was, but what he should have been;

But the poor Dog, in life the firmest friend,
The first to welcome, foremost to defend;
Whose honest heart is still his master's own,
Who labours, fights, lives, breathes, for him alone,
Unhonour'd falls, unnoticed all his worth,
Denied in Heaven the soul he held on earth;

While man, vain insect! Hopes to be forgiven,
And claims himself a sole exclusive Heaven!
Oh, man! Thou feeble tenant of an hour,
Debased by slavery, or corrupt by power,
Who knows thee well, must quit thee with disgust
Degraded mass of animated dust!

Thy love is lust, thy friendship all a cheat,
Thy smiles hypocrisy, thy words deceit!
By nature vile, ennobled but by name,
Each kindred brute might bid thee blush for shame.
Ye! Who, perchance, behold this single Urn
Pass on —- it honours none you wish to mourn:

To mark a Friend's remains these stones arise,
I never knew but one, and here he lies.

DOGS FOR DISPOSAL

Margaret Mackprang Mackay

My dog is a nuisance, an absolute pest;
With him in the house there is truly no rest.
He leaves dirty tracks on the mirror-bright floor,
And scratches the paint from the tidy front door.

He slobbers his water and spills half his food;
The rugs are all gnawed and slippers are chewed.
He sheds tufts of hair and he scatters his fleas;
He buries his bones under bushes and trees.

He keeps us awake every night with his yaps;
The neighbors all curse him for spoiling their naps.
I'll stand it no longer. I'm getting fed up.
I won't be a slave to that bothersome pup!

Er — Pardon — Excuse me, but what did you say?
You ask if I'm giving the puppy away?
You've the nerve to suggest that you'll take him with pleasure!
Well, certainly not! He's an absolute treasure!

FATHER'S WAY

Eugene Field

My father was no pessimist,
　　　　He loved the things of earth,
Its cheerfulness and sunshine,
　　　　Its music and its mirth.
He never sighed or moped around—
　　　　Whenever things went wrong.
I warrant me he'd mocked at fate,
　　　　With some defiant song.
But, being he warn't much on tune,
　　　　Whenever times were blue—
He'd whistle softly to himself,
　　　　The only tune he knew.

Now, mother when she learned that tune,
　　　　Which father whistled so,
Would say, "There's something wrong today,
　　　　With Ephraim, I know.
He never tries to make believe
　　　　He's happy that ere way
But that I'm certain as can be,
　　　　Some trouble is to pay."
And so, betimes, quite natural like,
　　　　To us observant youth,
There seemed suggestion in that tune,
　　　　Of deep, pathetic truth.

When Brother William joined the war,
　　　　A lot of us went down—
To see the gallant soldier boys,
　　　　Right gaily out of town.
A-coming home poor mother cried,
　　　　As if her heart would break.
And all us children, too, for hers'
　　　　And not for Williams sake!
But father, trudgin' on ahead,
　　　　His hands behind him so,
Kept whistlin' to himself,
　　　　So sort of solemn-like and low.

And when my eldest sister, Sue,
     Was married and went West,
Seemed like it took the tuck right out
     Of mother and the rest.
She was the sunlight in our home,
     Why, father used to say,
It wouldn't seem like home at all,
     If Sue should go away.
Yet, when she went, a-leavin' us,
     All sorrow and all tears,
Poor father whistled lonesome like,
     And went to feed the steers.

When crops were bad and other ills
     Befell our homely lot,
He'd sit around and try to act
     As if he minded not.
And when came death and bore away,
     The one he worshiped so,
How vainly did his lips belie
     The heart benumbed with woe!
You see the telltale whistle told
     The mood he'd not admit,
He'd always quit his whistlin'
     When he thought we noticed it.

I'd like to see that stooping form,
     And hoary head again.
To see the honest, hearty smile,
     That cheered his fellow men.
Oh, could I kiss the kindly lips,
     That spake no creature wrong,
And share the rapture of that heart,
     That overflowed with song.
Oh, could I hear the little tune,
     He whistled long ago,
When he did battle with the griefs,
     He would not have us know.

GUILTY OR NOT GUILTY?

Author Unknown

She stood at the bar of justice,
A creature wan and wild,
In form too small for a woman,
In feature too old for a child.
For a look so worn and pathetic
Was stamped on her pale young face,
It seemed long years of suffering
Must have left that silent trace.

"Your name," said the judge, as he eyed her,
With kindly look, yet keen,
"Is—" "Mary Maguire, if you please, sir."
"And your age?" "I am turned fifteen."
"Well, Mary," — then from a paper
He slowly and gravely read—
"You are charged here—I am sorry to say it—
With stealing three loaves of bread.

"You look not like an old offender,
And I hope that you can show
The charge to be false. Now, tell me,
Are you guilty of this, or no?"
A passionate burst of weeping
Was at first her sole reply;
But she dried her tears in a moment,
And looked in the judge's eye.

"I will tell you just how it was, sir:
My father and mother are dead,
And my little brothers and sisters
Were hungry, and asked me for bread.
At first I earned it for them,
By working hard all day,
But somehow the times were hard, sir,
And the work all fell away.

"I could get no more employment;
The weather was bitter cold;
The young ones cried and shivered
(Little Johnnie's but four years old);
So what was I to do, sir?
I am guilty, but do not condemn;
I took—O! was it stealing?—
The bread to give to them."

Every man in the courtroom—
Graybeard and thoughtless youth—
Knew, as he looked upon her,
That the prisoner spoke the truth.
Out from their pockets came kerchiefs,
Out from their eyes sprung tears,
And out from old, faded wallets
Treasures hoarded for years.

The judge's face was a study,
The strangest you ever saw,
As he cleared his throat and murmured
Something about the law.
For one so learned in such matters,
So wise in dealing with men,
He seemed, on a simple question,
Sorely puzzled just then.

No one blamed him, or wondered
When at last these words they heard.
"The sentence of this young prisoner
Is for the present deferred."
And no one blamed him or wondered
When he went to her and smiled,
And tenderly led from the courtroom,
Himself, the "guilty" child!

TWO SINNERS

Ella Wheeler Wilcox

There was a man it is said one time
Who went astray in his youthful prime.
Can the brain keep cool and the heart keep quiet
When the blood is a river that's running riot?
And boys will be boys, the old folks say,
And the man is the better who's had his day.

The sinner reformed, and the preacher told
Of the prodigal son who came back to the fold.
And Christian people threw open the door
With a warmer welcome than ever before.
Wealth and honor were his to command,
And a spotless woman gave him her hand.

And the world strewed their pathway with flowers abloom,
Crying, "God bless lady and God bless groom."

There was a maiden who went astray
In the golden dawn of her life's young day.
She had more passion and heart than head,
And she followed blindly where fond Love led.
And love unchecked is a dangerous guide
To wander at will by a fair girl's side.

The woman repented and turned from sin,
But no door opened to let her in.
The preacher prayed that she might be forgiven,
But told her to look for mercy in Heaven.
For this is the law of the earth, we know,
That the woman is stoned, while the man free may go.

A brave man wedded her after all,
But the world said, frowning, "We shall not call."

FABLE

Ralph Waldo Emerson

The mountain and the squirrel
Had a quarrel,
And the former called the latter
"Little Prig";
Bun replied,
"You are doubtless very big;
But all sorts of things and weather
Must be taken in together,
To make up a year
And a sphere.
And I think it no disgrace
To occupy my place.
If I'm not so large as you,
You are not so small as I,
And not half so spry.
I'll not deny you make
A very pretty squirrel track;
Talents differ; all is well and wisely put;
If I cannot carry forests on my back,
Neither can you crack a nut."

GENERAL DELIVERY, ALASKA!

Bill Foster

The big swinging doors of the Red Dog Saloon
Have witnessed some almighty binges;
But nothing to equal the night in '06
When Jake tore them off of their hinges.

The flakes in the pan of that downtrodden man,
Stayed scarce and his future looked bleak;
So that's why I tried to convince him to go
Prospecting on Salty Dog Creek.

"Salty Dog Creek?" said Jake with a roar,
And fetched me a wicked straight left.
He hit me so hard on my belly of lard,
That I thought that my palate was cleft.

"Say, hold it," I said, as his fist hit my head,
And I sunk to my knees in the gravel.
"There's something about that small area, Jake,
That you, Pal, and I might unravel."

I said, "There's a rumor that up on that creek,
There's nuggets as big as a bucket."
Jake said, "Well, I'll try it, but buddy, look out,
By Friday if I haven't struck it."

We got to the creek at the first of the week,
Jake carried the shovels we stole;
He handed me one and said, "Just for fun,
Go find me a big "glory hole;"

Beneath the strong roots of a fallen down fir,
I found the bonanza he sought.
I yelled to him, "Jake, get yourself up here quick.
He asked me, "Ol' friend, what you got?"

"A glory hole, Jake," I said with a laugh.
There's nuggets as big as a turkey,
And all of them lying on top of the ground,
Not down in the water so murky."

So Jake he came running to look at the sight;
He hung his old head and he cried,
"A glory hole's something I did hope to find
Some day just before I had died.

But now that you've found it, my dreams I can't have."
It cut him like the blade of a knife.
That poor old prospector, I'd hurt him for sure.
It seemed I had ruined his life.

"But think of the party, Jake, that you can hold;"
I told him and he said, "You're right!"
Tomorrow the party, 'rehearsal' today,
Can you but envision the sight?"

He ripped off the doors of the Red Dog Saloon;
The weather outside it was cool.
Said, "Bring in the burro that carries my sacks;
'I'm buying a drink for my mule!"

A party was started, I could not believe,
Amid the old burro's loud brays.
And big Jake McGraw, he bought rounds for the house;
It lasted for twenty-one days.

And then on that day the old bartender said,
"The bar bill is now eighty grand.
I cannot continue to serve you, friend Jake,
Till I see some gold here in my hand."

The bartender opened up one of the sacks,
And roared, "Do not think me most bold,"
But there'll be a hanging in this place tonight!
These sacks are all filled with 'fool's gold'!"

"What?" roared old Jake, a stunned look on his face,
And he pointed his finger at me.
I dashed out the door, through the woods I did soar,
And jumped a big forty foot tree.

I'm hiding tonight in the frozen frontier.
The wind and the bitter cold chill me.
For Jake McGraw says that if ever I'm found,
That he'll be the man who will kill me.

'Don't know how it happened, I just tried to help;
For Jake McGraw once was my friend;
But trouble, it travels the roads that I walk
And waits for me round every bend.

Here in the high lonesome, the weather is cruel;
Survival itself is so hard.
If anyone out there should read my sad tale,
Perhaps you could send me a card.

I know you can't write me without an address,
So just in case someone should ask ya,
The only one that I can safely give out
Is — "General Delivery" — Alaska!

GUNGA DIN

Rudyard Kipling

(Recited by Mrs. Langtry)

You may talk o' gin an' beer
When you're quartered safe out 'ere,
An' you're sent to penny-fights an' Aldershot it;
But when it comes to slaughter
You will do your work on water,
An' you'll lick the bloomin' boots of 'im that's got it.

Now in Injia's sunny clime,
Where I used to spend my time
A-servin' of 'Er Majesty the Queen,
Of all them black-faced crew
The finest man I knew
Was our regimental bhisti, Gunga Din.

He was "Din! Din! Din!"
You limping lump o' brick dust, Gunga Din!
Hi! Slippy hitherao!
Water, get it! Panee lao!
You squidgy nosed old idol, Gunga Din!"

The uniform 'e wore
Was nothin' much before,
An' rather less than 'arf o' that be'ind,
For a twisty piece o' rag
An a goatskin water-bag
Was all the field equipment 'e could find.
When the sweatin' troop-train lay
In a sidin' through the day,
Where the 'eat would make your bloomin' eyebrows crawl,
We shouted "Harry By!"
Till our throats were bricky-dry,
Then we wopped 'im 'cause 'e couldn't serve us all.

It was "Din! Din! Din!"
You 'eathen where the mischief 'ave you been?
You put some juldee in it,
Or I'll marrow you this minute
If you don't fill up my helmet, Gunga Din!"

"E would dot an' carry one
Till the longest day was done,
An' 'e didn't seem to know the use o' fear,
If we charged or broke or cut,
You could bet your bloomin' nut,
'E'd be waitin' fifty paces right flank rear.
With 'is mussick on 'is back,
'E would skip with our attack,
An' watch us till the bugles made "Retire."
An' for all 'is dirty 'ide
'E was white, clear white, inside
When 'e went to tend the wounded under fire.

It was "Din! Din! Din!"
With the bullets kickin' dust spots on the green
When the cartridges ran out,
You could 'ear the front files shout:
"Hi! Ammunition-mules an' Gunga din!"

I shan't forgit the night
When I dropped be'ind the fight
With a bullet where my belt-plate should 'a' been.
I was chokin' mad with thirst,
An' the man that spied me first
Was our good old grinnin', gruntin' Gunga Din.
'E lifted up my 'ead,
An he plugged me where I bled,
An' 'e guv me 'arf-a-pint o' water—green:
It was crawlin' and it stunk,
But of all the drinks I've drunk,
I'm gratefullest to one from Gunga Din.

It was "Din! Din! Din!
'Ere's a beggar with a bullet through 'is spleen;
'E's chawin' up the ground,
An' 'e's kickin' all around:
For Gawd's sake git the water, Gunga Din!"

'E carried me away
To where a dooli lay,
An a bullet come an' drilled the beggar clean,
'E put me safe inside,
An' just before 'e died:
"I 'ope you liked your drink," sez Gunga Din.
So I'll meet 'im later on
In the place where 'e is gone—
Where it's always double drill and no canteen;
'E 'll be squattin on the coals,
Givin' drink to pore damned souls,
An' I'll get a swig in Hell from Gunga din!

Yes, Din! Din! Din!
You Lazarushian-leather Gunga din!
Tho' I've belted you an' flayed you,
By the livin' Gawd that made you,
You're a better man than I am, Gunga Din!

HELL IN TEXAS

Author Unknown

The Devil, we're told, in hell was chained,
And a thousand years he there remained.
And he never complained, nor did he groan,
But determined to start a hell of his own
Where he could torment the souls of men
Without being chained to a prison pen.

So he asked the Lord if He had on hand
Anything left when He made the land.
The Lord said, "Yes, I had plenty on hand,
But I left it down on the Rio Grande.
The fact is, old boy, the stuff is so poor,
I don't think you could use it in hell any more.

But the devil went down to look at the truck
And said if it came as a gift, he was stuck;
For after examining it careful and well
He concluded the place was too dry for hell.
So in order to get it off His hands,
God promised the devil to water the lands.

For he had some water, or rather some dregs,
A regular cathartic that smelt like bad eggs.
Hence the deal was closed and the deed was
given,
And the Lord went back to His place in Heaven.
And the devil said, "I have all that is needed
To make a good hell," and thus he succeeded.

He began to put thorns on all of the trees,
And he mixed the sand with millions of fleas.
He scattered tarantulas along all the roads,
Put thorns on the cacti and horns on the toads.
He lengthened the horns of the Texas steers
And put an addition on jackrabbit's ears.

He put little devils in the bronco steed
And poisoned the feet of the centipede.
The rattlesnake bites you, the scorpion stings,
The mosquito delights you by buzzing his wings.
The sand burrs prevail, so do the ants,
And those that sit down need half soles on their pants.

The devil then said that throughout the land
He'd manage to keep up the devil's own brand,
And all would be mavericks unless they bore
The marks of scratches and bites by the score.
The heat in the summer is a hundred and ten,
Too hot for the devil and too hot for the men.

The wild boar roams through the black chaparral;
It's a hell of a place he has for a hell.
The red pepper grows by the bank of the brook,
The Mexicans use it in all that they cook.
Just dine with a Greaser and then you will shout,
"I've a hell on the inside as well as without."

I SHALL NOT PASS
THIS WAY AGAIN

Author Unknown

Through this toilsome world, alas
Once and only once I pass;
If a kindness I may show,
If a good deed I may do
To a suffering fellow man,
Let me do it while I can.
No delay, for it is plain
I shall not pass this way again.

HE'S JUST A DOG

Joseph M. Anderson

Here is a friend who proves his worth
Without conceit or pride of birth;
Let want or plenty play the host,
He gets the least and gives the most –
        He's just a dog.

He's ever faithful, kind and true,
He never questions what I do;
And whether I may go or stay,
He's always ready to obey –
        'Cause he's a dog.

He watches me all through the day,
And nothing coaxes him away,
And through that night-long slumber deep,
He guards the home wherein I sleep –
        And he's a dog.

As mortals go, how few possess
Of courage, trust and faithfulness,
Enough for which to undertake,
Without some borrowed traits, to make
        A decent dog!

HONEST CONFESSIONS

Author Unknown

"I know what you're going to say," she said,
   And she stood up, looking uncommonly tall;
   "You are going to speak of the hectic fall,
And say you're sorry the summer's dead.
   And no other summer was like it, you know,
   And can't I imagine what made it so?
Now, aren't you, honestly?" "Yes," I said.

"I know what you're going to say," she said;
   "You are going to ask if I forget
   That day in June when the woods were wct,
And you carried me: — here she dropped her head –
   "Over the creek: you are going to say—
   Do I remember that horrid day?
Now, aren't you, honestly?" "Yes," I said.

"I know what you're going to say," she said;
   "You are going to say that since that time
   You have rather tended to run to rhyme,
And" – here her glance fell and her cheek grew red –
   "And I have noticed your tone was queer?
   "Why, everybody has seen it here!
Now, aren't you, honestly?" "Yes," I said.

"I know what you're going to say," I said:
   "You're going to say you've been much annoyed.
   I am short of tact, you will say devoid,
And I'm clumsy and awkward, and call me Ted;
   And I bear abuse like a dear old lamb,
   And you'll have me anyway, just as I am.
Now, aren't you, honestly?" "Yeeeees," she said.

HOW MUCH DO I LOVE YOU?

Sonja Christina

How much do I love you?
Count each tear from every eye.
How much do I love you?
Count each sigh you ever sigh.

How much do I love you?
Count each soul t'was ever near.
How much do I love you?
Count each word you ever hear.

How much do I love you?
Count each step that passes you by.
How much do I love you?
Count each star that dots the sky.

How much do I love you?
Count the fish that swim the sea.
How much do I love you?
Count all the hours of eternity.

How much do I love you?
Count the waves upon the shore.
And when you find the final total,
Know I love you so much more!

HIGH FLIGHT

John Gillespie Magee Jr.

*(This poem was written while in flight over England
during World War II . He was killed in 1941 while
serving with the Royal Canadian Air Force.)*

Oh, I have slipped the surly bonds of Earth
And danced the skies on laughter-silvered wings:
Sunward I've climbed, and joined the tumbling mirth
Of sun-split clouds—and done a hundred things
You have not dreamed of—wheeled and soared and swung
High in the sunlit silence: hov'ring there,
I've chased the shouting wind along, and flung
My eager craft through footless halls of air.
Up, the long, delirious, burning blue
I've topped the windswept heights with easy grace
Where never lark, or even eagle flew—
And, while the silent lifting mind I've trod
The high untrespassed sanctity of space,
Put out my hand and touched the face of God.

LONELY

— Walker

A little whimper, next a patient sigh,
And then a sniff—(Oh, dear, there's no reply).
A little patter on the landing floor,
A gentle scratching at my study door,
Another pause, and then, "Well, who is that?"
The door swings open, there upon the mat

He stands expectant: "Please, it's only me.
There's nobody downstairs; I thought I'd see
If you were lonely, too. Please, may I stay?
I promise you I won't be in the way."
Then at our feet contentedly he lies,
A world's devotion in two doggy eyes.

HOW PADDY STOLE THE ROPE

Author Unknown

There was once two Irish labouring men to England they came over;
They tramped about in search of work, from Liverpool to Dover.
Says Pat to Mick, "I'm tired of this; we're both left in the lurch;
And if we don't get work, bedad, I'll go and rob a church."
"What, rob a church!" says Mick to Pat, "How dare you be so vile?
There's something sure to happen as you're treading down the aisle.
But if you go I go with you; we'll get out safe, I hope;"
So if you'll listen, I'll tell you here how Paddy stole the rope.

So off they went with theft intent, the place they wanted finding;
They broke into a country church which nobody was minding.
They scraped together all they could and then prepared to slope,
When Paddy cries out, "Hold on, Mick, what shall we do for rope?
We've got no bag to hold the swag, and e'er we get outside,
With something stout and strong, my lad, the bundle must be tied."
Just then he spies the old church bell, and quick as an antelope,
He scrambled up the belfry high to try and steal a rope.

Now when Paddy up the belfry got, "Ah-hah, bedad, but stop;
To get a piece that's long enough, I must climb up to the top."
So, like a sailor, up he went, and 'neath the top, says he,
"I think the piece that's underneath quite long enough will be."
So, holding by one arm and leg, he drew his clasp knife out,
And right above his big fat head he cut the rope so stout.
He quiet forgot it held him up, and, by the Holy Pope,
Down to the bottom of the church fell Paddy and the rope.

"Come out of that," says Mick to Pat, as he on the floor lay groaning,
"If that's the way you cut a rope, no wonder now you're moaning.
I'll show you how to cut a rope, so just lend me the knife."
Be very careful," cries out Pat, "or else you'll lose your life."
He clambered up the other rope, and, like an artful thief,
Instead of cutting it above, he cut it underneath.
The piece fell down and left poor Mick alone up there to cope;
Says he, "Bad luck unto the day when we came stealing rope."

Now with Paddy groaning on the floor and Mick hung up on high,
Says Pat, "Come Down." "I can't," cried Mick, "for if I do, I die."
The noise soon brought the beadle round, the sexton and police,
And although they set poor Micky free, they gave them no release.
They marched them to the county jail where their conduct now they rue,
And if they'd got no work before, they've plenty now to do;
And for their ingenuity they now have larger scope
Than when they broke into a church to try and steal a rope.

HOW DO I LOVE THEE?
LET ME COUNT THE WAYS

Elizabeth Barrett Browning

How do I love thee? Let me count the ways.
I love thee to the depth and breadth and height
My soul can reach, when feeling out of sight
For the ends of Being and ideal Grace.
I love thee to the level of every day's
Most quiet need; by sun and candlelight
I love thee freely, as men strive for Right;
I love thee purely, as they turn from Praise.
I love thee with the passion put to use
In my old griefs, and with my childhood's faith.
I love thee with a love I seemed to lose
With my lost saints, —I love thee with the breath.
Smiles, tears, of all my life! — and, if God choose,
I shall but love thee better after death.

HOW SALVATOR WON

Author Unknown

(Recited by Nina Farrington)

The gate was thrown open, I rode out alone,
　　　　More proud than a monarch who sits on a throne;
I am but a jockey, but shout upon shout
　　　　Went up for the people who watched me ride out,
And the cheers that rang forth from the warm-hearted crowd
　　　　Were as earnest as those to which monarch e'er bowed.

My heart thrilled with pleasure, so keen it was pain,
　　　　As I patted my Salvator's soft, silken mane;
And a sweet shiver shot from his hide to my hand
　　　　As we passed by the multitude down to the stand.
The great waves of cheering came billowing back,
　　　　As the hoofs of brave Tenny ran swift down the track.

And he stood there beside us, all bone and all muscle,
　　　　Our noble opponent, well trained for the tussle
That waited us there on the smooth, shining course.
　　　　My Salvator, fair to the lovers of horse,
As a beautiful woman is fair to man's sight —
　　　　Pure type of the thoroughbred, clean limbed and bright,
Stood taking the plaudits as only his due
　　　　And nothing at all unexpected or new.

And then there before us the bright flag is spread,
　　　　There's a roar from the grand stand, and Tenny's ahead;
At the sound of the voices that shouted "a go!"
　　　　He sprang like an arrow shot straight from the bow.
I tighten the reins on Prince Charlie's great son;
　　　　He is off like a rocket, the race is begun.
Half way down the furlong, their heads are together,
　　　　Scarce room 'twixt their noses to wedge in a feather.
Past grand stand and judges, in neck-too-neck strife,
　　　　Ah, Salvator, boy! 'tis the race of your life.

I press my knees closer, I coax him, I urge —
      I feel him go with a leap and a surge;
I see him creep on, inch by inch, stride by stride;
      While backward, still backward, falls Tenny beside.
We are nearing the turn, the first quarter is passed —
      'Twixt leader and chaser the daylight is cast;
The distance elongates, still Tenny sweeps on,
      As graceful and free limbed and swift as a fawn,
His awkwardness vanished, his muscles all strained,
      A noble opponent, well born and well trained.

I glanced o'er my shoulder; ha! Tenny, the cost
      Of that one second's flagging will be – the race lost
One second's weak yielding of courage and strength,
      And the daylight between us has doubled its length.
The first mile is covered, the race is mine –no!
      For the blue blood of Tenny responds to a blow.
He shoots though the air like a ball from a gun,
      And the two lengths between us are shortened to one.

My heart is contracted, my throat feels a lump —
      For Tenny's long neck is at Salvator's rump;
And now, with new courage, grows bolder and bolder.
      I see him once more running shoulder to shoulder,
With knees, hands and body I press my great steed,
      I urge him, I coax him, I pray him to heed!
Oh, Salvator! Salvator! List to my calls,
      For blow of my whip will hurt both if it falls.
There's a roar from the crowd like the ocean in storm,
      As close to my saddle leaps Tenny's great form;
One more mighty plunge, and, with knee, limb and hand
      I lift my horse first by a nose past the stand;
We are under the string now – the great race is done —
      And Salvator, Salvator, Salvator won!

Cheer, hoary-headed patriarchs; cheer loud, I say;
      'Tis the race of the century witnessed today!
Though ye live twice the space that's allotted to men,
      Ye never will see such a grand race again.
Let the shouts of the populace roar like the surf,
      For Salvator, Salvator, king of the turf!

He has rivaled the record of thirteen long years,
　　　He has won the first place in the vast line of peers;
'Twas a neck-to-neck contest, a grand, honest race,
　　　And even his enemies grant him the place;
Down in the dust let old records be hurled,
　　　And hang out 2:05 in the gaze of the world.

I PITY THE MAN

Author Unknown

I pity the man who never has known
The pleasure of owning a pup,
Who never has watched his funny ways
In the business of growing up.

I pity the man who enters his gate
Alone and unnoticed at night,
No dog to welcome him joyously home
With his frantic yelps of delight.

I pity the man who never receives,
In hours of bitterest woe,
Sympathy shown by a faithful dog
In a way only he seems to know.

I pity the man with a hatred of dogs;
He is missing from life something fine;
For the friendship between a man and his dog
Is a feeling almost divine.

I AM THE TEARS

Sherry Sharp

He taught me many lessons,
Gave me unconditional love.
We just seemed to fit together,
I was the hand and he, the glove.

For unknown reasons we parted,
And thought we'd meet no more,
But each time he would come rushing back,
He was the ocean, I, the shore.

In times of heartbreak I would wither,
He helped me grow despite the pain.
He was the sunshine in my soul,
I was the flower. He was the rain.

When life's trail was steep and I stumbled,
He lifted me up and held me tight.
He helped me soar ever higher,
He was the wind and I the kite.

He shared my hopes and dreams with me,
There was a side of him I alone know.
He was my past, my future all,
I was the color and he the rainbow.

He was here but for a moment,
Seems he's been gone so many years.
He was life's promise, smiles and laughter.
Now I'm left. I am the tears.

I HAD BUT FIFTY CENTS

Author Unknown

I took my girl to a fancy ball; it was a social hop;
We waited till the folks got out, and the music it did stop.
Then to a restaurant we went, the best one on the street;
She said she wasn't hungry, but this is what she eat:
A dozen raw, a plate of slaw, a chicken and a roast,
Some applesass and sparagrass, and soft-shelled crabs on toast.
A big box stew, and crackers too; Her appetite was immense!
When she called for pie, I thought I'd die,
For I had but fifty cents.

She said she wasn't hungry and didn't care to eat,
But I've got money in my clothes to bet she can't be beat;
She took it in so cozy, she had an awful tank;
She said she wasn't thirsty, but this is what she drank:
A whisky skin, a glass of gin, Which made me shake with fear,
A ginger pop, with rum on top, a schooner then of beer,
A glass of ale, a gin cocktail; she should have had more sense;
When she called for more, I fell on the floor,
For I had but fifty cents.

Of course I wasn't hungry and didn't care to eat,
Expecting every moment to be kicked into the street.
She said she'd fetch her family round, and some night we'd have fun;
When I gave the man the fifty cents, this is what he done:
He tore my clothes, he smashed my nose, he hit me on the jaw.
He gave me a prize of a pair of black eyes and with me swept the floor.
He took me where my pants hung loose and threw me over the fence;
Take my advice, don't try it twice
If you've got but fifty cents.

I REMEMBER CHRISTMAS

Sherry Sharp

I remember a lovely Christmas,
Not so very long ago.
A Christmas that was cold and crisp,
A Christmas white with snow.

I remember how you walked the woods,
To find that special tree,
Though its branches were sparse and bowed to all
It was special; it was just for me.

I remember the Christmas magic,
A fire in the fireplace.
I remember the love and laughter.
I remember your precious face.

I remember the Christmas mistletoe,
And that special Christmas kiss.
I remember your mischievous laughter,
And your eyes so hard to resist.

Now the tinsel has lost its glitter.
The lights have lost their glow.
The evergreens seem to be mourning,
Their branches bowed on low.

The jingle bells are silent.
I hear no silver bells ring.
The carolers' mouths are moving,
But I can't hear them sing.

Christmas isn't coming this year.
I know that this is true.
How could there be a Christmas?
It's not Christmas without you.

JEALOUS OF YOU

Author Unknown

(From A Prison Wall)

Now my wife and me lived together
Without chick or child as it were.
Last week a pair she presented me,
So I says 'old on there ol' girl.

Jealous of you? Jealous of you?
Lloyd George is jealous of you!
In twenty long years, no baby appears,
And now you presents me with two?
My pals all agree, they don't look like me,
So you must have been false and untrue;
For while one's quite alack,
The other bugger's black,
And that's why I'm finished with you.

My wife's got a nose that's a beauty.
She feeds it on Guinness and Bass.
There ain't nothin' worse, than when she's got a thirst,
For her consumption has never been surpassed.

Jealous of you? Jealous of you?
The fishes are jealous of you!
On Guinness I've tried to keep you supplied
And Bass has worked overtime too!
You've a hole in your throat
Like the hold in a boat,
You can knock back a pint dear or two,
And through drinking gin, you've had the bailiffs called in,
And that's why I'm finished with you.

Now my wife, she keeps getting' younger,
If you allow for the liberty she takes.
Her birthdate keeps changing
By her own rearranging,
But you could light up all a London with her cakes.

Jealous of you? Jealous of you?
Maggie, I'm certainly not!
You've got a glass eye, and at night bye and bye
Your teeth you drop into a pot.
You're almost renig; your hair is a wig,
Your leg is a wooden one too.
I've splinters by gum, from my toes to my thumbs,
And that's why I'm finished with you!

So pull up a glass an' we'll make this our last
An' we'll drink to the good times we 'ad.
(An' the more beer I'm movin'
'Er looks keep on improvin'
So I'll keep 'er an' she'll pay the tab.)

MY DOG

Burr McIntosh

He's my dog –

Four legs and a tail,
A reckless vagabond out of jail.
Just a lot of dog, no pedigree,
All kinds of branches on his family tree.
Shoe button eyes, nose too long;
Makes your head ache when he sings his song.
His legs are gangly, he has knock-knees,
Tears up slippers, and harbors fleas.
Wild and wooly, likes to run away,
Knocks you down when he wants to play.
Is fond of "rassling" with gloves and hats,
Tears up flower beds and chases cats.
Sleeps all day, eats like a hog,
Absolutely worthless – but,

He's my dog!

JIM

James Whitcomb Riley

He was jes' a plain, ever'day, all-round kind of a jour,
  Consumpted lookin' — but la!
The jokiest, wittiest, story-tellin', song-singing,
  Laughinest, jolliest
  Feller you ever saw!

Worked at jes' coarse work, but you kin bet
  He was fine enough in his talk,
  And his feelin's, too!
Lordy! Ef he was on'y back on his bench agin today
  A-carryin' on
  Like he ust to do!

Any shopmate'll tell you there never was on top o' dirt
  A better feller'n Jim!
You want a favor — and couldn't git it anywheres else —
  You could git it o' him!
Most free hearted-est man thataway in the world, I guess!
  Give ever' nickel he's worth—
And, ef you'd a wanted it and named it to him
  And ef it was his,
  He'd agive you the earth!

Allus areachin' out, Jim was,
  And ahelping some poor feller onto his feet.
He'd anever akeered how hungry he was hisse'f
  So's the feller got somepin to eat!
Didn't make no difference at all to him
  How he was dressed,
  He ust to say to me:
"You tog out a tramp purty comfortable in wintertime,
  And he'll git along!" says he.

Jim didn't have, nor never could git ahead so overly much
  O' this world's goods at a time—
'Fore now I've saw him, more'n onc't, lend a dollar and ha'f to
  Turn 'round and borry a dime!

Mebby laugh and joke about hisse'f fer awhile
  Then jerk his coat
  And kind o' square his chin,
Tie his apern, and squat hisse'f on his old shoe bench
  And go peggin' agin.

Patientest feller, too, I reckon, 'at ever jes' naturally
  Coughed hisse'f to death!
Long enough after his voice was lost he'd laugh and say,
  He could git ever'thing but his breath.
"You fellers," he'd sort o' twinkle his eyes and say,
  "Is apilin' onto me
A mighty big debt for that air little weak chested
  Ghost o' mine to pack
  Through all eternity!"

Now there was a man 'at jes' 'peared like to me,
  'At ornt't anever died!
"But death hain't ashowin no favors," the old boss said,
  "On'y to Jim," and cried;
And Wigger, 'at put up the best sewed work in the shop,
  Er the whole blamed neighborhood,
He says, "When God made Jim, I bet you
  He didn't do anything else that day
  But jes' set around and feel good!"

JIM BLUDSO

Col. John Hay

Wall, no, I can't tell where he lives,
　　　　Because he don't live, you see;
Leastways, he's got out of the habit
　　　　Of livin' like you and me.
Whar have you been for the last three years,
　　　　That you haven't heard folk tell
How Jimmy Bludso pass'd in his checks
　　　　The night on the "Prairie Belle?"

He warn't no saint – them engineers
　　　　Is all pretty much alike;
One wife in Natchez – under-the-hill,
　　　　And another one here in Pike.
A careless man in his talk was Jim,
　　　　And an awkward man in a row-
But he never pinked, and he never lied;
　　　　I reckon he never knowed how.

And this was all the religion he had
　　　　To treat his engine well,
Never be passed on the river,
　　　　To mind the pilot's bell,
And if ever the "Prairie Belle" took fire,
　　　　And a thousand times he swore
He'd hold her nozzle agin the bank
　　　　Till the last soul got ashore.

All boats has their day on the Mississip',
　　　　And her day came at last;
The Movastar was a better boat,
　　　　But the Belle she wouldn't be passed,
And so came tearin' along that night,
　　　　The oldest craft on the line,
With a deck hand squat on her safety valve,
　　　　With her furnaces crammed, rosin and pine.

The fire bust out as she cl'ared the bar,
       And burnt a hole in the night,
And quick as a flash she turned, and made
       For that willerbank on the right.
There was runnin' and cursin',
       But Jim yelled out over all the infernal roar,
"I'll hold her nozzle agin the bank
       Till the last galoot's ashore."

Thro' the hot, black breath of the burnin' boat
       Jim Bludso's voice was heard,
And they all had trust in his cussedness
       And know'd he would keep his word.
And sure's you're born, they all got off
       Afore the smokestacks fell,
And Bludso's ghost went up alone
       In the smoke of the "Prairie Belle."

He warn't no saint—but at judgement,
       I'd run my chance with Jim,
'Longside of some pious gentlemen
       That wouldn't shook hands with him.
He'd seen his duty a dead sure thing,
       And went for it thar and then;
And Christ ain't a-going to be too hard
       On a man that died for men.

JUST DOGS

Charlotte Becker

"Why's all that fuss?" the sergeant said,
      "To 'ear them scudding feet –
Just dogs a-comin' back again—
      Sancho an' Pat an' Pete."

Just dogs? Why, Sancho saved ten lives
      Half buried by a shell.
He dug them out with bleeding paws
      Where blinding shrapnel fell.

And little Pat bore under fire
      His Red Cross water can,
Quenching the cruel, burning thirst
      Of many a wounded man.

Pete tugged grenades at Loos,
      As brave as any soldier there;
The general knelt them all
      To give his Croix de Guerre.

Just dogs? Why, scarce a soldier gone
      Would find his heaven complete
Unless he heard beside his own
      That sound of scudding feet!

LET US SMILE

Wilbur D. Nesbit

The thing that goes the farthest
Toward making life worthwhile,
That costs the least and does the most
Is just a pleasant smile.
That smile that bubbles from the heart
That loves its fellow men,
Will drive away the clouds of gloom
And coax the sun again.
It's full of worth and goodness, too,
With manly kindness blent;
It's worth a million dollars,
And it doesn't cost a cent.

There is no room for sadness
When we see a cheery smile;
It always has the same good look;
It's never out of style;
It nerves us on to try again
When failure makes us blue;
The dimples of encouragement
Are good for me and you.
It pays the highest interest—
For it is merely lent;
It's worth a million dollars,
And it doesn't cost a cent.

A smile comes very easy—
You can wrinkle up with cheer
A hundred times before
You can squeeze out a salty tear;
It ripples out, moreover,
To the heartstrings that will tug,
And always leaves an echo
That is very like a hug.
So, smile away! Folks understand
What by a smile is meant;
It's worth a million dollars,
And it doesn't cost a cent.

LITTLE BREECHES

Colonel John Hay

I don't go much on religion,
    I never ain't had no show,
But I've got a middlin' tight grip, sir,
    On the handful of things I know.
I don't pan out on the prophets,
    And free-will, an' that sort of thing;
But I b'lieve in God an' the angels,
    Ever since one night last spring.

I come into town with some turnips,
    And my little Gabe came along;
No four-year-old in the county
    Could beat him, for purty an' strong.
Peart, an' chipper, an' sassy,
    Allus ready to swear an' fight.
An' I learnt him to chaw terbaccer,
    Just to keep his milk teeth white.

The snow came down like a blanket,
    As we passed by old Taggart's store.
I went in for a jug of molasses,
    And I left the old team at the door.
They skeered at something an' started,
    I heard one little squall,
And hell-to-split over the prairie
    Went team, Little Breeches, an' all.

Hell-to-split over the prairie—
    I was almost froze with skeer;
But we mustered up some torches,
    An' we searched for 'em far an' near.
At last we found hosses an' wagon,
    Snowed under a soft white mound,
Upset, dead beat—but of little Gabe,
    No hide or hair was found.

Now, here all hope soured on me,
　　Of my fellow-critter's aid.
I jest dropped down on my marrow bones,
　　Crotch deep in the snow, an' I prayed.
At last the torches, they all gin out,
　　An me 'n Isrial Parr
Went off for some wood to a sheep-fold,
　　That he said was somewhere thar.

We found it at last, a little place,
　　Where they shut up the lambs at night.
I peeped in, an' saw 'em all huddled thar,
　　So warm, so sleepy, an' white.
And thar sot Little Britches, an' chirped,
　　As peart as ever you see,
"I want a chew of terbaccer,
　　An' that's what's the matter with me!

How did he git thar? Angels!
　　He never could walk so far.
They jest scooped down, an' they toted him,
　　To where it was safe an' warm.
An I think that savin' a little child,
　　And bringin' him back to his own,
Is a derned sight better bizness,
　　Than loafin' 'round the throne!

LIGHT SHINING OUT
OF DARKNESS

William Cowper

God moves in a mysterious way,
　　　　His wonders to perform;
He plants his footsteps in the sea,
　　　　And rides upon the storm.

Deep in unfathomable mines
　　　　Of never-failing skill,
He treasures up his bright designs,
　　　　And works his sovereign will.

Ye fearful saints fresh courage take,
　　　　The clouds ye so much dread
Are big with mercy and shall break
　　　　In blessings on your head.

Judge not the Lord by feeble sense,
　　　　But trust him for his grace;
Behind a frowning providence,
　　　　He hides a smiling face.

His purposes will ripen fast,
　　　　Unfolding ev'ry hour;
The bud may have a bitter taste,
　　　　But sweet will be the flow'r.

Blind unbelief is sure to err
　　　　And scan his work in vain;
God is his own interpreter,
　　　　And he will make it plain.

LITTLE LOST PUP

Arthur Guiterman

He was lost! – Not a shade of a doubt of that;
     For he never barked at a slinking cat,
But stood in the square where the wind blew raw,
     With a drooping ear and a trembling paw,

And a mournful look in his pleading eye
     And a plaintive sniff at the passer-by
That begged as plain as a tongue could sue,
     "O Mister! Please may I follow you?"

A lorn wee waif of a tawny brown,
     Adrift in the roar of a heedless town.
Oh, the saddest of sights in a world of sin,
     Is a little lost pup with his tail tucked in!

Now he shares my board and he owns my bed,
     And he fairly shouts when he hears my tread;
Then, if things go wrong, as they sometimes do,
     And the world is cold and I'm feeling blue,

He asserts his right to assuage my woes
     With a warm, red tongue and a nice, cold nose
And a silky head on my arm or knee
     And a paw as soft as a paw can be.

When we rove the woods for a league about
     He's as full of pranks as a school let out,
For he romps and frisks like a three months colt,
     And he runs me down like a thunderbolt.

Oh, the blithest of sights in the world so fair
Is a gay little pup with his tail in the air!

LITTLE MEG AND I

C. T. Murphy

You ask me, mates to spin a yarn
  Before we go below;
Well, as the night is calm and fair,
  And no chance for a blow,
I'll give you one, a story as true
  As ever yet was told;
For, mates, I wouldn't lie about the dead'
  No, not for all the gold.
The story's of a maid and lad,
  Who loved in days gone by.
The maiden was Meg Anderson,
  The lad, messmates, was I.

A neater, trimmer craft than Meg
  Was very hard to find;
Why, she could climb a hill
  And make five knots agin the wind;
And as for larnin, hulks and spars!
  I've often heard it said,
That she could give the scholars points
  And then come out ahead:
The old schoolmaster used to say,
  And mates, it made me cry,
That the smartest there was little Meg,
  The greatest dunce was I.

But, what cared I for larnin then,
  While she was by my side?
For tho' a lad, I loved her, mates,
  And for her would have died.
And she loved me, the little lass,
  And often have I smiled,
When she said, "I'll be your little wife"—
  'Twas the prattle of a child.
For there lay a gulf between us, mates,
  With the water running high,
On one side stood Meg Anderson,
  On the other side stood I.

Meg's fortune was twelve ships at sea,
        And houses on the land,
While mine—why, mates,
        You might have held my fortune in your hand.
Her father owned a vast domain,
        For miles along the shore.
My father owned a fishing smack,
        A hut and nothing more.
I knew that Meg I ne'er could win,
        No matter how I try,
For on a couch of down lay she,
        On a bed of straw lay I.

I never thought of leaving Meg,
        Or Meg of leaving me,
For we were young and never dreamed
        That I should go to sea.
'Till one bright morning father said,
        "There's a whale ship in the bay,
I want you, Bill, to make a cruise;
        You go aboard today."
Well, mates, in two weeks from that time,
        I bade them all goodbye,
While on the dock stood little Meg,
        And on the deck stood I.

I saw her oft before we sailed,
        When ere I came on shore,
And she would say, "Bill, when you're gone,
        I'll love you more and more,
And I'll promise to be true to you,
        Through all the coming years."
But while she spoke her bright blue eyes
        Would fill with pearly tears;
Then as I whispered words of hope
        An' kissed her eyelids dry,
Her last words were, "God speed you, Bill!"
        So parted Meg and I.

Well, mates, we cruised for four long years,
        Till at last one summer day,
Our good ship, the Minerva,
        Cast anchor in the bay;

Oh! How my heart beat high with hope,
     As I saw her home once more,
And on the pier stood hundreds
     To welcome us ashore;
But heart sank down within me
     As I gazed with anxious eye—
No little Meg stood on the dock
     As on the dock stood I.

Why, mates, it nearly broke my heart
     When I went ashore that day,
For they told me little Meg had wed,
     While I was far away.
They told me too, they forced her to't,
     And wrecked her fair young life;
Just think, messmates, a child in years,
     To be an old man's wife!
But her father said it must be so,
     And what could she reply,
For she was only just sixteen,
     Just twenty-one was I.

Well, mates, a few short years from then—
     Perhaps it mighta been four—
One blustering night Jack Glynn and I
     Were rowing to the shore,
When right ahead we saw a sight,
     That made us hold our breath,
There floating in the pale moonlight
     Was a woman cold in death;
I raised her up—Ah! God, messmates,
     That I had passed her by,
For in the bay lay little Meg,
     And over her stood I.

Next day I laid poor Meg away;
     And nightly on the wave,
My spirit wanders forth to keep
     A watch beside her grave;

Her father knows not where she lies,
        Nor he who her betrayed;
There's no one but Bill who knows
        Where little Meg is laid.
In a quiet grove of willows,
        Her father's house hard by,
There sleeps in peace my little Meg,
        And here, messmates, am I.

THE BRIDGE BUILDER

W. A. Dromgoole

An old man traveling a lone highway
Came at the evening, cold and gray,
To a chasm, vast and deep and wide
Through which was flowing a sullen tide.
The old man crossed in the twilight dim—
The sullen stream held no fear for him—
But he turned when he reached the other side
And built a bridge to span the tide.

"Old man," said a fellow pilgrim near,
"You are wasting your strength in building here.
Your journey will end with the ending day—
You never again will pass this way.
You have crossed the chasm, deep and wide.
Why build you this bridge at the eventide?"

The builder lifted his old gray head.
"Good friend, in the path I have come," he said
"There followeth after me today
A youth whose feet must pass this way.
This chasm that has been naught to me,
To that fair-haired youth may a pitfall be.
He, too, must cross in the twilight dim.
Good friend, I am building the bridge for him."

MA'S OLD GALVANIZED WASHTUB

Author Unknown

Did you ever have to take a Saturday bath
An' try to wash an' scrub,
While squattin' down on your haunches,
In a galvanized washing tub?
If not, than you ain't missed a thing,
But now I'm tellin' you what's right,
I done it 'til I wuz almost grown
An' every doggone Saturday night!

In summer it was bad enough,
But, in winter it was rough;
Spreading papers, buckets and kettles
An' all that sort of stuff.
Getting' ready for that ordeal
Was only half the rub
Of takin' a bath on Saturday night
In a galvanized washin' tub.

Did you ever stand there stripped to the skin,
A wood stove bakin' your hide?
A dreadin' to put your dern foot in
Fer fear you'd be burned alive?
Finally you'd git the' temperature right,
An' you'd slink in the tub like a frog,
That cold steel tank 'ud touch your skin
An' you'd squeal like a fresh stuck hog!

Then you'd get outa that tub next to the stove
And there drippin' and shakin',
The front of your body is freezing to death
While the back of your body is a bakin'.
Shiverin' 'n shakin', burnin' 'n' bakin',
That's the price I had to pay.
That awful ordeal'll haunt me
Until I'm old and gray.

I ain't done yet . . . there's somethin' else
That I've been wantin' to say.
I wuz the youngest of all us kids
Who bathed on Saturday.
We all bathed accordin' to age
And I fell last in order,
Which meant I had to wash myself
In their dad-blamed dirty water.

Now, I'm a guy of clean habits
And believe in a bath a week,
It helps to keep me healthy
And freshen my physique.
But if I had my druthers,
I'd rather eat a bug
Than to have to take my Saturday bath
In a galvanized washin' tub!

NATURE CALLING

Robert X. Leeds

I yearn for the days of long ago
In a log cabin lit by a wood fire's glow,
Without the acid rain and fog,
Without the traffic. Without the smog.

Take me back to a bygone day
Where the buffalo roamed and the antelope played,
When birds announced the time to rise,
Home grown food and home-made pies.

Return me to nature's pastoral scenes,
Pristine fields and trout laden streams.
Give me wild flowers, birds and towering trees,
My forefather's life, but indoor plumbing, please.

MALICE AFORETHOUGHT

John Large

The P.I. gazed upon the girl,
And sized her up like this:
"Apparently, you're half my age,
A pretty teenage miss;

Your hair is chic and really blonde,
Your garb is class, per se.
The sum of which defines you as
An evil stalker's prey."

"Amazing!" sighed the pretty miss.
"Not really," he denied.
"My observation's rather keen,
My knowledge very wide."

"I mean," said she, "amazing that
Someone could be so wrong.
I'm thirty-nine, my hair is dyed,
The clothes cost me a song."

"Oh, well," he said, offhandedly,
"I'm slightly out of line,
But trust me lady, if you please
And make your problem mine."

"I have a constant urge," said she,
"To rub all lawyers out,
To murder every one of them
'Til there's not one about!"

"I think you'd better heed my words,"
Advised the private eye.
"I can't control your wicked yen,
But let's give this a try:

Kill all the lawyers, save the one
You'll find in the twilight zone,
For at your trial, you're going to need
A Clarence Darrow clone."

MISMATCHED

Nancy Rustici

They met in spring when life was a force,
    And youth made them sure of their future's course.
They wed in the fall when the leaves were red
    And snuggled up close for the cold ahead.
        But Ben was a doer of quiet deeds,
        And she loved a golden word.

For barely a year while love was new,
    They buried their difference, and faith was true.
But restless for comfort, she dreamed of song,
    And blind to her wanting, he plodded along.
        For Ben was doer of quiet deeds,
        And she loved a golden word.

He built her a home of the strongest oak
    And mourned at her careless ways.
She sang less and less, for she shriveled inside
    Then finally, wandered away.
        For Ben was a doer of quiet deeds,
        And she longed for a golden word.

Ben found him a woman, silent and bland,
    Who cooked, scrubbed, and worked with a will.
She found her a poet, with crooning sighs,
    Who cared not for working at all.
        Now Ben had a doer of quiet deeds,
        And she'd found the golden words.

Ben found that his own work no longer would please,
    And he dreamed of her carefree song.
She worried and worked for her poet and self
    And dreamed of Ben, quiet and strong.
        She longed for a doer of golden deeds;
        Ben yearned for her quiet words.

Did they reunite in tearful joy
    And promise to love and forget?
Not likely, for life's not so easy to fix;
    And love, losing twice, hard to give.
        Now she dreams of the doer of quiet deeds.
        Whilst Ben dreams of her quiet words.

Mc CAFFERY

Author Unknown

(From A Prison Wall)

When I was eighteen years of age
Into the army I did engage.
I left my job with good intent
To join the Forty-Second Regiment.

To Fullford Barracks I did go
To spend my time at that depot.
And during that time I came to know
That Captain Hammond was my foe.

As I was stationed on guard one day,
Three comrades' children came out to play.
My Captain from his quarters came,
And ordered me to take their parents' names.

I took one name instead of three.
With neglect of duty he then charged me.
And when my papers they were signed,
Fourteen days to barracks I was then confined.

And when off duty I was disengaged,
My head and mind all filled with rage,
With loaded rifle I did prepare
To shoot my Captain on the Barracks Square.

I did the deed. I shed his blood.
At Liverpool Assizes my trial I stood;
And the judge he said, "McCaffery,
Prepare yourself for the Gallows Tree.

I have no father to take my part.
Nor no fond mother to break her heart,
But I have one friend and a girl is she,
Who would lay down her life to set McCaffery free.

Now all you young soldiers take a warning from me.
Treat all your officers with civility.
For if you don't it will be too late
And you'll share the sad fate of young McCaffery.

NEVER SPEND THE PRINCIPAL

Rosalie Kramer

I hear it more now every day.
From heaven above I hear him say,
"Remember you promised dear old Ray,
You'd never spend the principal."

I'm hearing his voice when in the shower.
I even heard him in the Eiffel Tower,
Repeating his warning on the hour,
"Don't you dare spend the principal!"

My stock has tripled over the years,
Yet I am constantly immersed in tears
When dealing with my silly fears
That I might spend the principal.

I want to give my children a gift
And now my face sure needs a lift,
But here I sit knowing he'd be miffed
If he guessed I'd spent the principal.

After I'm gone I see it clear:
A Corvette for my daughter dear,
A Rolls Royce for my son, I fear,
'Cause I didn't spend the principal.

I hope my children will want to save
Enough for flowers to cover my grave
After they've spent every cent we made,
Both the interest and the principal!

MR. McJONES

Faith Frances Berlin

As fine a man as ever there was,
    As ever a man alive,
Was my dear 'usband, Mr. McJones.
    Long may 'is memory thrive.

For forty years the two of us shared
    A flat an' a small bathroom.
For forty years we managed, an' that
    'E called our " 'oneymoon".

There was ten more years of 'im belchin' 'is beers.
    "I'm sure to see ninety," 'e said.
But 'e carried a chair from 'ere to there
    One day, an' 'e dropped down dead.

So I props 'im up on the chair right there
    For I 'ated to see 'im sprawl
On the kitchen floor where a minute before
    I'd seen a cockroach crawl.

I props 'im up with a twelve-ounce mug
    In 'is fist, like 'e'd sat all 'is nights,
An' the twelve-inch telly on top of 'is belly,
    The channel tuned in to the fights.

And 'e looked so fine, that 'usband of mine,
    So fine that I tied 'im in.
While I had my tea and some cake, for we'd
    Just opened a brand new tin.

An' 'e loved 'em so. Sweet cakes, ya know;
    Adored 'em when 'e was alive,
So I shoved one into 'is face in case
    'E felt 'e was bein' deprived.

It crumbled a bit, but I let 'im sit
    With icing a-smear on 'is shirt
'Cause I knew 'ow 'e'd hate to be caught with a plate
    Like some *"fancy,"* for 'e preferred dirt.

Oh yes, but 'e did! An' quite often 'e 'id
      A sandwich inside of 'is pants
In 'is pocket an' when 'e got 'ungry again,
      'E'd eat it . . . along with some ants.

'E wasn't the kind to be stiff or refined
      Drinkin' wine? No! 'E liked 'is cheap ales.
An' I never, by God, saw a mountain of sod
      As was under that man's fingernails.

'E bathed now an' then, but I can't think of when
      Was the last time 'e 'onored the tub.
Must 'ave been last July when 'is buddies stopped by
      For a beer, all 'is pals from the pub.

Celebratin' 'is birthday, 'e said, an' I served
      'Em all chicken an' spuds by the sack,
Wond'rin' all of the while where 'e'd got such a pile?
      Robbed a bank? Won a bet at the track?

Well, 'e never explained. When I later complained,
      'E back-'anded me one, an' one more.
"I found it," 'e laughed, "in yer bag." Then 'e asks
      What the 'ell I'd be needin' it for.

"Don' I pay all the bills? Don' I buy all yer pills?
      Don' I see there's a roof over'ead?
Don' ya take me to task, lovey duck, 'n don' ask
      Me again or yer better off dead!"

Quite the gentleman, 'e. But 'e's through knockin' me
      Now, said I, an' I whacked 'im a blow
As 'e sat in 'is chair dead as dust, and I swear
      I'd of cried if I weren't laughin' so.

Then I left 'im to rest in 'is gravy-stained vest
      After stoppin' to open 'is eyes.
Dead or not, 'e'd be sore if I touched 'im once more
      So I stopped brushin' off all them flies.

Ah, 'e sat in that chair like a wormy-eyed bear
　　　　'Til the smell of 'im knocked ya flat.
An' the neighbors all swore somewhere under the floor
　　　　Was the carcass of Fogarty's cat.

An' the days they went past. . .an' each one was the last
　　　　I would say. . .but 'e still claimed the chair.
An' 'e started to rot, just a bit, but I got
　　　　Used to that an' 'is followin' stare.

An' I laughed at the flies layin' eggs in 'is eyes.
　　　　An' I laughed at the nits in 'is nose.
An' I laughed at the bugs crawlin' out of the rugs
　　　　For a feast on the yeast in 'is toes.

When they dragged 'im away in a body bag, say
　　　　They was pinchin' their lips an' their noses.
Oh, I'll tell you his mess could make pris'ners confess,
　　　　But to me 'twas the sweet smell of roses.

An' they made me go into a ward where the Doc
　　　　Comes to talk, but I've nothin' to say.
All 'is friends, 'ow they grieved. An' they never believed
　　　　This ol' story I'm tellin' today.

For as fine a man as ever there was,
　　　　As ever a man could be,
Was my dead 'usband, Mr. McJones.
　　　　Accordin' to them. . . Not me!

MY MALAMUTE DOG

Bill Foster

His flying feet skim o'er the jagged ice clumps,
With razor sharp edges that cut.
They bred him to run in this icy frontier,
With half frozen fish in his gut.

His veins hold a flood of the malamute blood;
His teeth show no yellow of age.
An' his flanks, long and lean and his eyes have that sheen
Like the scars that adorn his rib cage.

He runs at the head of a husky dog sled
Like wind through the powdered snowdrifts.
The mightiest dog that has ever been born,
He scoffs at Alaska's high cliffs.

He feels not the clip of the cold rawhide whip.
He's immune to the loud cry of "Mush."
He's anxious to run for the joy and the fun
Through the ice and the snow and the slush.

His hair seems to glow when it's forty below
As he jogs with the North in his face.
He thrives on the sting that a sleet storm can bring,
While the wind sprays his eyes with her mace.

My God, see his beauty, he's wild and he's free,
A true, "land bound eagle" in flight.
His huge muscles ripple beneath the taut hide
As he twists like the tail of a kite.

God bless his beauty and God bless his cry
That long lonesome howl and whine.
And God bless the card game in Fairbanks that night,
That made this big malamute mine!

MY SWEETHEART OF LONG AGO

Herbert H. Taylor

That is her picture standing there,
　　The one with the full round face
And the laughing mouth and dark-brown hair
　　And the handsome throat and the lace.
And I almost seem to hear her speak,
　　For again I feel the spell
Of the music sweet that her lips have sung—
　　The songs that I loved so well.

In dreamland I often see her face
　　And it always grieves me so
To think she is lost to me evermore,
　　My sweetheart of long ago.
But these are the things that we must expect
　　As our hearts with memories fill.
A silver cup may be dimmed by neglect;
　　It will always be silver still.

When someone tells her the old, old tale
　　That I have so often told,
When someone binds on her dainty hand
　　A circlet of graven gold,
Will she give one thought to the vanished years,
　　Thinking of what is to be,
Knowing so well what she's always been
　　And will always be to me?

For whatever may come or whatever may go,
　　Though the picture may fade year by year,
There's a very warm spot in my heart I know
　　For the girl that I loved so dear.
And so I can say and always will
　　God bless her—I love her so
With all my heart, for she is still
　　My sweetheart of long ago.

O CAPTAIN! MY CAPTAIN!

Walt Whitman

(Written after the assination of President Lincoln)

O Captain! my Captain! our fearful trip is done,
The ship has weather'd every rack, the prize we sought is won,
The port is near, the bells I hear, the people all exulting,
While follow eyes the steady keel, the vessel grim and daring;
But O Heart! Heart! Heart!
  O the bleeding drops of red,
     Where on the deck my Captain lies,
       Fallen cold and dead.

O Captain! my Captain! rise up and hear the bells;
Rise up—for you the flag is flung—for you the bugle trills,
For you bouquets and ribbon'd wreaths—
                 For you the shores a-crowding,
For you they call, the swaying mass, their eager faces turning;
  Here Captain! dear father!
    This arm beneath your head!
      It is some dream that on the deck,
        You've fallen cold and dead.

My Captain docs not answer, his lips are pale and still,
My father does not feel my arm, he has no pulse nor will,
The ship is anchor'd safe and sound,
               Its voyage closed and done,
From fearful trip the victor ship comes in with object won;
  Exult O shores, and ring O bells!
    But I with mournful tread,
      Walk the deck my Captain lies,
        Fallen cold and dead.

OLD IRONSIDES

Oliver Wendell Holmes

(In 1830, eighteen years after U. S. frigate Constitution distinguished itself in the War of 1812, the federal govenment declared its intention to scrap the famous ship. Holmes penned this verse which swayed the conscience of the nation and the ship was saved. Her ensign still flies and she can still be viewed in Boston Harbor.)

Ay, tear her tattered ensign down!
 Long has it waved on high,
And many an eye has danced to see
That banner in the sky;
Beneath it rung the battle shout,
And burst the cannon's roar, —
The meteor of the ocean air
Shall sweep the clouds no more!

Her deck, once red with heroes' blood,
Where knelt the vanquished foe,
When winds were hurrying o'er the flood,
And waves were white below,
No more shall feel the victor's tread,
Or know the conquered knee; —
The harpies of the shore shall pluck
The eagle of the sea!

O, better that her shattered hulk
Should sink beneath the wave;
Her thunders shook the mighty deep,
And there should be her grave;
Nail to the mast her holy flag,
Set every threadbare sail,
And give her to the god of storms,
The lightning and the gale!

OLD JOHN HENRY

James Whitcomb Riley

Old John's jes' made o' the commonest stuff—
    Old John Henry.
He's tough, I reckon—but none too tough—
"Too much, though, 's better than not enough!"
    Says old John Henry.
He does his best; and when his best's bad,
He don't fret none, ner he don't get sad—
He simply 'lows it's the best he had,
    Old John Henry.

His doctern's jes' o' the plainest brand—
    Old John Henry.
"A smilin' face and a hearty hand
'S a religen 'at all folks understand,"
    Says old John Henry.
He's stove up some with rheumatiz,
And they hain't no shine on them shoes o' his
And his hair hain't cut, but his eye teeth is!
    Old John Henry.

He feeds hisself when the stock's all fed—
    Old John Henry.
And "sleeps like a babe" when he goes to bed—
"And dreams o' heaven and home made bread!"
    Says old John Henry.
He hain't refined as he'd ort to be
To fit the statutes of Poetry,
Nor his clothes don't fit him—but he fits me—
    Old John Henry.

'OSTLER JOE

George R. Sims

(Made famous by Mrs. James Brown Potter)

I stood at eve when the sun went down
  By a grave where a woman lies,
Who lured men's souls to the shores of sin
  With the light of wanton eyes;
Who sang the song that the siren sang
  On the treacherous Lunley height,
Whose face was as fair as a summer's day,
  And whose heart was as black as night.

Yet a blossom I fain would pluck today
  From the garden above her dust.
Not the languorous lily of soulless sin,
  Nor the blood red rose of lust.
But a sweet white blossom of holy love
  That grew in that one green spot,
In the arid desert of Phryne's life
  Where all else was parched and hot.

In the summer, when the meadows
  Were aglow with blue and red,
Joe, the 'ostler of "The Magpie,"
  And fair Annie Smith were wed;
Plump was Annie, plump and pretty,
  With a face as fair as snow,
He was anything but handsome,
  Was the "Magpie's" 'ostler Joe.

But he won the winsome lassie,
  The'd a cottage and a cow,
And her matronhood sat lightly
  On the village beauty's brow;
Sped the months, and came a baby—
  Such a blue-eyed baby boy!
Joe was working in the stables
  When they told him of his joy.

He was rubbing down the horses—
      Gave them then and there,
All a special feed of clover,
      Just in honor of his heir;
It had been his great ambition
      (And he told the horses so)
That the fates would send a baby
      Who might bear the name of Joe.

Little Joe, the child was christened
      And like babies grew apace,
He'd his mother's eyes of azure,
      And his fathers honest face;
Swift the happy years went over,
      Years of blue and cloudless sky,
Love was lord of that small cottage
      And the tempest passed them by.

Down the lane by Annie's cottage
      Chanced a gentleman to roam,
He caught a glimpse of Annie
      In her bright and happy home;
Thrice he came and saw her sitting
      By the window with her child,
And he nodded to the baby,
      And the baby laughed and smiled.

So at last it grew to know him
      (Little Joe was nearly four),
He would call the pretty "gemplum"
      As he passed the open door;
And one day he ran and caught him
      And in child's play pulled him in,
And the baby Joe had prayed for
      Brought about the mother's sin.

'Twas the same old wretched story
      That for ages bards have sung,
"Twas a woman, weak and wanton,
      And a villain's tempting tongue;
'Twas a picture deftly painted
      For silly creature's eyes,
Of the Babylonian wonders
      And the joy that in them lies.

Annie listened and was tempted—
     Was tempted and she fell,
As the angels fell from heaven
     To the blackest depth of hell;
She was promised wealth and splendor
     And a life of gentle sloth,
Yellow gold for child and husband—
     And the woman left them both.

Home one eve came Joe, the 'ostler,
     With a cheery cry of "wife!"
Finding that which blurred forever
     All the story of his life;
She had left a silly letter,
     Through the cruel scrawl he spelt,
Then he sought the lonely bedroom,
     Joined his horny hands and knelt.

"Now, O Lord, forgive her,
     For she ain't to blame," he cried;
"For I ought to seen her trouble
     And a-gone away and died;
Why a girl like her—God bless her—
     'Twasn't likely as her'd rest
With her bonny head forever
     On a 'ostler's ragged vest.

"It was kind o' her to bear with me,
     All the long and happy time,
So for my sake please to bless her,
     Though you count her deed a crime;
If so be I don't pray proper,
     Lord forgive me, for you see
I can talk all right to 'osses,
     But I'm kinder o' strange with Thee."

Ne'er a line came to the cottage
     From the woman who had flown,
Joe, the baby died that winter
     And the man was left alone;
Ne'er a bitter word he uttered,
     But in silence kissed the rod,
Saving what he told his horses,
     Saving what he told his God.

Far away in mighty London
  Rose the wanton into fame,
For her beauty won men's homage
  And she prospered in her shame;
Quick from lord to lord she flitted,
  Higher still each prize she won,
And her rivals paled beside her
  As the stars beside the sun.

Next she trod the stage half-naked
  And she dragged a temple down
To the level of a market
  For the women of the town;
And the kisses she had given
  To poor 'ostler Joe for naught,
With their gold and priceless jewels
  Rich and titled rousers bought.

Went the years with flying footsteps
  While her star was at its height.
Then the darkness came on swiftly
  And the gloaming turned to night;
Shattered strength and faded beauty
  Tore the laurels from her brow,
Of the thousands who had worshipped,
  Never one came near her now.

Broken down in health and fortune
  Men forgot her very name,
Till the news that she was dying
  Woke the echoes of her fame;
And the papers in their gossip
  Mentioned how an actress lay
Sick to death in humble lodgings,
  Growing weaker every day.

One there was who read the story
  In a far-off country place,
And that night the dying woman woke
  And looked upon his face;
Once again the strong arms clasped her
  That had clasped her long ago,
And the weary head lay pillowed
  Upon the breast of 'ostler Joe.

All the past he had forgiven—
        All the sorrow and the shame,
He had found her sick and lonely
        And his wife he now could claim;
Since the grand folks who had known her
        One and all had slunk away,
He could clasp his long-lost darling
        And no man could say him nay.

In his arms death found her lying,
        From his arms her spirit fled,
And his tears came down in torrents
        As he knelt beside his dead;
Never once his love had faltered,
        Through her sad unhallowed life,
And the stone above her ashes
        Bears the sacred name of wife.

That's the blossom I fain would pluck today
        From the garden above her dust,
Not the languorous lily of soulless sin,
        Nor the blood-red rose of lust;
But a sweet white blossom of holy love
        That grew in the one green spot,
In the arid desert of Phryne's life
        Where all else is parched and hot.

PALS

Charles F. Doran

When you're feeling sad and lonely
   And your "friends" all pass you by,
When there doesn't seem a single thing
   But to crawl away and die,

When the world is black and hollow,
   When you're buried in your woes —
Then, there comes a bark of welcome
   And a touch of a wet, cold nose.

While two hairy paws are clawing
   To scramble on your knees,
And a bushy tail is wagging,
   Two brown eyes say, "Master, please,

Let me crawl upon your bosom,
   Let me take my rightful place,"
And trying hard to lick the tear
   That's streaming down your face.

Could you find a better fellow
   If you searched the whole world through,
Who would stand by you in trouble
   And would always be truc-blue?

In his mind there is no question
   If or not the Master's right —
He's your pal if you're a pauper
   Or if you're a man of might.

Feed him then and give him shelter.
   Water when the sun is hot;
Do not be a self-made heathen.
   What would you do, if God forgot?

You're his God, friend, please be mindful,
   Do not let your memory clog.
Folk will know how large your soul is,
   By the way you treat a dog!

THE POLITICIAN

Michele S. Kurlander

He fills his lungs with air and struts
On stage—in full proud voice;
His pinstriped starched and blustery self
Masquerades as choice.

His public person tries to hide
His not-so-private bloat.
He tells us why he is the best
And asks us for our vote.

We want so much to find a man
To govern well and strong.
Unfortunately all we find
Are creatures crass and wrong.

Where are the statesmen, men of pride
Whose heads and hearts are good?
There once were men whose public words
Said truly where they stood.

But now the public figure is
Concerned alone with "spin."
His policies irrelevant,
His only goal to win.

The smell of money permeates
The marble walls of power.
The men who really care won't dare
To leave their ivory tower.

THE POPULAR SONG

By Herbert H. Taylor

If you want a receipe for that popular mystery
Known to the world as a popular song,
Take a fake story from newspaper history,
Get a soubrette to help push it along.

Never write sense; if you do you will rue it,
For no one will learn it or sing it for long;
Every bum actor will always go through it,
For he is the one who is making the song.

Never write words one could ever call clever,
For audiences never expect such a thing;
Then let 'em screech 'em forever and ever,
For who the hell hears what the chorus girls sing?

Let 'em have goblets, pretend to pour wine in 'em,
Then let 'em sing anything they durn please;
Dress 'em in tights if they only look fine in 'em,
People will then think of nothing but these.

As for the music, you'll manage that easily;
Get a few songs that were written before;
Swipe 'em and change 'em and have 'em sung breezily;
Get an arranger, you'll want nothing more.

A showman to publish your song is superior;
He'll force himself where a decent man will duck.
No thin cuticle mars a performer's exterior,
He's got the nerve and the devil's own luck.

So take my advice, throw your paper and ink away
If a big hit for next season you'd write;
Don't be afraid or endeavor to slink away,
Bow in response to your call the first night.

Though musicians may sneer at your work
And poo poo it all,
You needn't mind — not a line did you write;
You can laugh in your sleeves at their knocks
While you through it all fight for your royalties.*

*And boy do you fight!

121

OUR TWO OPINIONS

James Whitcomb Riley

Us two wuz boys when we fell out,
      Nigh to the age uv my youngest now;
Don't rec'lect what 'twuz about,
      Some small difference, I'll allow.
Lived next neighbors twenty years,
      A-hatin' each other, me 'nd Jim;
He havin' his opinyin uv me,
      'Nd I havin' mine uv him!

Grew up together 'nd wouldn't speak,
      Courted sisters, 'nd marr'd 'em, too;
'Tended same meetin'-house oncet a week,
      A-hatin' each other, through and through!
But when Abe Linkern asked the West
      F'r soldiers, we answered, me and Jim,
He havin' his opinyin uv me,
      'Nd I havin' mine of him!

But down in Tennessee one night
      Ther wuz sound uv firin' ou' way.
'Nd the Sergeant allowed there'd be a fight
      With the Johnnie Rebs some time nex'
day;
'Nd as I wuz thinkin' uv Lizzie 'nd home,
      Jim stood afore me, long 'nd slim;
He havin' his opinyin uv me,
      'Nd I havin' mine uv him!

Seemed like we knew there wuz gin' to be
      Serious trouble f'r me and him;
Us two schuck hands, did Jim 'nd me,
      But never a word from Jim or me!
He went his way, 'nd I went mine,
      'Nd into the battle roar went we,
I havin' my opinyin uv Jim,
      'Nd he havin' his of me.

Jim never come back from the war again,
  But I hain't forgot that last, last night,.
When waitin' f'r orders, us two men
  Made up 'nd schuck hands afore the fight.
'Nd after all, it's soothin' to know
  That here I be, 'nd yond'rs Jim,
He havin' his opinyin uv me,
  'Nd I havin' mine uv him!

OUTSIDE ARE DOGS

Bertha A. Ellis

Outside the gates, the pearly gates,
  They wait, above the stars,
Peering with eager, wistful eyes
  Between the golden bars.
Hoping the man they loved on earth
  Or the little boy who died,
May wander to the gates and pat
  The little heads outside.

I do not feel that I could rest
  Within the gates of gold,
Knowing those loving, faithful hearts
  Were waiting in the cold.
So when the call for me shall come
  To cross the great divide,
Perhaps the Lord will let me have
  A little place outside.

PARSON SNOW'S HINT

Author Unknown

The sermon was affecting
And so many hearers wept,
That no dust would have arisen,
Had the floor just than been swept.
In fact a score of brothers
Were impressed to that extent,
That they didn't see the "sasser"
When it on its mission went.

When the preacher had concluded,
He looked 'round upon the crowd,
And he said, "I'll make a few remarks
If I may be allowed.
I'm not used to mincin' matters,
And what I'm about to say,
Will be addressed to you, my friends,
In my accustomed way.

This is my fust sarmon 'mongst you,
And it pleases me to see
That the fountains ob your feelings
Am so broke up so easily;
But dar's one thing I has noticed,
That hab filled me wid unrest,
And left the knife ob discontent
A stickin' in my breast.

I understands de salaries
Ob preachers down dis way,
Come frum de contribution box.
Now, what I've seen today
Hab sowed some seeds ob doubt,
And fear within my aged breast,
Dat hab done commenced a-growin'
In a way dat I can't rest.

124

Although old age hab somewhat dimmed
        De keeness ob my sight,
It hain't had no effect,
        As yet, upon my appetite.
And anything dat threatens
        To decrease my bread an' meat,
Just takes me by the tender ha'r,
        And lif's me off my feet.

Let your sympathetic tears, my fren's,
        In de future freshly flow—
Don't run in onions on me—
        Don't use de old man so.
Wid all de brudders weepin',
        An' de sisters wid red eyes,
I feel like I could see saved souls
        A-mountin' to de skies.

But de best tings in dis worl', my friends,
        Can all be overdone,
An dis weepin' ober sarmons,
        We must all admit is one,
Use your handerchuffs wid judgement,
        And no mattah who you are,
Keep a dry eye on the sasser;
        Let us now unite in prayer!"

PAUL REVERE'S RIDE

Henry Wadsworth Longfellow

Listen my children, and you shall hear
Of the midnight ride of Paul Revere,
On the eighteenth of April, in Seventy-five;
Hardly a man is now alive
Who remembers that famous day and year.

He said to his friend, "If the British march
By land or sea from the town tonight,
Hang a lantern aloft in the belfry arch
Of the North Church tower a signal light,—
One, if by land, and two if by sea;
And I on the opposite shore will be,
Ready to ride and spread the alarm
Through every Middlesex village and farm,
For the country folk to be up and to arm."

Then he said, "Good night!" and with muffled oar
Silently rowed to the Charlestown shore,
Just as the moon rose over the bay,
Where swinging wide at her moorings lay
The *Somerset*, British man-of-war;
A phantom ship, with each mast and spar
Across the moon like a prison bar,
And a huge black hulk, that was magnified
By its own reflection in the tide.

Meanwhile, his friend through alley and street
Wanders and watches, with eager ears,
Till in the silence around him he hears
The muster of men at the barrack door,
The sound of arms, and the tramp of feet,
And the measured tread of the Grenadiers,
Marching down to their boats on the shore.

Then he climbed the tower of the Old North Church,
By the wooden stairs, with stealthy tread,
To the belfry-chamber overhead,
And startled the pigeons from their perch
On the sombre rafters, that round him made
Masses and moving shapes of shade,—

By the trembling ladder, steep and tall,
To the highest window in the wall,
Where he paused to listen and look down
A moment on the roofs of the town
And the moonlight flowing over all.

Beneath in the churchyard, lay the dead,
In their night-encampment on the hill,
Wrapped in silence so deep and still
That he could hear, like a sentinel's tread
The watchful night-wind, as it went
Creeping along from tent to tent,
And seeming to whisper, "All is well!"
A moment only he feels the spell
Of the place and the hour, and the secret dread
Of the lonely belfry and the dead;
For suddenly all his thoughts are bent
On a shadowy something far away,
Where the river widens to meet the bay,
A line of black that bends and floats
On the rising tide, like a bridge of boats.

Meanwhile, impatient to mount and ride
Booted and spurred, with a heavy stride
On the opposite shore walked Paul Revere.
Now he patted his horse's side,
Now gazed at the landscape far and near,
Then, impetuous, stamped the earth,
And turned and tightened his saddle girth;
But mostly he watched with eager search
The belfry's tower of the Old North Church,
As it rose above the graves on the hill,
Lonely and spectral and sombre and still.
And lo! As he looks, on the belfry height
A glimmer, and then a gleam of light!
He springs to the saddle, the bridle he turns,
But lingers and gazes, till full on his sight
A second lamp in the belfry burns!

A hurry of hoofs in a village street,
A shape in the moonlight, a bulk in the dark,
And beneath, from the pebbles, in passing, a spark
Struck out by a steed flying fearless and fleet;

That was all! And yet, through the gloom and the light,
The fate of a nation was riding that night;
And the spark struck out by that steed, in his flight
Kindled the land into flame with its heat.
He has left the village and mounted the steed,
And beneath him, tranquil and broad and deep,
Is the Mystic, meeting the ocean tides;
And under the alders that skirt its edge,
Now soft on the sand, now loud on the ledge,
Is heard the tramp of his steed as he rides.

It was twelve by the village clock,
When he crossed the bridge into Medford town.
He heard the crowing of the cock,
And the barking of the farmer's dog,
And he felt the damp of the river fog,
That rises after the sun goes down.

It was one by the village clock,
When he galloped into Lexington.
He saw the gilded weathercock
Swim in the moonlight as he passed,
And the meeting-house windows, blank and bare,
Gaze at him with a spectral glare,
As if they already stood aghast
At the bloody work they would look upon.

It was two by the village clock,
When he came to the bridge in Concord town.
He heard the bleating of the flock,
And the twitter of birds among the trees
And felt the breath of the morning breeze
 Blowing over the meadows brown.
And one was safe and asleep in his bed
Who at the bridge would be first to fall,
Who that day would be lying dead,
Pierced by a British musket-ball.

You know the rest. In books you have read,
How the British Regulars fired and fled,—
How the farmers gave them ball for ball,

Chasing the redcoats down the lane,
Then crossing the fields to emerge again
Under the trees at the turn of the road,
And only pausing to fire and load.
So through the night rode Paul Revere;
And so through the night went his cry of alarm
To every Middlesex village and farm,—
A cry of defiance, and not of fear,
A voice in the darkness, a knock at the door,
And a word that shall echo for evermore!
For, borne on the night-wind of the Past,
Through all our history, to the last,
In the hour of darkness and peril and need,
The people will waken and listen to hear
The hurrying hoof-beats of that steed,
And the midnight message of Paul Revere.

PAW MARKS

W. J. Hickmott, Jr.

On the floor I see the marks of muddy footprints.
      My favorite chair is graced with long grey hair.
The windowpane has smudgy little nose marks.
      But you know – I love to see those dear marks there.

There's a bone behind the davenport, I fancy.
      A rubber doll lies lonesome on the floor.
A little leather harness on the table,
      A dog leash on the handle of the door.

I know they're out of place and look untidy,
      But yet, I think I like them on the whole.
They make a house a home —a place that's happy,
      A little puppy's paw marks on your soul.

POOR HUSBAND WHEN HIS WIFE'S AWAY

William Jerry Ayers

Poor husband when his wife's away,
Seems every hour is a lonely day.
TV-dinners, stale pizza and moldy cheese,
Dusty furniture that makes him sneeze.
Up at dawn, poor fellow can't sleep.
Blankets on the floor and freezing feet.
Dirty dishes and pots and stains on the rug,
No one there to tease and hug.

No one to fuss or tell him how,
To hang up his clothes and "Do it now."
No one there to pout and scold
Or to cheer him when he's feeling old.
He gets her letters full of woman talk,
But misses her song, her familiar walk.
Just to watch her fix her hair,
Rocking back and forth in her favorite old chair.

Poor husband without his loving wife,
Empty days and empty nights.
Oh, happy day when she comes back,
Goodbye blues. Farewell insomniac.
Come back sunshine, back home to stay.
Whatever's for dinner, it's Okay.
For there's one thing he cannot bare,
His home's not home when she's not there.

PRISON WALLS

Author Unknown

(From A Prison Wall)

I wish I had someone to love me;
Someone to call my own.
I wish I had someone to live with,
Cause I'm tired of living alone.

Please meet me tonight in the moonlight.
Please meet me tonight all alone;
'Cause I have a story to tell you,
A story that's never been known.

I'll be carried to a new jail tomorrow,
Leaving my poor darling alone,
With the cold prison bars all around me,
And my head on a pillow of stone.

I have a ship on the ocean,
All laden with silver and gold.
Before my poor darling shall suffer,
That ship will be anchored and sold.

If I had the wings of an angel,
O'er these prison walls I would fly.
I would fly to the arms of my darling,
And there I'd be willing to die.

(There are probably a thousand verses and versions of this prison poem. Sometimes it is sung. Sometimes it is recited. Ironically, in many prisons it is considered a "bad luck omen", and inmates are dissuaded from either reciting or singing the verses.)

QUIET! . . PLEASE

Faith Frances Berlin

Marvin Mathers was a very
        Quiet man, so solitary
        No one ever thought he'd marry,
        But when Cupid arched his bow
Marvin's heart capitulated,
        Though his future wife was gaited
        Faster, and articulated
        Endlessly, he loved her so.

Oh, but Marvin's soul required
        Silence. Nothing so inspired
        Joy within him as, when tired,
        He foresaw his evening's rest
As a priceless interlude
        Of peacefulness and quietude
        Where conversations don't intrude.
        But he was fruitless in this quest.

Therefore Marvin's marriage soured
        Shortly after love had flowered,
        For his dear beloved showered
        Endless words upon his ears.
 Blithely talking while ignoring
        That her mate pretended snoring.
        Dull as dirt and deathly boring
        Words can drive a man to tears.

Could it then have been surprising
        That he found no peace on rising
        As she rattled on advising
        Him on how to run his life?
In the bathroom while he's shaving,
        It was silence he was craving.
        As he listened to her raving
        He began to hate his wife.

And the topic didn't matter.
        Drivel, drivel, chatter, chatter.
        He began to want to splatter
        All her brains against the wall.

Solitude and contemplation
    Murdered by her conversation
    Over gas or constipation,
    And she made no sense at all.

Twenty years of talk unceasing;
    Volume rising and increasing,
    Marvin never once releasing
    Angry words to stem the flow.
Biting tongue and clamping down on
    Words society would frown on;
    Rages deep enough to drown on,
    Marvin never let them go.

Twenty years of words a-tumble
    From her lips, a mindless jumble,
    Marvin lived within a jungle,
    Snarled in verbs; a wall of vines.
And then suddenly it happened.
    Something deep in Marvin snapped and
    There she lay – her jaw still flappped and
    Quivered.   She forgot her lines.

Wrap the rope around her tighter!
    Take your trusty pocket lighter,
    Flick the Bic and then ignite her!
    He delighted in her screams.
Axed her into fifty pieces,
    Then, still feeling quite capricious,
    Boiled her down to bones and greases,
    Going somewhat to extremes.

Had his passion then abated?
    Was his thirst for silence sated?
    No! He never hesitated
    With the work that he was at.
And without a shred of pity,
    Marvin hummed a catchy ditty
    As he called, "Come here, my pretty"
    And he fed her to the cat.

Neighbors call? She's on vacation.
    Missing? Bah! Express vexation.
    Keep the light of your elation
    Hidden in your hooded eyes.

Move and leave them no addresses.
    All they've got is talk and guesses.
    He's a fool if he confesses.
    Smile and learn to love your lies.

Years elapse, and Marvin tarries
    With a lady whom he marries,
    But this time the action varies
    As the blush fades from the bloom.
At the slightest indication
    Of his new wife's inclination
    To indulge in conversation,
    Marvin seals her like a tomb.

With a single glance so chilling
    She is suddenly unwilling
    To continue. Piercing, killing,
    Is the silent look he throws.
While it so far has deterred her
    From excess, with every word her
    Husband's contemplating murder
    Number two, for now he knows.

Life, regrettably is short for
    Second wives who fail to seize
    What is meant when Marvin Mathers
    Turns to murmur, "Quiet! . . . Please."

PALS

Mae Norton Morris

When I see a boy who hasn't a dog,
    Or a dog that hasn't a boy—
    I think of the lot they are missing
    Of frolic and genuine joy.

Some parents think dogs are a nuisance,
    Just something to bark and annoy—
They can't know how badly a boy needs a dog
    Or how sadly a dog needs a boy.

THE COVERED BRIDGE

Author Unknown

Tell the fainting soul in the weary form,
    There's a world of the purest bliss
That is linked as the soul and form are linked
    By a covered bridge like this.

Yet to reach that realm on the other shore,
    We must pass through a transient gloom,
And must walk unseen, unhelped and alone,
    Through that covered bridge—the tomb.

But we all pass over on equal terms
    For the universal toll
Is the outer garb, which the hand of God
    Has flung around the soul.

Though the eye is dim, and the bridge is dark
    And the river it spans is wide,
Yet faith points through to a shining mount
    That looms on the other side.

To enable our feet in the next day's march
    To climb up that golden ridge,
We must all lie down for a one night's rest
    Inside of the covered bridge.

RAGS

Edmund Vance Cooke

We called him "Rags".   He was just a cur,
But twice, on the Western Line,
That little old bunch of faithful fur
Had offered his life for mine.
And all that he got was bones and bread,
Or the leavings of soldier-grub,
But he'd give his heart for a pat on the head,
Or a friendly tickle and rub.

And Rags got home with the regiment,
And then, in the breaking away —
Well, whether they stole him, or whether he went,
I am not prepared to say.
But we mustered out, some to beer and gruel,
And some to sherry and shad,
And I went back to the Sawbones School,
Where I still was an undergrad.

One day they took us budding M.D.'s
To one of those institutes
Where they demonstrate every new disease
By means of bisected brutes.
They had one animal tacked and tied
And slit like a full-dressed fish,
With his vitals pumping away inside
As pleasant as one might wish.

I stopped to look like the rest, of course,
And the beast's eyes leveled mine
His short tail thumped with a feeble force,
And he uttered a tender whine.
It was Rags, yes, Rags! Who was martyred there,
Who was quartered and crucified,
And he whined that whine which is doggish prayer
And he licked my hand – and died.

And I was no better in part nor whole
Then the gang I was found among,
And his innocent blood was on the soul
Which he blessed with his dying tongue.
Well! I've seen men go to courageous death
In the air, on sea, on land!
But only a dog would spend his last breath
In a kiss for his murderer's hand.

And if there's no Heaven for love like that,
For such four-legged fealty — well!
If I have any choice, I tell you flat,
I'll take my chance in Hell.

MR. BONES

Dixie Wilson

An open door and a patch of sun
Where a comrade used to be,
And a little phantom brown-eyed tramp
Is somewhere waiting the step of me.

They say Heaven's light is beyond the dark
And there's peace beyond compare;
So tell me, shall a joyous bark
And a gladsome tail be there?

With my first strange unfamiliar steps
In a wide and far-off land,
Dare I know a small cold friendly nose
Will be reaching for my hand?

I ask no mansions wrought of gold,
Nor streets of precious stones . . .
Dear God, build just a little house,
For me – and Mr. Bones.

RETROSPECTION

Author Unknown

In the heart of Massachusetts there's a city I recall
    With a longing for my wayward boyhood days,
And a retrospective musing as the evening shadows fall
    Merges sad regrets and useless tears always.

But to everyone there's some place that he likes to know as "home",
    And that is why here in New York today
(Though I love it clear from Harlem down to Pulitzer's old dome)
    That I write of Worcester on the "B. and A."

And my earliest remembrance is it took about an hour
    To ride out on the old "New Worcester" car;
We had no electric motor — it was run by Jackass power,
    And the driver I recall was David Barr.

And when father gave me seven cents for carfare to the store,
    As soon as he had placed it in my hand
I used to start and walk down town and wish that I had more
    To spend at Charlie Goodwin's peanut stand.

The amusement I remember most enjoyed about that date
    There are others that since pleased me more, I think),
Was to be allowed to enter and to have the price to skate
    At H. H. Bigalow's roller-skating rink.

I remember Burnham Wardwell gave a lecture in that rink
    (I believe they wouldn't let him speak elsewhere),
But if he elected Hades as a place to speak, I think,
    Bigelow said he'd build a rink for Burnham there.

"Old Settler" writes me of two men he used to know of then,
    Whose canine appellations he believes
Of "bulldog" and of "pointer" have no reference to the men,
    Who were popularly (?) called "the forty thieves".

Then referring to the members of the Worcester County Bar
    (Of whom he makes me but a brief report),
He alludes to Geo F. Verry, F. T. Blackmer, Bacon, Hoar,
    And Judge Williams of the Central District court.

And he speaks about a law-suit that occurred once in this place
      Where General Spargue was plaintiff – years ago,
And Bigelow got Ben Butler up to help defend the case,
      But Butler failed to land the knock-out blow.

Then how Baron Hoyt, the truckman, his disgrace in teas attested
      When "Georgie" stole a horse and ran away;
His grief was most pathetic til he was himself arrested
      For stealing from the Commonwealth Café.

Our police force was imposing in those days in very truth
      When Col. J. M. Drennan held full sway,
And the shrewdness of the Pinkertons and cunning of Old Sleuth
      Were embodied in Detective Pat O'Day;

And I won't forget to mention in my worse than wretched rhymes,
      How Christy said he didn't care a damn
For all the Does and Baldwins, nor the Worcester Daily Times,
      And regaled us with the Sunday Telegram,

Which reported to its readers how a gorgeous wedding looked;
      Harry Smith I know it said had drawn a prize,
And the Telegram conceded that the victuals were well cooked
      And the horses all had diamonds 'stead of eyes.

Well, here's to good old Worcester – you are better there than here,
      And may the Lord have mercy on your souls,
For me a large plain lobster and a stein or two of beer
      And a plate of Mrs. Morgan's home-made rolls.

SAM THE CLAM'S DISCO

Robert X. Leeds

(With apologies to Tony Bennett)

Sam the Clam was a crusty crustacean
Who lived at the bottom of the sea.
A lady's man. . . (and if she swam)
You can bet that's where Sam the Clam'd be.

Now Ollie the Oyster was by gender the same
But by nature quite different indeed.
For nightlife and women just wasn't his game
A mollusk, though not the same breed.

So who can explain that life's little game
Would divine these sea urchins to meet?
But isn't it fact that opposites attract
Though they met in a subterranean leat?

Now Ollie the Oyster spent his time in the brine
In schools as good mollusks do,
While Sam (it is said) went from bed to bed to bed,
And his evenings might be considered as lewd.

But with some misgivin', Ollie envied the livin'
His friend Sam would bring him each day.
And although not restrained, he always refrained
From "going too far" (as they say).

As the years passed on through, their friendship just grew
And they both took an oath never to be parted.
That despite all that may, they would always find a way
To go on the same way they started.

But alas and alack, Sam the Clam took a track
That led him to beds and regret.
For he found a surprise and his sudden demise
In the grasp of a fisherman's net.

Sam the Clam found too late that we all have a date,
And in the end there is no magic Genie.
For he soon would be missed when he ended up dished
With some friends on a plate of linguini.

"St. Peter," Sam pleaded, "I did what was needed,
I was simply good will in a shell."
"Maybe so, we concede, but you exceeded the need,"
And St. Peter wished him better luck in Hell.

And Ollie the Oyster withdrew in a shell
And his remorse was certainly stellar.
He knew he was jaded when he ended up plated
And served up as Oysters Rockefeller.

The Gate was opened wide when Ollie arrived
And St Peter ushered him through when he landed.
A virtuous life, free of sin and of strife
Was the passport that heaven demanded.

"Now here are your wings and among other things
Here's a halo to wear o'er your crown.
They both are attached, so they won't come unlatched
And they'll go with your celestial gown.

Here's a gold harp for your care and I bid you beware,
For to lose it would be a great sin.
You must never forget it, or you'll sorely regret it
Because if outside, you'll ne'er get back in."

Though pleasures abounded, St. Pete was astounded
Poor Ollie found nothing to please him.
He withdrew in a shell, 'cause he so missed his pal
That St. Peter decided to treat him.

"Just what can we do? We would try if we knew,
Enjoy heaven! Come out of your shell!"
Ollie told his sore tale, how he missed his old pal
And would spend with him one week in Hell.

With such a request, St. Pete tried his best,
But no other option would pass.
So he agreed to the deal, he would let Ollie feel
The heat and the torment he asked.

"Take your harp and use care and I bid you beware,
For to lose it would be a great sin.
You must never forget it, or you'll sorely regret it,
Because from Hell you will never get back in."

In a flash it was rendered and Ollie was entered
To an inferno of fire frothing frogs.
So he made his own way to a noise down the way,
To a familiar voice coming out of the smog.

Ollie gasped in surprise at the sight 'fore his eyes,
A nightclub, blaring piano and drum,
With a bright neon sign and he read the design,
It read "Sam The Clam's Disco – Welcome."

There were spirits galore, in bottles, on floor,
And Sam, he was tending the bar,
And a six-fingered frog sang a strange dialogue
As he plucked on an eight stringed guitar.

An Elvis impersonator, in the form of a 'gator
Sang love songs and swiveled his hips,
And little fish swooned to the words that he crooned
And the waitress loved their fish and tips.

When the two saw each other, like two long lost brothers
They fell into each other's arms.
Old times were renewed, and some stories too lewd,
To be recounted with all of their charms.

For seven long days they relived their ways,
With dancing and girls and brine-ale.
And for seven short nights they renewed the delights
Till the time caught them short on their trail.

Ollie awoke the eighth day, and to his dismay,
He was standing before Heaven's gate.
But he didn't go far, for his pathway was barred
By St. Peter who appeared most irate.

Ollie's mind did a twist; there was something he'd missed,
He remembered and then he did know,
The warning was plain and he sang out in pain —
Oops!   "I left my harp in Sam The Clam's Disco. . ."

SHE IS MORE TO BE PITIED THAN CENSURED

William B. Gray

At the old concert hall on the bowery
Round the table were seated one night
A crowd of young fellows carousing;
With them life seemed cheerful and bright.
At the very next table was seated
A girl who had fallen to shame.
All the young fellows jeered at her weakness
Till they heard an old woman exclaim:

She is more to be pitied then censured,
She is more to be helped than despised,
She is only a lassie who ventured
On life's stormy path ill advised.
Do not scorn her with words fierce and bitter,
Do not laugh at her shame and downfall;
For a moment just stop and consider
That a man was the cause of it all.

There's an old-fashioned church round the corner,
Where the neighbors all gathered one day
While the parson was preaching a sermon
O'er a soul that had just passed away.
'Twas the same wayward girl from the Bow'ry,
Who a life of adventure had led—
Did the clergyman jeer at her downfall?
No—he asked for God's mercy and said:

She is more to be pitied than censured,
She is more to be helped than despised,
She is only a lassie who ventured
On life's stormy path ill-advised.
Do not scorn her with words fierce and bitter,
Do not laugh at her shame and downfall;
For a moment just stop and consider
That a man was the cause of it all!

SHERRY

Author Unknown

(A Lady's Toast)

Here's to your health in amber wine,
    And a lifetime brief but merry;
I tip you a kiss from this glass of mine
    And pledge Young Love in sherry!
You may sing the praise of your rare old port,
    And your extra dry, my Honey;
But the cup I lift is the gods' own gift
    And can't be bought with money.
They may chant of the "crystal," sparkling, bright,
    And the moss-covered bucket at leisure;
But the cup for quaffing that gladdens my sight
    Is the chalice of passion and pleasure!

    Oh, 'tis so. Don't I know?
    You're in for it, once you begin it.
    As with wine, so with love, you'd better go slow,
    For the devil himself is in it!

Mon Cher, 'midst the smoke of your fragrant cigar,
    (Yes, I'm fond of that sort of thing –very),
I touch your glass for a "Here's how you are!"
    In this draught ('tis the third) of old sherry!
You may trust, mark my words, any man that you please,
    If you're made with a heart, and are human;
You may drink of love's sacrament, down to the lees,
    Provided, of course, you're a woman.

You may give him the blood from your heart—yes, 'tis
so—
    And starve everyday while you pet him;
But just make up your mind, from the very word Go,
    He'll drain that heart dry, if – you'll let him!
Then turn on his heel as he leisurely strikes
    A match, for "the smoke" that comes after;
And your pleading is flattery such as he likes,

Oh, 'tis so. Don't I know?
You're in for it, once you begin it.
As with love, so with wine, you'd better go slow,
For the devil himself is in it!

But 'tis better to "smile" than to sigh all the while,
  Life's brief, and so ought to be merry;
To live as you go is a pretty good style,
  (So, my boy, just a little more sherry!)
You'll be loath to believe it until you're a goner;
   But the peace in your heart (the branch from your dove)
    Will fill out but little, 'pon honor!
You may tell about trusting a man out of sight:
  All that kind of thing at your pleasure—
My ideas are more forcible, far, than polite;
  But a man, after all, he's a treasure!

  Oh, 'tis so. Don't I know?
  You're in for it, once you begin it.
  As with wine, so with love, you can't seem to go slow,
  Tho' you know that the devil is in it!

So here's to the life, for all sorrows and sighs,
  And here's to the night that is dying—
I quaff to that ominous flame in your eyes,
  And the sweets on your lips that are lying!
We'll drink to the joy, though' it's partly alloy—
  It is truc, though it's singular – very;
But life as I view it, 's no failure, my boy,
So long as there's kisses and – sherry!

SLEEPIN' AT THE FOOT O' THE BED

Luther Patrick

Did ye ever sleep at the foot o' the bed
      When the weather wuz whizzin' cold,
When the wind wuz a-whistlin' aroun' the house
      An' the moon wuz yeller ez gold,
An give yore good warm feathers up
      To Aunt Lizzie and Uncle Fred-
Too many kinfolks on a bad, raw night
      And you went to the foot o' the bed-
      Fer some dern reason the coldest night o' the season
An' you wuz sent to the foot o' the bed?

I could allus wait till the old folks et
      An' then eat the leavin's with grace.
The teacher could keep me after school,
      An' I'd still hold a smile on my face.
I could wear the big boys' wore-out clothes
      Er let sister have my sled,
But it allus did git my nanny goat
      To have to sleep at the foot o' the bed.
      They's not a location topside o' creation
That I hate like the foot o' the bed.

'Twuz fine enough when the kinfolks come
      The kids brought brand-new games.
You could see how fat all the old folks wuz,
      An' learn all the babies' names.
Had biscuits an' custard and chicken pie,
      An' allus got Sunday fed,
But you knowed dern well when night come on
      You wuz headed fer the foot o' the bed;
      You couldn't git by it, they wuz no use to try it,
You wuz headed fer the foot o' the bed.

They tell me that some folks don't know whut it is
      To have company all over the place,
To rassel fer cover thru a long winter night
      With a big foot settin' in your face,

Er with cold toenails a-scratchin' yore back
        An' a footboard a-scrubbin' yore head.
I'll tell the wide world you ain't lost a thing
        Never sleepin' at the foot o' the bed.
        You can live jest as gladly an' die jest as sadly
'N never sleep at the foot o' the bed.

I've done it, an' I've done it a many uv a time
        In this land o' brave an' the free,
An' in this all-fired battle uv life
        It's done left its mark upon me.
Fer I'm allus a-strugglin' around at the foot
        Instead of forgin' ahead,
An I don't think it's caused by a doggone thing
        But sleepin' at the foot o' the bed.
        I've lost all my claim on fortune an' fame
A-sleepin' at the foot o' the bed.

ONE FINGERED JAKE

Author Unknown

One-fingered Jake
Thus spake:
"Bill — he wuz raw —
He said 'twas a buzz saw;
I said he lied,
'N then I tried
T' p'int out to him
Along its rim
There was no teeth in sight —
Zipp!
Flipp!
Bill was right."

STRIVE ON

Robert X. Leeds

(I dedicate this poem to all the thousands of poets, philosophers, lecturers, writers, business tycoons, seminar leaders, politicians, and teachers whose quotations I've borrowed for this here poem of inspiration. I shore hope we help you more than we helped me.)

It seems I bought a million books
And was at every "How To" fair.
'Bout "How to Succeed In Business"
And "How To Become A Zillionaire."

But somethin' shore did not work out,
And it weren't for lack a strivin'
Cause I listened good to all I could
And I never gave up tryin'.

I even made up a mighty list
A the things I needed to remember.
I begun in the January of my life,
An' I'm still trying in December.

So, I figger I might not a done somethin' right,
An I wouldn' want you to err too.
So here's a list of what I larned,
An' my closin' opinion too:

"Persevere against the obvious,"
"Ride again when you're tossed aloft."
"If your ship of state is full a holes,
Get in, stand up, cast off."

"When the score is a hundred to nothing
And there's one more inning ta play,
Have faith there's a home run lurking,
In your strike-out king that day."

148

When you fail, and fail, and fail again,
Just take comfort in the tale,
That "Someone else succeeded,
When he stayed the failure's trail."

"Just build a better mouse trap,
And the world'll beat a path to your door."
(The house of the guy who did it,
Is now an interstate corridor.)

"There's a pot at the end of every rainbow."
"Just follow each yellow brick road."
"Don't look back at the facts or the failures,
Just keep failing and you'll somehow grow."

So I've writ my own kind of encouragement:
"If you tried an' you didn't succeed,
Remember the mightiest — Mightiest Oaks
Were just nuts once like you and me!"

OUR LIPS AND EARS

Author Unknown

If you your lips would keep from slips,
Five things observe with care:
Of whom you speak, to whom you speak,
And how and when and where.

If you your ears would save from jeers,
These things keep meekly hid:
Myself and I and mine and my
And how I do and did.

THAT COCKER SPANIEL MUTT

Bo Tandy Magruder

As I set and relax, my mind journeys back
To my youth in rural Tennessee,
Wearin' cutoff Levi's an' a hikin' backpack,
I'd go fishin' an' hikin' an' roamin' free.

But on this fine day in the hot summer heat,
Like a country lad, I chose to have fun,
By swimmin' in the creek in my altogether,
An' tonin' my tan in the noonday sun.

But a smilin' figure snuck up from behind,
An' her cocker spaniel mutt by her side.
'Twas the girl that had lately been on my mind,
An' I woke with a dent in my pride.

To heck with the days when men were bold,
I was young 'n I jus' wanted to die.
An' to her it musta' been a sight to behold,
As I ran for my cutoffs nearby.

But her mutt made a dive for my cutoff Levi's,
An' she yelled but that dog wouldn' mind her.
It grabbed hold of my pants and proceeded to prance,
An' took off with me chasing that cur.

For a small, mangy hide it had a mighty great stride,
An' I chased her through meadow an' glen.
In my state mortified, I begged and I cried,
As I saw lands where I'd never been.

The farmers stopped plowin', an' the kids all were shoutin',
They railed at the mighty pursuit;
As I screamed and I yelled an' I cursed her to Hell,
But that darn dog ran on with her loot.

I coaxed her an' promised the meal of her life,
A steak every night for her dinner.
But by then she was a swimmer of the Cumberland River,
An' on the far bank a crowd crowned her the winner.

As I reached the far shore, I was embarrassed and more,
Till some kind soul covered my butt.
I just smiled all around. 'Said, "I shoulda got her a hound
'Stead o' that doggoned li'l Cocker Spaniel mutt!"

THE NUISANCE

Margaret Mackprang Mackay

My dog is a nuisance, an absolute pest;
With him in the house there is truly no rest.
He leaves dirty tracks on the mirror-bright floor
And scratches the paint of the tidy front door.

He slobbers his water and spills half his food;
The rugs are all gnawed and slippers are chewed.
He sheds tufts of hair and he scatters his fleas;
He buries his bones under bushes and trees.

He keeps us awake every night with his yaps;
The neighbors all curse him for spoiling their naps.
I'll stand it no longer. I'm getting fed up.
I won't be a slave to that bothersome pup!

Er — Pardon — Excuse me, but what did you say — ?
You ask if I'm giving the puppy away?
You've the nerve to suggest that you'll take him with pleasure?
Well, certainly not! He's an absolute treasure!

THAT QUEEN

Author Unknown

The Judge was a Christian and played on the square.
    But, he figured the cards pretty close!
He would call off your hand every time to a pair,
    And lay down a "full" when he chose

The Colonel could play a more difficult game,—
    I don't mean to say he would cheat,
But he held the top card when the big betting came,
    And some hands that couldn't be beat.

Coming home from Chicago, the two chanced to meet—
    They were very old friends—on the cars;
And as neither the other at poker could beat,
    They played euchre, five points for cigars.

The cards ran along pretty evenly, too.
    Till the Judge turned a moment his head,
When the Colonel, in shuffling, slipped the deck through,
    And the Judge cut a cold one instead.

'Twas euchre, of course, but the Judge was amazed
    When he lifted four kings in a lump;
But the Colonel, not seeming a particle dazed,
    Turned up a red queen for a trump.

"You say—do you pass, Judge? The Colonel called out,
    "Look here," said the limb of the law,
"I've mighty queer cards, if you're in for a bout,
    We'll play this one hand out at draw."

The Colonel considered and wriggled his neck—
    "I, too, have a very odd hand.
If you'll give me that queen from the top of the deck,
    We'll play out the cards as they stand."

"Agreed," said the Judge, for he saw at a glance,
    The Colonel had one of two things—
Full, or four queens, and he hadn't a chance
    To rake down the pot from four kings.

The Judge chipped with fifty; The colonel came back;
    The Judge answered him with a raise.
Of the bets the two made, I could never keep track,
    But they piled up like gals on a chaise.

At last says the Judge, "Here, I'm hunting no more
    Four kings! Reach over that pot!"—
"Hold on," says the Colonel, "I, too, have found four,
    And they're four little aces I've got."

The Judge took the cards and looked over them well,
    Fetched a breath from his trouser's waistband—
"Well, what I'd like to know is, what in hell
    That queen had to do with that hand?"

PITY THE MAN

Russell Wragg

A man may smile and bid you hail,
    Yet wish you to the devil.
But when a good dog wags his tail,
    You know he's on the level.
Pity the man who knows no pattering paws
Who wins no welcoming bark for his return,
Who never sees the scratch of little claws
Upon his polished floors. Pray he may earn
    The adoration of clear eyes that see
    Within a master's face their deity.

THE ACE IN THE HOLE

Al Wilson

Now you'll meet a lot of guys
Who think they're mighty wise
        All because they know a thing or two;
You'll find them every day
Strolling up and down Broadway,
        Telling of the wonders they can do;
There's common and there's booters,
There's cardsharps and crapshooters;
        They congregate around the Metropole,
They wear flashy ties and collars,
But where'd they get their dollars
        If they'd lose that old ace down in the hole?

Some of them write to their old forks for coin;
        That is their ace in the hole.
While others skip bells on the old tenderloin;
        That is their ace in the hole.
They'll tell you of trips they are going to make
To Italy or the North Pole,
But their names will be mud,
Like a chump playing stud,
        If they lose that old ace in the hole.

Now the more you stroll around
In this good old New York town,
        You'll find that what I'm telling you is true.
They'll greet you with a smile,
But you'll know all the while,
        They're only trying to slip it onto you.
To you they will be telling
Of Lemons they are selling
        And money they have spent in buying clothes.
But you know that they are lying
It's the ace that does the buying,
        That clothes them from their heads down to their toes.

Some of them write to their old folks for coin;
That is their ace in the hole.
While others skip bells on the old tenderloin;
That is their ace in the hole.
They'll tell you of trips they are going to make
To Italy or the North Pole,
But their names will be mud,
Like a chump playing stud,
If they lose that old ace in the hole.

THE SOLDIER

Rupert Brooke

If I should die, think only this of me;
That there's some corner of a foreign field
That is forever England. There shall be
In that rich earth a richer dust concealed,
A dust whom England bore, shaped, and made aware,
Gave once her flowers to love, her ways to roam
A body of England's, breathing English air,
Washed by the rivers, blest by the aura of home.

And think, this heart, all evil shed away.
A pulse in the eternal mind, no less
Gives somewhere back the thoughts by England given:
Her sights and sounds, dreams happy as her day,
And laughter learnt of friends and gentleness
In hearts at peace under an English heaven.

THE BALLAD OF ME AND SOURDOUGH DAN

James Ploss

Now sourdough Dan was the strangest man
     Our mining town'd ever known;
On Saturday nights he shunned the lights
     Preferring ta set alone.
From where he'd came or his las' name
     Not one'a us wanted ta know.
And none'a us cared how sourdough fared,
     We jes' watched him come 'n go.

He homed in a shack, setup away back
     Up near to th' Mountain's crown.
Just once a week he'd cross No Luck Creek
     And make his way ta town.
He'd ne'r would meet a friend on the street,
     But Dan didn't seem ta care:
To the General Store, Bogan's Bar 'n no more,
     Then back ta his shack up there.

Ya never would see Dan with a she,
     An' the townfolk began ta fear
That they'd welcomed in a man a sin,
     A giant sized, bushy-beard'd queer!
I thought 'at way too – What else could I do?
     Till one day I 'Howdyed' the man
To find out that he was straight as could be,
     We grew friendly, me 'n sourdough Dan.

Now when once a week Dan crossed No Luck Creek,
     He'd meet me in Bogan's bar.
There big Dan 'n me, Well, we'd have us a spree,
     'N we'd end up with a big fat cigar.
We'd sit all alone at a table of our own
     Ignoring my frien's 'at I'd see,
And when mellowed with beer, Dan'd bend my ear,
     An' he ne'r spoke to no one but me.

Dan confided in me; he was rich as could be
    From some strikes he'd made some time before.
His partners all died 'n I dunno if he lied,
    But he said they left him all the hoard.
So he homed in his shack, 'at was set way far back
    So no one'd guess or know,
An' there he counted his gold, thru the long winters snow
    An' it comforted him no matter the cold.

He tol' me a story what I heard tol' before
        How a man an' his money were parted.
He met a young beauty in a cathose one day,
        An' 'at was the way what it started.
He'd plied her with money to his very las' cent,
        An' she promised her love would be straight.
But she dumped on him for a gambler named slim,
        And Dan's love was turned into hate!

So he off'd with that life and dreams of a wife
    An' North to our northland he came.
There he settled on down in our li'l mining town
    Where nobody know'd of his name.
So I learned right there why he'd no use of the fair,
    An' I couldn't blame ol' Sourdough none.
For your heart to be broke is the Devil's own joke
    An' it sure ain't a man's idea of fun!

Dan made me swear what he told me there
    Over booze was between jus' us two,
An' I promised that I would give up an' die
    Than repeat it, and our friendship grew.
For it was Dan, by heck, who'd pick up the check
    For our blowouts in Bogan's bar;
He was grateful, ya see, for just havin' me
    To talk to and share drinks and cigar.

Then gradually (it was easy to see)
    The townsfolk avoided me, too,
And the rumors they spread made me wish I was dead,
    Though there wasn't a word that was true.

Then I moved in with Dan and they said to a man,
    "You see? What we figured was true!
That Sourdough Dan is a queer, not a man!
    Now he's making one out of Jim, too!"

Then the dern General Store wouldn't sell anymore
    Supplies to Sourdough an' me,
So we jus' had to mush fifty miles through the slush
    For our bacon, our beans, and our tea.
Sourdough Dan and I, our throats parched an' dry
    (Since Bogan's was refusing us, too,)
Refused to give in, though the ice grew purty thin,
    Till we fermented our own batch of brew!

Things came to a head, when Dan was in bed
    An' I was long gone for supplies:
When a snotnosed brat, nothing more than that,
    Spread around a black passel of lies
Of what Sourdough had done to that snotnose in fun,
    An' the whole town rose up righteous with hate.
I returned from the trail, to that outpost of hell
    Got back to our shack, but too late!

Believing that kid, the townfolk all did
    A deed that'd curl a bald man's hair;
They stripped Sourdough Dan, then hanged the bare man,
    An' they left him cold, stiff hanging there.
When I arrived back to our 'cross-the-creek shack,
    I found my ol' friend swingin' there.
He was naked and froze from his head to his toes,
    There was hoarfrost in his black bushy hair.

I buried Dan back of our mountaintop shack
    And covered his gave with some stone.
I set fire to that shack and without looking back,
    Left that town like I'd come there, alone.
After nosing around, The good people found
    That that snotnose had lied 'bout poor Dan;
An' Dan 'ad never been no practitioner of sin,
    They was sorry right down to the last man.

Well they nosied aroun' till they tracked me on down,
      And they begged me to forgive and come back;
They fell to their knees bleating eloquent pleas,
      Offered me work and to rebuild my shack.

But I tol' them, forget it, in Hell they'll regret it.
         I'll not return to where they murdered my friend!
And all sad of face, they left my new place
    With their penitential business at an end.

I recall those gory days through a likkered-up haze,
    While holding forth in the Purple Fan Bar;
And so I won' freeze, naked gals perch on my knees
    And I puff on the best ten-cent cigars.
Ya see, 'fore I burned that old shack, I returned
    To the Mother Lode hidden by Dan,
And I found where 'twas hid and filtch it I did;
    Now I live like a state-side gentleman!

And if any ol' time you be up in my clime,
    Be sure to drop in at The Purple Fan:
If you're so dry you can't blink, well, I'll buy you a drink
    To the memory of Sourdough Dan!
Cuz Dan, you can see, proved more than a friend to me
    When them moralists hanged him that night.
For his golden stash bought all the comforts I sought
    An' its nice he ain't hanging 'round up-tight.

THE SIGH

Author Unknown

There's a sigh for a yes,
And a sigh for a no,
And a sigh for, "I can't bear it."

Oh what shall be done;
Shall I stay or run?
Oh! Cut the sweet apple and share it.

THE BALLAD OF READING GAOL

Oscar Wilde

He did not wear his scarlet coat,
    For blood and wine are red,
And blood and wine were on his hands
    When they found him with the dead,
The poor dead woman whom he loved,
    And murdered in her bed.

He walked amongst the Trial Men
    In a suit of shady grey;
A cricket cap was on his head,
    And his step seemed light and gay;
But I never saw a man who looked
    So wistfully at the day.

I never saw a man who looked
    With such a wistful eye
Upon that little tent of blue
    Which prisoners call the sky,
And at every drifting cloud that went
    With sails of silver by.

I walked, with other souls in pain,
    Within another ring,
And was wondering if the man had done
    A great or little thing,
When a voice behind me whispered low,
    "That fellow's got to swing."

Dear Christ! The very prison walls
    Suddenly seemed to reel,
And the sky above my head became
    Like a casque of scorching steel;
And, though I was a soul in pain,
    My pain I could not feel.

I only knew what hunted thought
    Quickened his step, and why
He looked upon the garish day
    With such a wistful eye;
The man had killed the thing he loved,
    And so he had to die.

Yet each man kills the thing he loves,
By each let this be heard,
Some do it with a bitter look,
Some with a flattering word,
The coward does it with a kiss,
The brave man with a sword!

Some kill their love when they are young,
And some when they are old;
Some strangle with the hands of Lust,
Some with the hands of Gold.
The kindest use a knife, because
The dead so soon grow cold.

Some love too little, some too long
Some sell, and others buy;
Some do the deed with many tears,
And some without a sigh:
For each man kills the thing he loves,
Yet each man does not die.

He does not die a death of shame
On a day of dark disgrace,
Nor have a noose about his neck,
Nor a cloth upon his face,
Nor drop feet foremost through the floor
Into an empty space.

He does not sit with silent men
Who watch him night and day;
Who watch him when he tries to weep,
And when he tries to pray;
Who watch him lest himself should rob
The prison of its prey.

He does not wake at dawn to see
Dread figures throng his room,
The shivering Chaplain robed in white,
The Sheriff stern with gloom,
And the Governor all in shiny black,
With the yellow face of Doom.

He does not rise in piteous haste
　　　To put on convict-clothes,
While some coarse-mouthed Doctor gloats and notes
　　　Each new and nerve-twitched pose,
Fingering a watch whose little ticks
　　　Are like horrible hammer-blows.

He does not know that sickening thirst
　　　That sands one's throat, before
The hangman with his gardener's gloves
　　　Slips through the padded door,
And binds one with three leathern thongs,
　　　That the throat may thirst no more.

He does not bend his head to hear
　　　The Burial Office read,
Nor, while the terror of his soul
　　　Tells him he is not dead,
Cross his own coffin, as he moves
　　　Into the hideous shed.

He does not stare upon the air
　　　Through a little roof of glass:
He does not pray with lips of clay
　　　For his agony to pass;
Nor feel upon his shuddering cheek
　　　The kiss of Caiaphas.

Six weeks our guardsman walked the yard,
　　　In the suit of shabby grey:
His cricket cap was on his head,
　　　And his step seemed light and gay,
But I never saw a man who looked
　　　So wistfully at the day.

I never saw a man who looked
　　　With such a wistful eye
Upon that little tent of blue
　　　Which prisoners call the sky,
And at every wandering cloud that trailed
　　　Its ravelled fleeces by.

He did not wring his hands, as do
     Those witless men who dare
To try to rear the changeling Hope
     In the cave of black Despair:
He only looked upon the sun,
     And drank the morning air.

He did not wring his hands nor weep,
     Nor did he peek or pine,
But he drank the air as though it held
     Some healthful anodyne;
With open mouth he drank the sun
     As though it had been wine!

And I and all the souls in pain,
     Who tramped the other ring,
Forgot if we ourselves had done
     A great or little thing,
And watched with gaze of dull amaze
     The man who had to swing.

And strange it was to see him pass
     With a step so light and gay,
And strange it was to see him look
     So wistfully at the day,
And strange it was to think that he
     Had such a debt to pay.

For oak and elm have pleasant leaves
     That in the spring-time shoot:
But grim to see is the gallows-tree,
     With its adder-bitten root,
And, green or dry, a man must die
     Before it bears its fruit!

The loftiest place is that seat of grace
     For which all worldlings try:
But who would stand in hempen band
     Upon a scaffold high,
And through a murderer's collar take
     His last look at the sky?

It is sweet to dance to violins
      When Love and Life are fair:
To dance to flutes, to dance to lutes
      Is delicate and rare:
But it is not sweet with nimble feet
      To dance upon the air!

So with curious eyes and sick surmise
      We watched him day by day,
And wondered if each one of us
      Would end the self-same way.
For none can tell to what red Hell
      His sightless soul may stray.

At last the dead man walked no more
      Amongst the Trial Men,
And I knew that he was standing up
      In the black dock's dreadful pen,
And that never would I see his face
      In God's sweet world again.

Like two doomed ships that pass in storm
      We had crossed each other's way:
But we made no sign, we said no word,
      We had no word to say;
For we did not meet in the holy night,
      But in the shameful day.

A prison wall was round us both,
      Two outcast men we were:
The world had thrust us from its heart
      And God from out His care:
And the iron gin that waits for Sin
      Had caught us in its snare.

In Debtors' Yard the stones are hard,
      And the dripping wall is high,
So it was there he took the air
      Beneath the leaden sky,
And by each side a Warder walked
      For fear the man might die.
Or else he sat with those who watched
      His anguish night and day;

Or else he sat with those who watched
     His anguish night and day;
Who watched him when he rose to weep,
     And when he crouched to pray;
Who watched him lest himself should rob
     Their scaffold of its prey.

The Governor was strong upon
     The Regulations Act:
The Doctor said that Death was but
     A scientific fact:
And twice a day the chaplain called
     And left a little tract.

And twice a day he smoked his pipe,
     And drank his quart of beer:
His soul was resolute, and held
     No hiding-place for fear;
He often said that he was glad
     The hangman's hands were near.

But why he said so strange a thing
     No Warder dared to ask:
For he to whom a watcher's doom
     Is given as his task,
Must set a lock upon his lips
     And make his face a mask.

Or else he might be moved, and try
     To comfort or console:
And what should Human Pity do
     Pent up in Murderers' Hole?
What word of grace in such a place
     Could help a brother's soul?

With slouch and swing around the ring
     We trod the Fool's Parade!
We did not care. We knew we were
     The Devil's Own Brigade;
And shaven head and feet of lead
     Make a merry masquerade.

We tore the tarry rope to shreds
      With blunt and bleeding nails;
We rubbed the doors, and scrubbed the floors,
      And cleaned the shining rails:
And, rank by rank, we soaped the plank,
      And clattered with the pails.

We sewed the sacks, we broke the stones,
      We turned the dusty drill:
We banged the tins, and bawled the hymns,
      And sweated on the mill:
But in the heart of every man
      Terror was lying still.

So still it lay that every day
      Crawled like a weed-clogged wave:
And we forgot the bitter lot
      That waits for fool and knave,
Till once, as we tramped in from work,
      We passed an open grave.

With yawning mouth the yellow hole
      Gaped for a living thing;
The very mud cried out for blood
      To the thirsty asphalt ring;
And we knew that ere one dawn grew fair
      Some prisoner had to swing.

Right in we went, with soul intent
      On death and Dread and Doom:
The Hangman, with his little bag,
      Went shuffling through the gloom:
And each man trembled as he crept
      Into his numbered tomb.

That night the empty corridors
      Were full of forms of Fear,
And up and down the iron town
      Stole feet we could not hear,
And through the bars that hide the stars
      White faces seemed to peer.

He lay as one who lies and dreams
    In a pleasant meadow-land,
The watchers watched him as he slept,
    And could not understand
How one could sleep so sweet a sleep
    With a hangman close at hand.

But there is no sleep when men must weep
    Who never yet have wept:
So we—the fool, the fraud, the knave—
    That endless vigil kept,
And through each brain on hands of pain
    Another's terror crept.

Alas! It is a fearful thing
    To feel another's guilt!
For, right within, the sword of Sin
    Pierced to its poisoned hilt,
And as molten lead were the tears we shed
    For the blood we had not spilt.

The Warders with their shoes of felt
    Crept by each padlocked door,
And peeped and saw, with eyes of awe,
    Grey figures on the floor,
And wondered why men knelt to pray
    Who never prayed before.

All through the night we knelt and prayed,
    Mad mourners of a corse!
The troubled plumes of midnight were
    The plumes upon a hearse:
And bitter wine upon a sponge
    Was the savour of Remorse.

The grey cock crew, the red cock crew,
    But never came the day:
And crooked shapes of Terror crouched,
    In the corners where we lay:
And each evil sprite that walks by night
    Before us seemed to play.

They glided past, they glided fast,
      Like travellers through a mist:
They mocked the moon in a rigadoon
      Of delicate turn and twist,
And with formal pace and loathsome grace
      The phantoms kept their tryst.

With mop and mow, we saw them go,
      Slim shadows hand in hand:
About, about, in ghostly rout
      They trod a saraband:
And the damned grotesques made arabesques,
      Like the wind upon the sand!

With the pirouettes of marionettes,
      They tripped on pointed tread:
But with flutes of Fear they filled the ear,
      As their grisly masque they led,
And loud they sang, and long they sang,
      For they sang to wake the dead.

"Oho!" they cried, "The world is wide,
      But fettered limbs go lame!
And once, or twice, to throw the dice
      Is a gentlemanly game,
But he does not win who plays with sin
      In the secret House of Shame."

No things of air these antics were,
      That frolicked with such glee:
To men whose lives were held in gyves,
      And whose feet might not go free.
Ah! wounds of Christ! They were living things,
      Most terrible to see.

Around, around, they waltzed and wound;
      Some wheeled in smirking pairs;
With the mincing step of a demirep
      Some sidled up the stairs:
And with subtle sneer, and fawning leer,
Each helped us at our prayers.

The morning wind began to moan,
        But still the night went on:
Through its giant loom the web of gloom
        Crept till each thread was spun:
And, as we prayed, we grew afraid
        Of the Justice of the Sun.

The moaning wind went wandering round
        The weeping prison-wall:
Till like a wheel of turning steel
        We felt the minutes crawl:
O moaning wind! What had we done
        To have such a seneschal?

At last I saw the shadowed bars,
        Like a lattice wrought in lead,
Move right across the whitewashed wall
        That faced my three-plank bed,
And I knew that somewhere in the world
        God's dreadful dawn was red.

At six o'clock we cleaned our cells,
        At seven all was still,
But the sough and swing of a mighty wing
        The prison seemed to fill,
For the Lord of Death with icy breath
        Had entered in to kill.

He did not pass in purple pomp,
        Nor ride a moon-white steed.
Three yards of cord and a sliding board
        Are all the gallows' need:
So with rope of shame the herald came
        To do the secret deed.

We were as men who through a fen
        Of filthy darkness grope:
We did not dare to breathe a prayer,
        Or to give our anguish scope:
Something was dead in each of us,
And what was dead was Hope.

For Man's grim Justice goes its way,
    And will not swerve aside:
It slays the weak, it slays the strong,
    It has a deadly stride:
With iron heel it slays the strong,
    The monstrous parricide!

We waited for the stroke of eight;
    Each tongue was thick with thirst.
For the stroke of eight is the stroke of Fate
    That makes a man accursed,
And Fate will use a running noose
    For the best man and the worst.

We had no other thing to do,
    Save to wait for the sign to come:
So, like things of stone in a valley alone,
    Quiet we sat and dumb:
But each man's heart beat thick and quick,
    Like a madman on a drum!

With sudden shock the prison-clock
    Smote on the shivering air,
And from all the gaol rose up a wail
    Of impotent despair,
Like the sound that frightened marshes hear
    From some leper in his lair.

And as one sees most fearful things
    In the crystal of a dream,
We saw the greasy hempen rope
    Hooked to the blackened beam,
And heard the prayer the hangman's snare
    Strangled into a scream.

And all the woe that moved him so
    That he gave that bitter cry,
And the wild regrets and the bloody sweats,
    None knew so well as I:
For he who lives more lives than one
More deaths than one must die.

There is no chapel on the day
      On which they hang a man:
The Chaplain's heart is far too sick,
      Or his face is far too wan,
Or there is that written in his eyes
      Which none should look upon.

So they kept us close till nigh on noon,
      And then they rang the bell,
And the Warders with their jingling keys
      Opened each listening cell,
And down the iron stair we tramped,
      Each from his separate Hell.

Out into God's sweet air we went,
      But not in wonted way,
For this man's face was white with fear,
      And that man's face was grey,
And I never saw sad men who looked
      So wistfully at the day.

I never saw sad men who looked
      With such a wistful eye
Upon that little tent of blue
      We prisoners called the sky,
And at every careless cloud that passed
      In happy freedom by.

But there were those amongst us all
      Who walked with downcast head,
And knew that, had each got his due,
      They should have died instead:
He had but killed a thing that lived,
      Whilst they had killed the dead.

For he who sins a second time
      Wakes a dead soul to pain,
And draws it from its spotted shroud,
      And makes it bleed again,
And makes it bleed great gouts of blood,
And makes it bleed in vain!

Like ape or clown in monstrous garb
With crooked arrows starred,
Silently we went round and round
The slippery asphalt yard;
Silently we went round and round
And no man spoke a word.

Silently we went round and round,
And through each hollow mind
The Memory of dreadful things
Rushed like a dreadful wind,
And Horror stalked before each man,
And Terror crept behind.

The Warders strutted up and down,
And kept their herd of brutes.
Their uniforms were spick and span,
And they wore their Sunday suits,
But we knew the work they had been at,
By the quicklime on their boots.

For where a grave had opened wide,
There was no grave at all:
Only a stretch of mud and sand
By the hideous prison-wall,
And a little heap of burning lime,
That the man should have his pall.

For he has a pall, this wretched man,
Such as few men can claim:
Deep down below a prison-yard,
Naked for greater shame,
He lies, with fetters on each foot,
Wrapt in a sheet of flame!

And all the while the burning lime
Eats flesh and bone away.
It eats the brittle bone by night,
And the soft flesh by day.
It eats the flesh and bone by turns,
But it eats the heart always.

For three long years they will not sow
      Or root or seedling there:
For three long years the unblessed spot
      Will sterile be and bare,
And look upon the wondering sky
      With unreproachful stare.

They think a murderer's heart would taint
      Each simple seed they sow.
It is not true! God's kindly earth
      Is kindlier than men know,
And the red rose would but blow more red,
      The white rose whiter blow.

Out of his mouth a red, red rose!
      Out of his heart a white!
For who can say by what strange way,
      Christ brings His will to light,
Since the barren staff the pilgrim bore
      Bloomed in the great Pope's sight?

But neither milk-white rose nor red
      May bloom in prison air;
The shard, the pebble, and the flint,
      Are what they give us there:
For flowers have been known to heal
      A common man's despair.

So never will wine-red rose or white,
      Petal by petal, fall
On that stretch of mud and sand that lies
      By the hideous prison-wall,
To tell the men who tramp the yard
      That God's Son died for all.

Yet though the hideous prison-wall
      Still hems him round and round,
And a spirit may not walk by night
      That is with fetters bound,
And a sprit may but weep that lies
      In such unholy ground,

He is at peace—this wretched man—
        At peace, or will be soon:
There is no thing to make him mad,
        Nor does Terror walk at noon,
For the lampless Earth in which he lies
        Has neither Sun nor Moon.

They hanged him as a beast is hanged:
        They did not even toll
A requiem that might have brought
        Rest to his startled soul,
But hurriedly they took him out,
        And hid him in a hole.

The stripped him of his canvas clothes,
        And gave him to the flies:
They mocked the swollen purple throat
        And the stark and staring eyes:
And with laughter loud they heaped the shroud
        In which their convict lies.

The Chaplain would not kneel to pray
        By his dishonoured grave:
Nor mark it with that blessed Cross
        That Christ for sinners gave,
Because the man was one of those
        Whom Christ came down to save.

Yet all is well; he has but passed
        To Life's appointed bourne:
And alien tears will fill for him
        Pity's long-broken urn,
For his mourners will be outcast men,
        And outcasts always mourn.

I know not whether Laws be right,
        Or whether Laws be wrong;
All that we know who lie in gaol
        Is that the wall is strong;
And that each day is like a year,
        A year whose days are long.

But this I know, that every Law
          That men have made for Man,
Since first Man took his brother's life,
          And the sad world began,
But straws the wheat and saves the chaff
          With a most evil fan.

This too I know—and wise it were
          If each could know the same—
That every prison those men build
          Is built with bricks of shame,
And bound with bars lest Christ should see
          How men their brothers maim.

With bars they blur the gracious moon,
          And blind the goodly sun:
And they do well to hide their Hell,
          For in it things are done
That Son of God nor son of Man
          Ever should look upon!

The vilest deeds like poison weeds,
          Bloom well in prison-air;
It is only what is good in Man
          That wastes and withers there:
Pale Anguish keeps the heavy gate,
          And the Warder is Despair .

For they starve the little frightened child
          Till it weeps both night and day:
And they scourge the weak and flog the fool
          And gibe the old and grey,
And some grow mad, and all grow bad,
          And none a word may say.

Each narrow cell in which we dwell
          Is a foul and dark latrine,
And the fetid breath of living death
          Chokes up each grated screen,
And all, but Lust, is turned to dust
          In Humanity's machine.

The brackish water that we drink
      Creeps with a loathsome slime,
And the bitter bread they weigh in scales
      Is full of chalk and lime,
And Sleep will not lie down, but walks
      Wild-eyed, and cries to Time.

But though lean Hunger and green Thirst
      Like asp with adder fight,
We have little care of prison fare,
      For what chills and kills outright
Is that every stone one lifts by day
      Becomes one's heart by night.

With midnight always in one's heart,
      And twilight in one's cell,
We turn the crank or tear the rope,
      Each in his separate Hell,
And the silence is more awful far
      Than the sound of a brazen bell.

And never a human voice comes near
      To speak a gentle word:
And the eye that watches through the door
      Is pitiless and hard.
And by all forgot, we rot and rot,
      With soul and body marred.

And thus we rust Life's iron chain
      Degraded and alone:
And some men curse, and some men weep,
      And some men make no moan:
But God's eternal Laws are kind
      And break the heart of stone:

And every human heart that breaks,
      In prison-cell or yard,
Is as that broken box that gave
      Its treasure to the Lord,
And filled the unclean leper's house
      With the scent of costliest nard.

Ah! Happy they whose hearts can break
        And peace of pardon win!
How else may man make straight his plan
        And cleanse his soul from Sin?
How else but through a broken heart
        May Lord Christ enter in?

And he of the swollen purple throat,
        And the stark and staring eyes,
Waits for the holy hands that took
        The Thief to Paradise;
And a broken and a contrite heart
        The Lord will not despise.

The man in red who reads the Law
        Gave him three weeks of life,
Three little weeks in which to heal
        His soul of his soul's strife,
And cleanse from every blot of blood
        The hand that held the knife.

And with tears of blood he cleansed the hand,
        The hand that held the steel:
For only blood can wipe out blood,
        And only tears can heal:
And the crimson stain that was of Cain
        Became Christ's snow-white seal.

In Reading gaol by Reading town
        There is a pit of shame,
And in it lies a wretched man
        Eaten by teeth of flame,
In a burning winding-sheet he lies,
        And his grave has got no name.

And there, till Christ call forth the dead,
        In silence let him lie:
No need to waste the foolish tear,
        Or heave the windy sigh:
The man had killed the thing he loved,
        And so he had to die.

And all men kill the thing they love,
    By all let this be heard,
Some do it with a bitter look,
    Some with a flattering word,
The coward does it with a kiss,
    The brave man with a sword!

THE BETROTHED

Rudyard Kipling

Open the old cigar-box,
    Get me a Cuba stout,
For things are running crossways,
    And Maggie and I are out.
We quarreled about Havanas—
    We fought o'er good cheroot,
And I knew she is exacting,
    And she says I am a brute.

Open the old cigar-box—
    Let me consider a space;
In the blue veil of the vapor,
    Musing on Maggie's face.
Maggie is pretty to look at—
    Maggie's a loving lass.
But the prettiest cheeks must wrinkle,
    The truest of loves must pass.

There's peace in a Laranaga,
    There's calm in a Henry clay,
But the best cigar in an hour
    Is finished and thrown away—
Thrown away for another
    As perfect and ripe and brown—
But I could not throw away Maggie
    For fear o' the talk o' the town!

Maggie, my wife at fifty—
    Gray and dour and old—
With never another Maggie
    To purchase for love or gold.
And the light of Days that have Been
    The dark of the Days that Are,
And Love's torch stinking and stale,
    Like the butt of a dead cigar—

The butt of a dead cigar
        You are bound to keep in your pocket
With never a new one to light
        Tho' it's charred and black to the socket.
Open the old cigar-box—
        Let me consider a while—
Here is a mild Manila—
        There is a wifely smile.

Which is the better portion—
        Bondage bought with a ring,
Or a harem of dusky beauties
        Fifty tied in a string?
Counselors cunning and silent—
        Comforters true and tried
And never a one of the fifty
        To sneer at a rival bride.

Thought in the early morning,
        Solace in time of woes,
Peace in the hush of the twilight,
        Balm ere my eyelids close.
This will the fifty give me,
        Asking nought in return
With only a Suttee's passion—
        To do their duty and burn.

This will the fifty give me.
        When they are spent and dead,
Five times other fifties
        Shall be my servants instead.
The furrows of far-off Java,
        The isles of the Spanish Main,
When they hear my harem is empty,
        Will send me my brides again.

I will take no heed to their raiment,
        Nor food for their mouths withal,
So long as the gulls are nesting,
        So long as the showers fall.

I will scent 'em with best vanilla,
        With tea will I temper their hides,
And the Moor and the Mormon shall envy
        Who read of this tale of my brides.

For Maggie has written a letter
        To give me my choice between
The wee little whimpering Love
        And the great god Nick o' Teen.
And I have been servant of Love
        For barely a twelve-month clear,
But I have been Priest of Partagas
        A matter of seven year;

And the gloom of my bachelor days
        Is flecked with the cheery light
Of stumps that I burned to Friendship
        And Pleasure and Work and Fight.
And I turn my eyes to the future
        That Maggie and I must prove,
But the only light on the marshes
        Is the Will-o'-the Wisp of love.

Will it see me safe through my journey,
        Or leave me bogged in the mire?
Since a puff of tobacco can cloud it,
        Shall I follow the fitful fire?
Open the old cigar-box,
        Let me consider anew—
Old friends, and who is Maggie
        That I should abandon you?

A million surplus Maggies
        Are willing to bear the yoke;
And a woman is only a woman,
        But a good cigar is a smoke.
Light me another Cuba;
        I hold to my first-sworn vows,
If Maggie will have no rival,
        I'll have no Maggie for spouse!

THE CHARGE
OF THE LIGHT BRIGADE

Alfred, Lord Tennyson

Half a league, half a league, half a league onward,
All in the Valley of Death rode the six hundred.
"Forward the Light Brigade! Charge for the guns!" he said.
Into the Valley of Death rode the six hundred.

"Forward, the Light Brigade!" Was there a man dismayed?
Not though the soldier knew someone had blundered.
Theirs not to make reply, theirs not to reason why,
Theirs but to do and die.
Into the Valley of Death Rode the six hundred.

Cannon to right of them, cannon to left of them,
Cannon in front of them volleyed and thundered;
Stormed at with shot and shell, boldly they rode and well
Into the jaws of Death,
Into the mouth of hell rode the six hundred.

Flashed all their sabres bare, flashed as they turned in air
Sabring the gunners there, charging an army, while
All the world wondered. Plunged through the line they broke;
Cossack and Russian reeled from the sabre-stroke
Shattered and sundered.
Then they rode back, but not, not the six hundred.

Cannon to right of them, cannon to left of them,
Cannon behind them volleyed and thundered;
Stormed at with shot and shell, while horse and hero fell.
They that had fought so well came through the jaws of Death,
Back from the mouth of hell,
All that was left of them, left of six hundred.

When can their glory fade? O the wild charge they made!
All the world wondered. Honor the charge they made!
Honor the Light Brigade,
Noble six hundred!

THE LAST
OF THE LIGHT BRIGADE

Rudyard Kipling

There were thirty million English
    Who talked of England's might.
There were twenty broken troopers
    Who lacked a bed for the night.
They had neither food nor money.
    They had neither service nor trade.
They were only shiftless soldiers,
    The last of the Light Brigade.

They felt that life was fleeting.
    They knew not that art was long.
That though they were dying of famine
    They lived in deathless song.
They asked for a little money
    To keep the wolf from the door;
And thirty million English
    Sent twenty pounds and four!

They laid their heads together
    That were scarred and lined and grey;
Keen were the Russian sabres,
    But want was keener than they.
And an old Troop-Sergeant muttered,
    "Let us go to the man who writes
The things on Balaclava
    The kiddies at school recites."

They went without bands or colours,
    A regiment ten-file strong,
To look for the Master-singer
    Who had crowned them all in song.
And, waiting his servant's order,
    By the garden gate they stayed,
A desolate little cluster,
    The last of the Light Brigade.

They strove to stand to attention,
      To straighten the toil-bowed back.
They drilled on an empty stomach,
      The loose-knit files fell slack;
With stooping of weary shoulders,
      In garments tattered and frayed,
They shambled into his presence,
      The last of the Light Brigade.

The old Troop-Sergeant was spokesman,
      And "Beggin' your pardon," he said,
"You wrote o' the Light Brigade, Sir.
      Here's all that isn't dead.
An' it's all come true what you wrote, sir,
      Regardin' the mouth of hell;
For we're all of us nigh to the workhouse,
      An' we thought we'd call an' tell.

No, thank you, we don't want food, Sir;
      But couldn't you take an' write
A sort of 'to be continued'
      And 'see next page' o' the fight?
We think that someone has blundered,
      An' couldn't you tell 'em how?
You wrote we were heroes once, Sir.
      Please write we are starving now."

The poor little army departed,
      Limping and lean and forlorn.
And the heart of the Master-singer
      Grew hot with the "scorn of scorn".
And he wrote for them wonderful verses
      That swept the land like flame
Till the fatted souls of the English
      Were scourged with the thing called Shame.

O thirty million English
      That babble of England's might,
Behold there are twenty heroes
      Who lack their food tonight.
Our children's children are lisping
      To "honor the charge they made—"
And we leave to the streets and the workhouse
      The charge of the Light Brigade!

THE CLINK OF THE ICE

Eugene Field

Notably fond of music,
    I dote on a sweeter tone
Than ever the harp has uttered,
    Or even the lute bass known.
When I awake at five in the morning
    With a feeling in my head
Suggestive of mild excesses
    Before I retired to bed.

When a small but fierce volcano
    Vexes me sore inside;
And my throat and mouth are furred
    With fur that seemeth a buffalo hide,
How gracious those dew of solace
    That over my senses fall
At the clink of the ice in the pitcher
    That the boy brings up the hall.

Oh! Is it the gaudy ballet
    With features I cannot name
That kindles in virile bosoms
    That slow but devouring flame!
Or is it the midnight supper,
    Eaten before we retire,
That presently, by combustion,
    Setteth us all on fire?

Or is it the cherry magnum?
    Nay, I'll not chide the cup
That maketh the meekest mortal
    Anxious to whoop things up.
Yes, what the cause soever,
    Relief comes when we call —
Relief with that rapturous clinkety-clink
    That clinketh alike for all.

I've dreamt of the fiery furnace
        That was one vast bulk of flame,
And That I was Abednego
        A-wallowing in that same;
And I've dreamt that I was a crater
        Possessed of a mad desire
To vomit molten lava
        And snort big gobs of fire;

I've dreamt I was Roman candles
        And rockets that fizzed and screamed,
In short, I've dreamt the cussedest dream
        That ever a human dreamed.
But all the red- hot fancies
        Were scattered quicker than a wink
When the spirit within that pitcher
        Went tapping its clinkety-clink.

Boy, why so slow in coming
        With that gracious saving cup?
Oh, haste thee to the succor
        Of the man who is burning up.
See how the ice bobs up and down,
        As if it wildly strove
To reach its grace to the wretch
        Who feels like a red-hot kitchen stove.

The piteous clink it clinks, methinks,
        Should thrill you through and through.
An erring soul is wanting drink
        And he wants it P.D.Q.
And lo! The honest pitcher, too,
        Falls in so dire a fret
That its pallid form is presently
        Bedewed with a chilling sweat.

May blessings be showered upon the man
        Who first devised this drink,
That happens along at five a.m.
        With its rapturous clinkety-clink.

I never have felt the cooling flood
      Go sizzling down my throat
But what I vow to hymn a hymn
      To that clinkety-clink devote.

So now in the prime of my manhood
      I polish this lyric gem
For the uses of all good fellows
      Who are thirsty at five a.m.
But 'specially for those fellows
      Who have known this pleasing thrall
Of the clink of the ice in the pitcher
      That the boy brings up the hall.

WHEN LOVELY WOMAN STOOPS TO FOLLY

Oliver Goldsmith

When lovely woman stoops to folly,
      And finds too late men betray,
What charm can soothe her melancholy,
      What art can wash her guilt away?

The only art her guilt to cover,
      To hide her shame from every eye,
To give repentance to her lover,
      And wring his bosom—is to die.

THE COUNTERSIGN WAS "MARY"

Margaret Eytinge

'Twas near the break of day, but still
  The moon was shining brightly,
The west wind as it passed the flowers
  Set each one swaying lightly.
The sentry slow paced to and fro,
  A faithful night-watch keeping,
While in the tents behind him stretched
  His comrades all were sleeping.

Slow to and fro the sentry paced,
  His musket on his shoulder,
But not a thought of death or war,
  Was with the brave young soldier.
Ah, ho! His heart was far away
  Where, on a western prairie,
A rose-twined cottage stood. That night
  The countersign was "Mary".

And there his own true love he saw,
  Her blue eyes kindly beaming.
Above them on her sunkissed brow,
  Her curls like sunlight gleaming.
And heard her singing, as she churned
  The butter in the dairy,
The song he loved the best. That night
  The countersign was "Mary".

"Oh, for one kiss from her!" he sighed,
  When up the lone road glancing,
He spied a form, a little form,
  With faltering steps advancing.
And as it neared him silently,
  He gazed at it in wonder,
Then dropped his musket to his hand,
  And challenged: "Who goes yonder?"

Still on it came. "Not one step more,
	Be you man, or child, or fairy,
Unless you give the countersign.
	Halt! Who goes there?" " 'Tis Mary,"
A sweet voice cried and in his arms
	The girl he'd left behind him
Half-fainting fell. O'er many miles,
	She'd bravely toiled to find him.

"I heard that you were wounded, dear,"
	She sobbed, "My heart is breaking.
I could not stay a moment, but,
	All other ties forsaking,
I traveled, by my grief made strong,
	Kind heaven watching o'er me,
Until—unhurt and well?" "Yes, love,"
	"At last you stood before me."

They told me that I could not pass,
	The lines to seek my lover
Before day fairly came; but I
	Pressed on ere night was over,
And as I told my name, I found,
	The way free as our prairie."
"Because, thank God! Tonight," he said,
	"The countersign is Mary".

THE CREMATION OF SAM McGEE

Robert Service

There are strange things done in the midnight sun
By the men who moil for gold;
The Artic trails have their secret tales
That would make your blood run cold;
The Northern Lights have seen queer sights,
But the queerest they ever did see
Was that night on the marge of Lake Lebarge
I cremated Sam McGee.

Now Sam McGee was from Tennessee,
Where the cotton blooms and blows.
Why he left his home in the South to roam
'Round the Pole, God only knows.
He was always cold, but the land of gold
Seemed to hold him like a spell;
Though he'd often say in his homely way
That he'd "sooner live in Hell."

On a Christmas Day we were mushing our way
Over the Dawson trail.
Talk of your cold! Through the parka's fold
It stabbed like a driven nail.
If our eyes we'd close, then the lashes froze
Till sometimes we couldn't see.
It wasn't much fun, but the only one
To whimper was Sam McGee.

And that very night, as we lay packed tight
In our robes beneath the snow,
And the dogs were fed, and the stars o'erhead
Were dancing heel and toe,
He turned to me, and "Cap," says he,
"I'll cash in this trip I guess;
And if I do, I'm asking you
Won't refuse my last request."

Well, he seemed so low that I couldn't say no;
Then he says with a sort of moan,
"It's the cursed cold, and it's got right hold
Till I'm chilled clean through to the bone.
Yet 'taint being dead — it's my awful dread
Of the icy grave that pains;
So I want you to swear that, foul or fair,
You'll cremate my last remains."

A pal's last need is a thing to heed,
So I swore I would not fail;
And we started on at the streak of dawn;
But God! He looked ghastly pale.
He crouched on the sleigh, and he rave all day
Of his home in Tennessee;
And before nightfall a corpse was all
That was left of Sam McGee.

There wasn't a breath in that land of death,
And I hurried horror-driven,
With a corpse half hid that I couldn't get rid,
Because of a promise given;
It was lashed to the sleigh, and it seemed to say:
"You may tax your brawn and brains,
But you promised true, and it's up to you
To cremate these last remains."

Now a promise made is a debt unpaid,
And the trail has its own stern code.
In the days to come, though my lips were dumb,
In my heart how I cursed that load!
In the long, long night, by the lone firelight,
While the huskies, round in a ring,
Howled out their woes to the homeless snows –
Oh God, how I loathed the thing!

And every day that quiet clay
Seemed to heavy and heavier grow;
And on I went, though the dogs were spent
And the grub was getting low.
The trail was bad, and I felt half-mad,
But I swore I would not give in;
And I'd often sing to the hateful thing,
And it hearkened with a grin.

Till I came to the marge of Lake Lebarge
And a derelict there lay;
It was jammed in the ice, but I saw in a trice
It was called the Alice May.
And I looked at it, and I thought a bit,
And I looked at my frozen chum;
Then "Here," said I, with a sudden cry,
"Is my cre-ma-tor-eum!"

Some planks I tore from the cabin floor,
And I lit the boiler fire;
Some coal I found that was lying around,
And I heaped the fuel higher;
The flames just soared, and the furnace roared—
Such a blaze you seldom see,
And I burrowed a hole in the glowing coal,
And I stuffed in Sam McGee.

Then I made a hike, for I didn't like
To hear him sizzle so;
And the heavens scowled, and the huskies howled
And the wind began to blow.
It was icy cold, but the hot sweat rolled
Down my cheeks, and I don't know why;
And the greasy smoke in an inky cloak
Went streaking down the sky.

I do not know how long in the snow
I wrestled with grisly fear;
But the stars came out and they danced about
Ere again I ventured near;
I was sick with dread, but I bravely said,
"I'll just take a peep inside.
I guess he's cooked, and it's time I looked."
Then the door I opened wide.

And there sat Sam, looking cool and calm,
In the heart of the furnace roar;
And he wore a smile you could see a mile,
And he said, "Please close that door.
It's fine in here, but I greatly fear
You'll let in the cold and storm –
Since I left Plumtree, down in Tennessee,
It's the first time I've been warm."

There are strange things done in the midnight sun
By the men who moil for gold;
The Arctic trails have their secret tales
That would make you blood run cold;
The Northern Lights have seen queer sights,
But the queerest they ever did see
Was that night on the marge of Lake Lebarge
I cremated Sam McGee.

THE MAN IN THE GLASS

Author Unknown

When you get what you want in your struggle for self
    And the world makes you king for a day,
Just go to the mirror and look at yourself,
    And see what that man has to say.

For it isn't your father or mother or wife
    Whose judgement upon you must pass.
The fellow whose verdict counts most in your life
    Is the one staring back from the glass.

You may be like Jack Horner and chisel a plum
    And think you're a wonderful guy.
But the man in the glass says you're only a bum
    If you can't look him straight in the eye.

He's the fellow to please – never mind all the rest,
    For he's with you clear to the end.
And you've passed your most dangerous, difficult test
    If the man in the glass is your friend.

You may fool the whole world down the pathway of years
    And get pats on the back as you pass.
But your final reward will be heartache and tears
    If you've cheated the man in the glass!

THE DANCER

Faith Frances Berlin

Ol' Jack 'ad a worm what 'e kept in a can what would
Crawl out and do us a dance on the bar.
Is that ridiculous? Sure! But it tickled us silly.
To us Winnie Worm was a star!

Whistlin' and clappin', we'd watch Winnie single-foot
Tap down the bar; a one-legged Astaire.
And we'd laugh and say, "Jees! She ain't even got knees!"
Man, I'd never believed it — if I wasn't there.

On Fridays we'd finish our shift and you'd find
Every one of us liftin' a beer in that dive.
Drawn to the place like a magnet was pullin' us;
All of us waitin' for Jack to arrive.

In 'e would stagger and nobody'd ask 'im,
But all of us 'eld the same thought to a man;
Sneakin' looks sideways and nudgin' and winkin';
And won'drin' if Jack had remembered the can.

After awhile someone caved in and shouted,
"Hey, Jack, 'ow about it? Where's Winnie tonight?"
And out came the can and then out wiggled Winnie;
A wonder of squirmy, earth-wormy delight.

String-like and skinny, I've never seen any
Of God's lowly creatures creative as she.
Lithe and gymnastic, she stretched like elastic,
More simply fantastic a worm couldn't be.

Loopin' and whirlin' and twirlin' ecstatic'ly,
She's acrobatic'ly tops in 'er field.
Watchin' 'er oddly-shaped pink naked body make
Shimmerin' circles your 'eart had to yield.

Oh sure, there was always some wise guy ta deal with,
A spoiler, a party-poop, you knows the kind,
Saying, "She's only squirmin' like any ol' worm an' if
You calls that dancin' you're drunk or you're blind!"

By rights that old bar was as dark as a dungeon,
So maybe we should'a left room for some doubt.
But somebody shoots out a fist for ol' Winnie,
And everyone cheers as we carries 'im out.

Week after week good ol' Winnie would do it.
We'd look forward to it, you know, and we'd sing
Some ol' song we remembered while she, soft and limber,
Would writhe to the rhythm — a magical thing.

There in awed silence, with just Jimmy whistlin',
We'd watch Winnie twirlin' around on her toe.
There in that dark smoky dive we'd stand squintin',
Our eyes, spillin' beer and enjoyin' the show.

But one night poor Freddie, 'e pulls out a flashlight.
"Let's give 'er a spotlight," 'e says with a laugh.
It showed 'er off swell as he 'eld it above 'er,
But some 'ow it fell, cutting Winnie in half.

"Ya killed her!" Jack screamed as we stared at the pieces,
A half-mangled mess only Jack could retrieve.
"Ya killed her!" He cradled the can, Winnie's coffin,
An' somebody wiped off the bar with 'is sleeve.

*　　　*　　　*　　　*

We di'n't see Jack for a month after that, and we
Knowed 'e was grievin' 'cause Winnie was dead.
Poor Freddie, 'e'd sit at the bar slowly turnin'
That death-dealin' flashlight and shakin' his 'ead.

And more than a few of us cried in our beer,
As we wondered if creatures like Winnie had souls.
"It's only a worm, fer Chrissake!" says the Barkeep.
Our eyes shot 'is blasphemous 'eart full'a 'oles.

Oh, Lord, 'ow we missed watching Winnie's sweet dancing;
Her mystical movements to simple refrains.
An' nobody's glass ever sullied the spot
On the bar where we wiped off poor Winnie's remains.

195

There wasn't much laughin' or talk anymore,
And like statues we'd sit starin' off into space.
It's strange 'ow you feel when you lose somethin' magic;
It's somethin' you knows nothin' real can replace.

We still came around for a beer every Friday,
But no use in foolin' ourselves, it was plain
We were right back to losers, to beer bums and boozers;
All yearnin' for somethin' we couldn't explain.

*   *   *   *

Then one night there's Jack strollin' in through the door
And 'e's slappin' 'igh-fives and 'e's walkin' on air.
"'Ey, Jack! Welcome back!" And he's got this ol' grin on
Like you've got an ace but 'e's 'oldin' a pair.

'E 'ikes up a stool and 'e's playing it cool
As 'e leans back and takes a long pull on 'is beer.
Then casually placin' 'is back to the bar till 'e's
Facin' us, "Fellas, I got somethin' 'ere. . ."

'E brings out the can; Winnie's can, you remember.
The sight of it rips out a gasp from the guys,
And just for a second I'm thinkin', "It's Winnie!
No — I saw 'er go — with me very own eyes."

A hush of excitement befalls us and I'm barely
Breathin'; we're all of us elbows and grins.
Jack tips out the can on the bar and 'e's tellin' us,
"Winnie's come back! An' she's twice what she's been."

And there on the bar, a bit short, and no wonder,
But up on their toes, two Winnies appear.
Can they dance? Aw, who cares?
Were too damn drunk and happy.
Twice the magic is back! "Ey, who's buyin' the beer?"

THE DEACON'S MASTERPIECE
(THE WONDERFUL "ONE HOSS SHAY")

A Logical Story by Oliver Wendell Holmes

Have you heard of the wonderful one-hoss shay,
That was built in such a logical way
It ran a hundred years to a day,
And then, of a sudden, it—ah, but stay,
I'll tell you what happened without delay,
Scaring the parson into fits,
Frightening people out of their wits,
Have you heard of that, I say?

Seventeen Hundred and Fifty Five.
Georgius Secundus was then alive,
Snuffy old drone from the German hive.
That was the year when Lisbon-town
Saw the earth open and gulp her down,
And Braddock's army was done so brown,
Left without a scalp to its crown.
It was on the terrible, Earthquake-day
That the Deacon finished the one-hoss shay.

Now in building of chaises, I tell you what,
There is always somewhere a weakest spot,
In hub, tire, felloe, in spring or thill,
In pancl, or crossbar, or floor , or sill,
In screw, bolt, thoroughbrace,—lurking still,
Find it somewhere you must and will,
Above or below, or within or without,
And that's the reason, beyond a doubt,
A chaise breaks down but doesn't wear out.

But the Deacon swore (as Deacons do,
With an "I dew vum," or an "I tell ycou")
He would build one shay to beat the taown
'N the keounty 'n' all the kentry raoun':
It should be so built that it couldn; break daown:
"Fur," said the Deacon, " 't's mighty plain
Thut the weakes' places mus' stan' the strain;
'N' the way t' fix it, uz I maintain, is only jest
T' make that place uz strong us the rest."

197

So the Deacon inquired of the village folk
Where he could find the strongest oak,
That couldn't be split nor bent nor broke,
That was for spokes and floor and sills;
He sent for lancewood to make the thills;
The crossbars were ash, from the straightest trees;
But lasts like iron for things like these;
The hubs of logs from the "Settler's ellum,
Last of its timber, they couldn't sell 'em,
Never an axe had seen their chips,
And the wedges flew from between their lips,
Their blunt ends frizzled like celery-tips;

Step and prop-iron, bolt and screw,
Spring, tire, axle, and linchpin too,
Steel of the finest, bright and blue;
Thoroughbrace bison-skin, thick and wide;
Boot, top, dasher, from tough old hide
Found in the pit where the tanner died.
That was the way he "put her through."
"There!" said the Deacon, "naow she'll dew!"

Do! I tell you, I rather guess
She was a wonder, and nothing less!
Colts grew horses, beards turned gray,
Deacon and deaconess dropped away,
Children and grandchildren—where were they?
But there stood the stout old one-hoss shay
As fresh as on Lisbon-earthquake-day!

Eighteen Hundred; — It came and found
The Deacon's masterpiece strong and sound.
Eighteen hundred increased by ten;
"Hahnsum kerridge" they called it then.
Eighteen hundred and twenty came;
Running as usual; much, the same.
Thirty and forty at last arrive,
And then come fifty, and fifty-five.
Little of all we value here
Wakes on the morn of its hundredth year
Without both feeling and looking queer.

In fact, there's nothing that keeps its youth,
So far as I know, but a tree and truth.
This is a moral that runs at large;
(Take it. You're welcome. No extra charge.)

First of November, the Earthquake-day.
There are traces of age in the one-hoss shay,
A general flavor of mild decay,
But nothing local as one may say.
There couldn't be,— for the Deacon's art
Had made it so like in every part
That there wasn't a chance for one to start,
For the wheels were just as strong as the thills,
And the floor was just as strong as the sills
And the panels just as strong as the floor,
And the whipple-tree neither less nor more,
And the back-crossbar as strong as the fore,
And spring and axle and hub encore.
And yet, as a whole, it is past a doubt
In another hour it will be worn out!

First of November, 'Fifty-five!
This morning the parson takes a drive.
Now, small boys, get out of the way!
Here comes the wonderful one-hoss shay,
Drawn by a rat-tailed, ewe-necked bay.
"Huddup!" said the parson. Off went they.
The parson was working his Sunday's text,
Had got to fifthly, and stopped perplexed
At what the —Moses – was coming next.

All at once the horse stood still,
Close by the meet'n'-house on the hill
First a shiver, and then a thrill,
Then something decidedly like a spill,
And the parson was sitting upon a rock,
At half-past nine by the meet'n'-house clock,
Just the hour of the earthquake shock!

What do you think the parson found,
When he got up and stared around?
The poor old chaise in a heap or mound,
As if it had been to the mill and ground!
You see, of course, if you're not a dunce,
How it went to pieces all at once,
All at once and nothing first,
Just as bubbles do when they burst.

End of the wonderful one-hoss shay.
Logic is logic. That's all I say.

THE PREACHER'S MISTAKE

William Croswell Doane

The Parish priest of austerity
Climbed up in a high church steeple
To be nearer God so that he might hand
His word down to His people.

When the sun was high, when the sun was low,
The good man sat, unheeding sublunary things.
From transcendency
Was he forever reading.

And now and again, when he heard the creak
Of the weather vane a-turning,
He closed his eyes and said, "Of a truth
From God I now am learning."

And in sermon script, he daily wrote
What he thought was sent from heaven;
And he dropped this down on his people's heads
Two times one day in seven.

In his age, God said, "Come down and die!"
And he cried out from the steeple,
"Where art thou, Lord?" and the Lord replied,
"Down here among my people."

THE DEFECTIVE MIRROR

Michele S. Kurlander

Who is this hag in the mirror
With cross and furrowed brow?
That aging crone with sagging flesh
Is not someone I know.

My eyes are weaker than they were;
They don't see things so clear.
I need to find my spectacles;
They must be somewhere near.

When I can see, I'll look again
And ask this stranger why
She's hiding in my bedroom mirror
And how she has come by.

Oh, there they are! I'll look again.
I'll sneak another take.
(She looks a little like my mom,
When she was first awake.)

Her eyes are baggy, wet, and tired.
There's blotches on her cheeks.
She seems to not have rested for
Several days or weeks.

Her tummy has that rounded look
That comes with middle age.
I tear my glasses off my face
In furious crimson rage.

Like all equipment sold today
That mirror is clearly broken.
I'll call a man to fix the thing,
Tomorrow, when I've woken!

THE DUEL

Eugene Field

The gingham dog and the calico cat
Side by side on the table sat;
'Twas half-past twelve, and (what do you think!)
Nor one nor t'other had slept a wink!
    The old Dutch clock and the Chinese plate
    Appeared to know as sure as fate
There was going to be a terrible spat.

*(I wasn't there; I simply state
what was told to me by the Chinese plate!)*

The gingham dog went, "bow-wow-wow!"
And the calico cat replied, "mee-ow!"
The air was littered, an hour or so,
With bits of gingham and calico,
    While the old Dutch clock in the chimney-place
    Up with its hands before its face,
For it always dreaded a family row!

*(Now mind: I'm only telling you
what the Old Dutch clock declares is true!)*

The Chinese plate looked very blue,
And wailed, "Oh, dear! What shall we do?"
But the gingham dog and the calico cat
Wallowed this way and tumbled that,
    Employing every tooth and claw
    In the awfullest way you ever saw—
And, oh! How the gingham and calico flew!

*(Don't fancy I exaggerate—
I got my news from the Chinese plate!)*

Next morning, where the two had sat
They found no trace of dog or cat
And some folks think unto this day
That burglars stole that pair away!
   But the truth about the cat and pup
   Is this: they ate each other up!
Now what do you really think of that!

(The old Dutch clock it told me so,and that
is how I came to know.)

TURN-ABOUT

W. Williams

Maybe I am quixotic,
Or, shall we say? Neurotic?
Well, here's a conundrum:
Why have men gift of tongue
When noble dogs are dumb?
Aye, that's the conundrum!
And if I could dispose it,
'Tis thus I would transpose it;
Our dogs should have the gift of tongue,
And every silly man be dumb!

THE DOG THAT WENT TO CHURCH

Hilda Van Stockum

Outside the church the dogs were waiting.
> Outside the magic door they knew
They could not enter. They were waiting
> For their masters to come through.

They discussed among each other
> How it was that only here
In this place, their owners left them,
> Would not tolerate them near.

Suddenly their chatter halted
> As with popping eyes they saw
How a great big grey police dog
> Calmly walked in as though HE was called.

"He'll be kicked out," they predicted.
> "Watch and see him howl with pain."
But though eagerly they waited,
> They didn't see the dog again.

He was sitting near the altar
> With a dignity unmatched,
While his little master, kneeling,
> Received Communion as he watched.

Then the dog with gentle movements
> Led the child back to his seat,
And later, when the Mass was over
> Out again into the street.

The other dogs there watched in silence,
> Moved aside to let them pass.
They understood. To aid the sightless,
> Even dogs may go to Mass.

THE FASTEST GOAT ALIVE

Bill Foster

Now I ain't one to boast or brag,
    But the fastest animal known
Was bought by Ol' Tom Murray,
    When only three-quarters grown.
He had outstanding qualities
    And were I to just pick one,
I'd have to name his greatest trait - -
    That goat could surely run.

We paced him with a Jeep one time,
    Me an' another guy,
An' our jeep was going eighty
    When that dern goat sailed on by.
I told the boys at Reilly's Bar,
    "Let's keep this under wrap,
An' we might make a little cash
    From some poor gambling sap."

So Ed and me, we went to see,
    A high bred gambler named Ted,
Seems like he owned some stable,
    And a champion thoroughbred.
We watched his big horse training
    And we sort of out loud said,
"He's sort a fast, but what a shame,
    His feet is made of lead."

This gambling man turned slow around,
    His face all strained an' red,
An he walks right up into my face,
    An' asks what I just said.
An' I all ups with apologies,
    An' admits his horse is fast.
An' finishes with a sad lament,
    "To bad he's so outclassed."

"Outclassed?" he screamed. "What do you mean?
    He's a champion thoroughbred!
He's beat the best from East and West,
    And never less than a head!"

"Well, that was in the past," I says,
　　　　"An' we ain't ones to gloat,
But, we could beat that horse of yours,
　　　　An' do it with our goat!"

I thought he'd drop a laughter,
　　　　An' he says, "Just what's he done?"
An' I told how him how he'd raced some turtles,
　　　　And came in number one.
I tol' him of a snail race,
　　　　That we held in our small town,
And how our goat came from behind,
　　　　And won the race hands down.

The dollar signs clicked within his eyes.
　　　　He said, "Let's make a bet."
He took the bait and then I says,
　　　　"Sir, what odds can we get?"
"Why, ten to one," he screamed with joy.
　　　　"We'll run a race at noon.
You've got two weeks to train your goat.
　　　　We'll meet the sixth of June!"

We raced on back to Reilly's Bar
　　　　We had to pick a trainer,
And Clancy claimed he should be named,
　　　　Cause he'd fished aboard a seiner.
He said, "Now you can't figure out,
　　　　How that's hooked up with goats?
Well, let me tell you time's all you have,
　　　　On anything that floats."

So, just so I'd be occupied
　　　　An' not go touched from the strains,
I read me books and one on goats
　　　　And how to pick their brains.
He said, "On top a that, my friends,
　　　　My mind is most inventive;
To make a goat run really fast,
　　　　He's got to have incentive!"

206

A master plan was thus conceived,
      For three days at a stretch,
We wouldn't feed the goat a thing,
      And then, here was the catch.
We'd take a great big garbage can
      And fill it to the top
With all the things a goat loves best,
      And round it off with slop.

On feedin' days we'd take that goat
      A mile down the road,
An' he'd take off a running,
      When the garbage can was showed.
By the fifth of June he was so fast
      He had to stop and skid
To give Ed time to jump aside
      When he would jerk the lid.

Now race day was a sight to see
      The boys from Reilly's Bar
Were takin' bets from gentry folk
      Who came from near and far.
They couldn't see the wall we'd built
      Surrounded by a moat,
Two miles beyond the race track
      Just to slow McMurray's goat.

An' at twelve o'clock, the race began;
      The horse, it took the lead.
McMurray's goat was super weak,
      (Of course, from lack of feed.)
The guy who owned the thoroughbred screamed,
      "I've won. I've won this race!"
His friends did gloat, and disparaged the goat,
      That could not even place.

Whilst I just leaned against the rail
      And did suppress a smile;
Oh, the thoroughbred was leading all right,
      But only by half a mile.
Now, no one seemed to notice
      When I raised and dropped my hand,
But Ed, he caught my signal
      And he raised the garbage can.

A thunderclap then rent the air,
   A mushroom cloud of dust.
Went spewing to the heavens,
   As I breathed, "In God We Trust."
I hoped the wall would slow him,
   Or the water in the moat
'Cause Tom was in the saddle,
   And here comes McMurray's Goat.

Now, fourteen inches from the wire,
   A blazing streak of white
Shot past that startled racehorse
   And disappeared from sight.
"McMurray's Goat has won,"
   We screamed; I thought I'd lose my head.
But the garbage can had disappeared
   And so had Tom and Ed.

Two miles beyond the race track
   The sound was heard by all,
Was like a blast of dynamite
   When that poor goat hit the wall.
Now late that night the telephone rang
   Down at Reilly's Bar.
'Twas Tom and Ed in Idaho:
   "Could someone bring a car?"

They'd finally got the goat to stop,
   One hundred miles from home.
I swear it's true. I'm telling you,
   I heard them on the phone.
Oh, I've been known to stretch the truth,
   And fancy up a fact,
But I confess I wouldn't mess
   With what happened on that track.

An' if you've doubts, at Reilly's Bar,
   Stop in and you will find,
Mc Murray's Goat with his handicap sheets
   And the Derby on his mind!
An' if its true, I'm telling you,
   Cash in your stocks and poke,
And bet with the boys at the window,
   On the long shot McMurray's Goat !

THE FEMALE OF THE SPECIES

Rudyard Kipling

When the Himalayan peasant
    Meets the he-bear in his pride,
He shouts to scare the monster,
    Who will often turn aside.
But the she-bear thus accosted
    Rends the peasant tooth and nail,
For the female of the species
    Is more deadly than the male.

When Nag, the basking cobra,
    Hears the careless foot of man,
He will sometimes wriggle sideways
    And avoid it if he can.
But his mate makes no such motion
    Where she camps beside the trail,
For the female of the species
    Is more deadly than the male.

When the early Jesuit fathers
    Preached to Hurons and Choctaws,
They prayed to be delivered
    From the vengeance of the squaws.
'Twas the women, not the warriors,
    Turned those stark enthusiasts pale.
For the female of the species
    Is more deadly than the male.

Man's timid heart is bursting
    With the things he must not say,
For the Woman that God gave him
    Isn't his to give away;
But when hunter meets with husband,
    Each confirms the other's tale—
The female of the species
    Is more deadly that the male.

Man, a bear in most relations—
    Worm and savage otherwise,—
Man propounds negotiations;
    Man accepts the compromise.

Very rarely will he squarely
        Push the logic of a fact
To its ultimate conclusion
        In unmitigated act.

Fear or foolishness impels him,
        Ere he lay the wicked low
To concede some form of trial
        Even to his fiercest foe.
Mirth obscene diverts his anger—
        Doubt and Pity oft perplex
Him in dealing with an issue—
        To the scandal of The Sex!

But the Woman that God gave him,
        Every fiber of her frame
Proves her launched for one sole issue,
        Armed and engined for the same;
And to serve that single issue,
        Lest the generations fail,
The female of the species
        Must be deadlier that the male.

She who faces Death by torture
        For each life beneath her breast
May not deal in doubt or pity—
        Must not swerve for fact or jest.
These be purely male diversions—
        Not in these her honour dwells.
She the Other Law we live by,
        Is that Law and nothing else.

She can bring no more to living
        Than the powers that make her great
As the Mother of the Infant
        And the Mistress of the Mate.
And when Babe and Man are lacking
        And she strides unclaimed to claim
Her right as femme (and baron),
        Her equipment is the same.

She is wedded to convictions—
        In default of grosser ties;
Her contentions are her children,
        Heaven help him who denies!—
He will meet no suave discussion,
        But the instant, white-hot, wild,
Wakened female of the species
        Warring as for spouse and child.

Unprovoked and awful charges—
        Even so the she-bear fights,
Speech that drips, corrodes, and poisons—
        Even so the cobra bites,
Scientific vivisection
        Of one nerve till it is raw
And the victim writhes in anguish—
        Like the Jesuit with the squaw!

So it comes that Man, the coward,
        When he gathers to confer
With his fellow-braves in council,
        Dare not leave a place for her.
Where, at war with Life and Conscience,
        He uplifts his erring hands
To some God of Abstract Justice—
        Which no woman understands.

And Man knows it! Knows, moreover,
        That the Woman that God gave him
Must command but may not govern—
        Shall enthrall but not enslave him.
And she knows, because She warns him,
        And Her instincts never fail,
That the Female of Her Species
        Is more deadly than the male.

THE GIRL WITH
THE BLUE VELVET BAN

Author Unknown

In that city of wealth, beauty and fashion,
Dear old Frisco where I first saw the light,
And the many frolics that I had there
Are still fresh in my memory tonight.

One evening while out for a ramble
Here or there without thought or design,
I chanced on a young girl, tall and slender,
At the corner of Kearney and Pine.

On her face was the first flush of nature,
And bright eyes seemed to expand;
While her hair fell in rich, brilliant masses
Was entwined in a Blue Velvet Band.

To a house of gentle ruination,
She invited me with a sweet smile;
She seemed so refined, gay and charming
That I thought I would tarry awhile.

She then shared with me a collection
Of wines of an excellent brand
And conversed in politest language
This girl with the Blue Velvet Band.

After lunch, to a well-kept apartment,
We repaired to the third floor above;
And I thought myself truly in Heaven
Where reigneth the Goddess of Love.

Her lady's taste was resplendent,
From the graceful arrangement of things,
From the pictures that stood on the bureau,
To a little bronze Cupid with wings.

But what struck me the most was an object
Designed by an artistic hand;
'Twas the costly "lay-out" of a hop-fiend,
And that fiend was my Blue Velvet Band.

On a pile of soft robes and pillows
She reclined, I declare, on the floor.
Then we both hit the pipe and I slumbered;
I ponder over and o'er.

'Tis months since the craven arm grasped me,
And in bliss did my life glide away,
From opium to "dipping" and thieving,
She artfully led day by day.

One evening, coming home wet and dreary
With the swag from a jewelry store,
I heard the soft voice of my loved one
As I gently opened the door.

"If you'll give me a clue to convict him,"
Said a stranger, in tones soft and bland,
"You'll then prove to me that you love me."
"It's a go," said my Blue Velvet Band.

Ah! How my heart filled with anger
At woman, so fair, false and vile,
And to think that I once true adored her
Brought to my lips a contemptible smile.

All ill-gotten gains we had squandered,
And my life was hers to command;
Betrayed and deserted for another—
Could this be my Blue Velvet Band?

Just a few moments before I was hunted
By the cops, who wounded me, too,
And my temper was none the sweetest
As I swung myself into their view.

And the copper, not liking the glitter
Of the "44" Colt in my hand,
Hurriedly left through the window,
Leaving me with my Blue Velvet Band.

What happened to me I will tell you;
I was "ditched" for a desperate crime.
There was hell in a bank about midnight,
And my pal was shot down in his prime.

As a convict of hard reputation,
Ten years of hard grind I did land;
And I often thought of the pleasures
I had with my Blue Velvet Band.

One night as bedtime was ringing,
I was standing close to the bars;
I fancied I heard a girl singing,
Far out in the ocean of stars.

Her voice had the same touch of sadness
I knew that but one could command;
It had the same thrill of gladness
As that of my Blue Velvet Band.

Many months have passed since this happened,
And the story belongs to the past;
I forgave her, but just retribution
Claimed this fair, but false one, at last.

She slowly sank lower and lower
Down through life's shifting sands,
'Till finally she died in a hop joint,
This girl with the Blue Velvet Band.

If she had been true when I met her,
A bright future for us was in store;
For I was an able mechanic,
And honest and square to the core.

But as sages of old have contended,
What's decreed us mortals must stand;
So a grave in the potter's field ended
My romance with the Blue Velvet Band.

Now, when I get out I will hasten
Back to my home town again
Where my chances are good for some dollars
All the way from a thousand to ten.

And if I'm in luck I'll endeavor
To live honest in some other land
And bid farewell to dear old Frisco
And the grave of my Blue Velvet Band.

WOMAN

Linda Robertson

The epitome of human kind,
She's elegance and grace.
The joy of being female
Is written on her face.

She walks in beauty all day through,
Her chores are done with pride.
Her love of those she holds so dear
Is always kept inside.

She shows her love through giving,
Through touch with loving hands.
She carries memories in her heart
That she alone understands.

She is the earth, the moon, the stars;
She is the soil and the sod;
She is the perfect gift to man;
She is the gift of God.

215

THE GREAT PROVIDER

Bill Foster

Sumac, alder, birch and maple,
Poplar, fir and spruce,
Beechnuts for the clucking grouse,
And willow shoots for moose.
Mushrooms mild for white-tailed deer,
And hazelnuts to bury,
There's a squirrel now, going by,
With all that he can carry.

Five inch earthworms in my garden,
Perfect size for trout,
God, you've thought of everything,
There's nothing you left out.
Rainy days to raise the brook
And sunshine for my corn,
You've been The Great Provider,
Since the day that I was born.

How'd you put that beaver pond
With setting sun behind it
One point eight miles from my door
And right where I could find it?
How come all those grouse last fall
Could not believe my luck?
I must have seen fourteen fly by
While sitting in my truck.

Lord, I've been neglectful;
I never once said Thanks,
For Fiddleheads that hide from me,
On flooded riverbanks
Or salmon laying where the Tay
Flows to the Nashwaak River.
I've always been recipient,
With you Lord, as the giver.

But right today all that will change,
And I won't need a prod
To say what burns within my heart,
A simple, Thank You, God.

THE MAN HE KILLED

Thomas Hardy

Had he and I but met
By some old ancient inn,
We should have sat us down to wet
Right many a nipperkin!

But ranged as infantry,
And staring face to face,
I shot at him as he at me,
And killed him in his place.

I shot him dead because —
Because he was my foe,
Just so: my foe of course he was;
That's clear enough; although

He thought he'd 'list, perhaps,
Off-hand – just as I –
Was out of work – had sold his traps –
No other reason why.

Yes; quaint and curious war is!
You shoot a fellow down
You'd treat if met where any bar is
Or help to half-a-crown.

THE HARPY

Robert Service

There was a woman, and she was wise,
Woefully wise was she.
She was old, so old, yet her years all told
Were but a score and three;
And she knew by heart, from finish to start,
The Book of Iniquity.

There is no hope for such as I
On earth, nor yet in Heaven;
Unloved I live, unloved I die,
Unpitied, unforgiven.
A loathed jade, I ply my trade,
Unhallowed and unshriven.

I paint my cheeks, for they are white,
And cheeks of chalk men hate.
Mine eyes with wine I make to shine
That man may seek and sate.
With overhead a lamp of red
I sit me down and wait.

Until they come, the nightly scum,
With drunken eyes aflame,
Your sweethearts, sons, ye scornful ones —
'Tis I who know their shame.
The gods, ye see, are brutes to me—
And so I play my game.

For life is not the thing we thought,
And not the thing we plan.
And Woman in a bitter world
Must do the best she can —
Must yield the stroke and bear the yoke
And serve the will of man,

Must serve his need and ever feed
The flame of his desire
Though be she loved for love alone,
Or be she loved for hire,
For every man since life began
Is tainted with the mire.

And though you know he loves you so
And sets you on love's throne,
Yet let your eyes but mock his sighs,
And let your heart be stone,
Lest you be left (as I was left)
Attainted and alone.

From love's close kiss to hell's abyss
Is one sheer flight I trow.
And wedding ring and bridal bell
Are will-o'-wisps of woe.
And 'tis not wise to love too well,
And this all women know.

Wherefore, the wolf-pack having gorged
Upon the lamb, their prey,
With siren smile and serpent guile
I make the wolf-pack pay —
With velvet paws and flensing claws,
A tigress roused to slay.

One who in youth sought truest truth
And found a devil's lies,
A symbol of the sin of man,
A human sacrifice.
Yet shall I blame on man the shame?
Could it be otherwise?

Was I not born to walk in scorn
Where others walk in pride?
The Maker marred and evil-starred
I drift upon His tide,
And He alone shall judge His own,
So I his judgement bide.

Fate has written a tragedy;
Its name is "The Human Heart".
The Theater is the House of Life,
Woman, the mummer's part.
The Devil enters the prompter's box,
And the play is ready to start.

THE HELL-BOUND TRAIN

Author Unknown

A Texas cowboy lay down on a barroom floor,
Having drunk so much he could drink no more;
So he fell asleep with a troubled brain
To dream that he rode on a hell-bound train.

The engine with murderous blood was damp
And was brilliantly lit with a brimstone lamp;
An imp, for fuel, was shoveling bones,
While the furnace rang with a thousand groans.

The boiler was filled with lager beer
And the devil himself was the engineer;
The passengers were a most motley crew—
Church member, atheist, Gentile, and Jew,

Rich men in broadcloth, beggars in rags,
Handsome young ladies, and withered old hags,
Yellow and black men, red, brown, and white,
All chained together—O God, what a sight!

While the train rushed on at an awful pace—
The sulphurous fumes scorched their hands and face;
Wider and wider the country grew,
As faster and faster the engine flew.

Louder and louder the thunder crashed,
Brighter and brighter the lightning flashed;
Hotter and hotter the air became
Till the clothes were burned from each quivering frame.

And out of the distance there arose a yell,
"Ha, ha," said the devil, "we're nearing Hell!"
Then oh, how the passengers all shrieked with pain
And begged the devil to stop the train.

But he capered about and danced for glee
And laughed and joked at their misery.
"My faithful friends, you have done the work,
And the devil never can a payday shirk.

You've bullied the weak, you've robbed the poor.
The starving brother you've turned from the door.
You've laid up gold where the canker rust
And have given free vent to your beastly lust.

You've justice scorned and corruption sown
And trampled the laws of nature down.
You have drunk, rioted, cheated, plundered, and lied,
And mocked at God in your hell-born pride.

You have paid full fare, so I'll carry you through,
For it's only right you should have your due.
Why, the laborer always expects his hire,
So I'll land you safe in the lake of fire,

Where your flesh will waste in the flames that roar,
And my imps torment you forevermore.
Then the cowboy awoke with an anguished cry,
His clothes wet with sweat and his hair standing high.

Then he prayed as he never had prayed till that hour
To be saved from his sin and the demon's power;
And his prayers and his vows were not in vain,
For he never rode the hell-bound train.

THE HOMECOMING

Royal L. Craig

All day long did our winsome Kate
Stare far out o'er the sea.
"Won't you come back
My handsome Jack
Come sailing home to me?"

Now Jack had signed on board the brig,
The square-sailed Columbine.
Two masts she bore,
Cannons four,
And twenty at the line.

Oh, Katey, Katey, bide a wee
Till your Jack returns to home.
I'll kiss you twice
And Hug you thrice,
And never more will roam.

A hurricane hit the Columbine
Close-reefed she ran before.
Her heart was oak
But still she broke,
Onto the rock-bound shore.

The sea was crashing all around;
The ship was sinking fast.
Though most were lost,
Her Jack was tossed
To a timber from the mast.

It took a month for word to reach
Our winsome Katey's ear.
The ship was gone,
Her Jack along
To a cold and watery bier.

Our Katey watched the boiling reef,
The gateway to the sea.
"My Jack. My Jack.
You can't come back,
I will keep you company!"

It took six months for Jack's return,
Back to his winsome Kate.
Her father sighed.
Her mother cried,
"Oh Jack, you've come too late."

Our Jack has never taken wife,
Nor sought another's hand.
Fresh roses wave
Above her grave
That overlooks the strand.

And one dark eve', upon the reef,
Jack cried aloud this plea,
"Oh, winsome Kate,
I cannot wait!"
And vanished in the sea.

If you go down to Watson's Walk
And phantom forms appear,
Just say a prayer
While walking there
And even shed a tear.

Two hearts driven by heartless fate
To surrender to the sea,
And loud and long
Hear Katey's song,
"My Jack's come back to me!"

THE INDIAN BURYING GROUND

Philip Freneau

In spite of all the learned have said,
  I still my old opinion keep;
The posture, that we give the dead,
  Points out the soul's eternal sleep.

Not so the ancients of these lands—
  The Indian, when from life released,
Again is seated with his friends
  And shares again the joyous feast.

His imaged birds and painted bowl
  And venison for a journey dressed,
Bespeak the nature of the soul,
  Activity, that knows no rest.

His bow, for action ready bent,
  And arrows, with a head of stone,
Can only mean that life is spent,
  And not the old ideas gone.

Thou, stranger, that shalt come this way,
  No fraud upon the dead commit.
Observe the swelling turf and say
  They do not lie, but here they sit.

Here still a lofty rock remains
  On which the curious eye may trace,
(Now wasted, half, by wearing rains)
  The fancies of a ruder race.

Here still an aged elm aspires
  Beneath whose far-projecting shade,
(And which the shepherd still admires),
  The children of the forest played!

There oft a restless Indian queen
  (Pale Shebah, with her braided hair)
And many a barbarous form is seen
  To chide the man that lingers there.

By midnight moons, o'er moistening dews
   In habit for the chase arrayed,
The hunter still the deer pursues,
   The hunter and the deer, a shade!

And long shall timorous fancy see
   The painted chief and pointed spear
And Reason's self shall bow the knee
   To shadows and delusions here.

THE ROAD TO VAGABONDIA

Dana Burnet

He was sitting on a doorstep
    As I went strolling by,
A lonely little beggar
    With a wistful, homesick eye.
And he wasn't what you'd borrow,
    And he wasn't what you'd steal;
But I guessed his heart was breaking
    So I whistled him to heel.

They had stoned him through the city streets,
    And naught the city cared;
But I was heading outward
    And the roads are sweeter shared.
So I took him for a comrade,
    And I whistled him away
On the road to Vagabondia,
    That lies across the way.

Yellow dog he was; but bless you,
    He was just the chap for me!
For I'd rather have an inch of mutt
    Than a mile of pedigree.
So we stole away together
    On the road that has no end
With all the new born day to fling away
    And all the stars to spend!

THE JUMBLIES

Edward Lear

They went to sea in a Sieve, they did,
      In a Sieve they went to sea.
In spite of all their friends could say,
On a winter's morn, on a stormy day,
      In a Sieve they went to sea!
And when the Sieve turned round and round,
And every one cried, "You'll all be drowned!"
They called aloud, "Our Sieve ain't big,
But we don't care a button! We don't care a fig!
      In a Sieve we'll go to sea!"
Far and few, far and few,
      Are the lands where the Jumblies live;
Their heads are green, and their hands are blue,
      And they went to sea in a Sieve.

The water it soon came in, it did,
      The water it soon came in.
So to keep them dry, they wrapped their feet
In a pinky paper all folded neat,
      And they fastened it down with a pin.
And they passed the night in a crockery-jar,
And each of them said, "How wise we are!
Though the sky be dark, and the voyage be long,
Yet we never can think we were rash or wrong,
While round in our Sieve we spin!"
      Far and few, far and few,
      Are the lands where the Jumblies live.
      Their heads are green and their hands are blue,
      And they went to sea in a sieve.

And all night long they sailed away;
      And when the sun went down,
They whistled and warbled a moony song
To the echoing sound of a coppery gong,
      In the shade of the mountains brown,
"O Timballo! How happy we are,
When we live in a sieve and a crockery-jar;
And all night long in the moonlight pale,
We sail away with a pea green sail,

In the shade of the mountains brown!"
Far and few, far and few,
Are the lands where the Jumblies live;
Their heads are green, and their hands are blue,
And they went to sea in a Sieve.

They sailed to the Western Sea they did,
To a land all covered with trees,
And they bought an Owl and a useful Cart
And a pound of Rice and a Cranberry Tart
And a hive of silvery Bees.
And they bought a Pig and some green Jack-daws
And a lovely Monkey with lollipop paws
And forty bottles of Ring-Bo-Ree,
And no end of Stilton Cheese.
Far and few, far and few,
Are the lands where the Jumblies live;
Their heads are green, and their hands are blue,
And they went to sea in a Sieve.

And in twenty years they all came back,
In twenty years or more,
And every one said, "How tall they've grown!
For they've been to the Lakes, and the Torrible Zone,
And the hills of the Chankly Bore."
And they drank their health and gave them a feast
Of dumplings made of beautiful yeast;"
And every one said, "If we only live,
We too will go to sea in a Sieve,—
To the hills of the Chankly Bore!"
Far and few, far and few,
Are the lands where the Jumblies live.
Their heads are green, and their hands are blue,
And they went to sea in a Sieve.

THE LEGEND OF THE ORGAN-BUILDER

Julia C. R. Dorr

Day by day the Organ-Builder in his lonely chamber wrought.
Day by day the soft air trembled to the music of his thought
Till at last the work was ended and no organ-voice so grand
Ever yet had soared responsive to the master's magic hand.

Ay, so rarely was it builded that whenever groom and bride,
Who in God's sight were well pleasing, in the church stood side by side.
Without touch or breath the organ of itself began to play,
And the very airs of heaven through the soft gloom seemed to stray.

He was young, the Organ-builder, and o'er all the land his fame
Ran with fleet and eager footsteps like a swiftly rushing flame.
All the maidens heard the story. All the maidens blushed and smiled,
By his youth and wondrous beauty and his great renown beguiled.

So he sought and won the fairest, and the wedding day was set.
Happy day — the brightest jewel in the glad year's coronet!
But when they the portal entered, he forgot his lovely bride—
Forgot his love, forgot his God, and his heart swelled high with pride.

"Ah!" thought he; "how great a master am I, when the organ plays,
How the vast cathedral arches will re-echo with my praise!"
Up the aisle the gay procession moved. The altar shone afar
With every candle gleaming through soft shadows like a star.

But he listened, listened, listened, with no thought of love or prayer
For the swelling notes of triumph from his organ standing there.
All was silent. Nothing heard he save the priest's low monotone,
And the bride's robe trailing softly o'er the floor of fretted stone.

Then his lips grew white with anger. Surely God was pleased with him
Who built the wondrous organ for His temple vast and dim!
Whose the fault, then? Hers, the maiden standing meekly at his side!
Flamed his jealous rage, maintaining she was false to him, his bride.

Vain were all her protestations, vain her innocence and truth.
On that very night he left her to her anguish and her ruth.
Far he wandered to a country wherein no man knew his name;
For ten weary years he dwelt there, nursing still his wrath and shame.

Then his haughty heart grew softer, and he thought by night and day
Of the bride he had deserted, till he hardly dared to pray.
Thought of her, a spotless maiden, fair and beautiful and good,
Thought of his relentless anger that had cursed her womanhood.

Till his yearning, grief, and penitence at last were all complete,
And he longed, with bitter longing, just to fall down at her feet.
Ah! How throbbed his heart when after many a weary day and night,
Rose his native towers before him, with the sunset glow alight!

Through the gates into the city, on he pressed with eager tread;
There he met a long procession—mourners following the dead.
"Now, why weep ye so, good people? And whom bury ye today?
Why do yonder sorrowing maidens scatter flowers along the way?

Has some saint gone up to heaven?" "Yes," they answered, weeping sore;
"For the Organ-Builder's saintly wife our eyes shall see no more;
And because her days were given to the service of God's poor,
From his church we mean to bury her. See, yonder is the door!"

No one knew him; no one wondered when he cried out, white with pain.
No one questioned when, with pallid lips, he poured his tears like rain.
" 'Tis someone whom she has comforted who mourns with us," they said,
As he made his way unchallenged and bore the coffin's head;

Bore it through the open portal, bore it up the echoing aisle,
Let it down before the altar where the lights burned clear the while.
When, Oh, hark! The wondrous organ of itself began to play
Strains of rare, unearthly sweetness never heard until that day!

All the vaulted arches rang with the music sweet and clear.
All the air was filled with glory as of angels hovering near.
And ere yet the strain was ended; he who bore the coffin's head,
With the smile of one forgiven, gently sank beside it, dead.

They who raised the body knew him, and they laid him by his bride.
Down the aisle and o'er the threshold they were carried, side by side,
While the organ played a dirge that no man ever heard before
And then softly sank to silence — silence kept for evermore.

THE LITTLE DOG ANGEL

Bur McIntosh

High up in the courts of heaven today
　　A little dog angel waits;
With the other angels he will not play,
　　But sits alone at the gates.
"For I know that my master will come," says he,
　　"And when he comes he'll call for me."

And his master, far down on the earth below,
　　As he sits in his easy chair,
Forgets sometimes, and he whistles low
　　For the dog that is not there.
And the little dog angel cocks his ears
　　And dreams that his master's call he hears.

And I know that at length when his master waits
　　Outside in the dark and cold,
For the hand of death to open the gates
　　That lead to these courts of gold,
The little dog angel's eager bark
　　Will comfort his soul while he's still in the dark.

THE LEVEL AND THE SQUARE

Robert Morris, LL.D.

We meet upon the Level and we part upon the Square.
What words sublimely beautiful those words Masonic are.
They fall like strains of melody upon the listening ears
As they've sounded Hallelujahs to the world three thousand years.

We meet upon the Level, though from every station brought,
The Monarch from his palace, the Laborer from his cot.
For the king must drop his dignity when knocking at our door,
And the poorest is his equal as he circles round the floor.

We act upon the Plumb; 'tis our Master's great command.
We walk upright in virtue's ways; we lean to neither hand.
The All-Seeing Eye that reads our hearts will bear us witness true,
That we shall try to honor God and give each man his due.

We part upon the Square, for the world must have its due;
We mingle with the ranks of man but keep our secrets true;
And the influence of our gatherings in memory is green,
And we long upon the Level to renew the happy scene.

There's a world where all are equal, we are hurrying toward it fast.
We shall meet upon the Level there, when the gates of Death are passed;
But right before the Orient and our Master will be there,
Our works to try, our lives to prove with God's unerring Square.

When we meet upon the Level there we never will depart.
There's a mansion bright and glorious set for the pure in heart.
There's a mansion and a welcome and a multitude is there,
Who in this world of sloth and sin did part upon the Square.

Let us meet upon the Level, then, while laboring patient here,
Let us meet and let us labor, though the labor be severe.
Already in the western sky the signs bid us prepare
To gather up our Working Tools and part upon the Square.

Hands round, then Brother Masons, gather in the golden chain.
We part upon the square below, to meet in Heaven again.
Each tie that has been broken here shall be cemented there,
And none be lost around God's throne who parted on the Square.

THE MAID

Sonja Christina

The maid was always sloppy,
And that's to say the least.
The only one who liked her
Was our dog, poor mongrel beast.

She took hours to do the dusting.
Took hours to get anything done,
And as for the dog, I wasn't surprised
'Cause he liked everyone.

That maid did terrible housework
And her energy lacked a lot;
She took hours to polish silverware,
And hours to do a pot.

Allowances were always made
When she frequently was late,
We made excuses for her absences,
But her language sealed her fate.

She used more sailors' gutter slang
Than I could bare to hear,
So on this day, she got her pay
And a notice to not re-appear.

Repentant? Not this truculent maid.
She just called for our dog to come round
Then withdrew from her purse and promptly disbursed
A five-dollar bill to the hound.

This action seemed so very odd,
I demanded the woman explain,
Why she'd share her wages with the dog,
Was she daft or just going insane?

Her smile was most contemptuous,
She lectured with a smirk,
"I always pays an honest wage
To them what helps me work."

"You see," says she, "Washin' dishes
Is the job I really hates,
So your dog was most obliging
When it came to cleaning plates!"

DRINK TO ME ONLY WITH THINE EYES

Ben Jonson

Drink to me only with thine eyes,
And I will pledge with mine;
Or leave a kiss but in the cup,
And I'll not look for wine.
The thirst that from the soul doth rise
Doth ask a drink divine;
But might I of Jove's nectar sup,
I would not change for thine.
I sent thee late a rosy wreath,
Not so much honoring thee
As giving it a hope that there
It could not withered be.
But thou thereon didst only breathe,
And sent' it back to me:
Since when it grows, and smells, I swear,
Not of itself, but thee.

THE MEN THAT DON'T FIT IN

Robert Service

There's a race of men that don't fit in,
A race that can't stay still;
So they break the hearts of kith and kin,
And they roam the world at will.
They range the field and they rove the flood,
And they climb the mountain's crest.
Theirs is the curse of the gypsy blood,
And they don't know how to rest.

If they just went straight, they might go far.
They are strong and brave and true;
But they're always tired of the things that are,
And they want the strange and new.
They say: "Couldn't I find my proper groove,
What a deep mark I would make!"
So they chop and change, and each fresh move
Is only a fresh mistake.

And each forgets as he strips and runs
With a brilliant, fitful pace,
It's the steady, quiet, plodding ones
Who win in the lifelong race.
And each forgets that his youth has fled,
Forgets that his prime is past
Till he stands one day with a hope that's dead
In the glare of the truth at last.

He has failed. He has failed.
He has missed his chance.
He has just done things by half.
Life's been a jolly good joke on him,
And now is the time to laugh.
Ha, ha! He is one of the Legion Lost;
He was never meant to win.
He's a rolling stone, and it's bred in the bone;
He's the man who won't fit in.

THE OYSTER'S LESSON

Author Unknown

There once was an oyster whose story I tell,
> Who found that some sand had got into his shell.
It was only a grain, but it gave him great pain,
> (For oysters have feelings, although they're so plain.)

Now, did he berate the harsh workings of fate
> That had brought him to such a deplorable state?
Did he curse at the government? Cry for election?
> Claim that the sea should have given him protection?

"No!" He said to himself as he lay on a shell,
> "Since I cannot remove it, I shall try to improve it.
Now the years have rolled 'round as the years always do,
> And he came to his ultimate destiny. . . Stew!

And the small grain of sand that had bothered him so
> Was a beautiful pearl, all richly aglow.
Now the tale has a moral for isn't it grand,
> What an oyster can do with a morsel of sand?

What couldn't we do if we'd only begin
With some of the things that get under our skin?

THE MILLS OF THE GODS

Author Unknown

He was the slave of Ambition and he vowed to the Gods above
To sell his soul to perdition for Fortune, Fame, and Love.
"Three Wishes," he cried and the Devil replied:
"Fortune is a fickle one, often wooed but seldom won,
Ever changing like the sun, still I think it can be done.
You have a friend, a rich one too; Kill him! His wealth is willed to
you."
Ambition fled. He paused awhile, but, daunted by the Devil's smile,
He killed his friend to gain his aim,
                Then bowed his head in grief and shame;
But the Devil cried, "It's all in the game.
You wanted Fortune, Love, and Fame, and so, I came.
Three wishes through your life shall run.
                Behold, I've given you Number One."

And the Gods on high, with a watchful eye,
                Looked down on the ways of man,
With their hopes and fears through the weary years
                Since the days of the world began
And the man, he prayed, for the soul betrayed
                Had breathed a parting call:
"Though the Mills of the Gods grind slowly,
                Yet they grind exceeding small."

Urged by the spur of Ambition, with the Devil still as his guide,
He now sought social position, for wealth had brought him pride.
"Bring Fame," cried the man, so the Devil began:
"Fame is but an accident, often sought but seldom sent;
                Still, I think we're on the scent.
You know a genius gone insane; go steal the product of his brain.
The man obeyed, then cried, "Begone!
                From crime to crime you lead me on,
To kill a friend whose smile was glad, to rob a genius driven mad,
Through want. Oh God! Am I that bad?"
But the Devil cried, "What luck you've had! You're famous, lad!
Three wishes run your whole life through,
                Behold, I've given you Number Two."

And the Gods looked down with an angry frown
   Till Satan fled their scorn.
For the Devil may play with the common clay,
   But genius is heaven born.
And the man grew bold with his Fame and Gold
   And cried, "Well, after all,
The mills of the Gods grind slowly
If they ever grind at all."

Men, good or bad, are but human and he, like the rest, wanted love.
So the Devil soon brought him the woman as fair as an angel above.
"I love you," he cried, but the woman replied,
   "Love is such an empty word.
Fancy, fleeting, like a bird. You have Wealth and Fame, I've heard-
   These are the things to be preferred."
He gave her both. The wealth she spent
And then betrayed him, so Fame went.

But Love came not, in his despair, she only smiled and left him there.
And he called her "The Woman Who Didn't Care."
But the Devil cried, "You've had your share; the game ends there.
Two of your wishes came through me,
   But the mighty Gods keep Number Three."

And the Gods grew stern as the Mills they turned
   That grind before they kill,
Till, staggering blind with wandering mind,
   And the glare of an imbecile.
From day to day he begs his way and whines his piteous call,
"The Mills of the Gods grind slowly,
Yet they grind exceeding small."

THE NEW DOG

I. B. Malleson

There's a new dog lies on the parlor rug
     Where the old dog used to lie,
A dog with a short white curly coat
     And a brown patch over his eye.
He takes his meals from the old dog's dish
     And sleeps on the old dog's chair,
And the rest have forgotten the Spaniel dog
     Who for ten long years slept there.

But at night when the house is fast asleep
     Sounds a step I used to know,
And the dog that I loved comes stealing back
     From the land where the Good Dogs go.
A dark shape opens the bedroom door;
     I hear a familiar whine,
There are two brown paws on the counterpane,
     And a dog's head close to mine.

There isn't a secret he keeps from me
     Of life in the Great Beyond.
There are shining seraphs to take him on walks,
     Real bones and a splendid pond;
And the Baby Angels throw balls for him,
     In the fields where the grass is sweet,
And he hasn't forgotten the strange brown stone
     That he used to lay at my feet.

He remembers the days in the grassy parks
     And the cats he used to chase.
(And yet they can talk of another dog
     Who shall take the old dog's place).
He tells me he looked for the old green chair
     Where his basket used to be,
But he found an intruder sleeping there,
     So he came to look for me.

Oh, the new dog is a faithful chap
And earns his daily bread
And the right to feed from the self-same dish
And sleep on the self-same bed.
And of course he must be on the parlor rug
Where the old chap used to lie,
But a brown dog visits me every night,
Pathetically asking why.

EPITAPH TO A CROW

Thomas Paine

Here lies the body of John Crow
Who once was high but now is low;
Ye brother crows take warning all
For as you rise, so must you fall.

*(This poem was written by Thomas Payne at the age of 8 Years.
On January 10, 1776, Paine published his famous fifty-page phamplet,
"Common Sense". The phamplet sold over 500,000 copies and is considered one
of the main causes for the issuance of the Declaration of Independence.)*

THE OLD STAGE QUEEN

Ella Wheeler Wilcox

Back in her box by the curtains shaded
She sits alone, by the house unseen;
Her eye is dim and her cheek is faded
She who once was the people's queen.

The Curtain rolls up, and she sees before her
A vision of beauty and youth and grace.
Ah! No wonder all hearts adore her,
Silver-throated and fair of face.

Out of her box she leans and listens;
O! Is it with pleasure or with despair
That her thin cheek pales and her dim eye glistens,
While that fresh young voice sings the grand old air?

She is back again in her past's bright splendor
When life was worth living and love was a truth!
Ere time had told her she must surrender
Her double dower of fame and youth.

It is she herself who stands there singing
To that sea of faces, that shines and stirs;
And the cheers on cheers that go up ringing
And rousing the echoes, are hers, all hers!

Just for one moment the sweet delusion
Quickens her pulse and blurs her sight
And wakes within her that wild confusion
Of joy that is anguish and fierce delight.

The curtain goes down, and the lights are gleaming
Brightly o'er circle and box and stall.
She starts like a sleeper who wakes from dreaming;
Her youth lies under Time's funeral pall.

Her day is dead, and her star descended
Never to rise or to shine again.
Her reign is over, her queenship ended —
A new name is sounded and sung by men.

All the glitter and glow and splendor
All the glory of that lost day
With the friends that seemed true
   And the love that seemed tender,
Why, what is it all but a dead bouquet!

She rises to go; has the night turned colder?
The new queen answers to call and shout,
And the old queen looks back over her shoulder
As all unnoticed, she passes out.

THE PURPLE COW

Gelett Burgess

I never saw a Purple Cow,
I never hope to see one;
But I can tell you, anyhow,
I'd rather see than be one.

THE PURPLE COW
(A Lament)
Gelett Burgess

Ah, yes! I wrote the "Purple Cow"—
I'm sorry, now, I wrote it!
But I can tell you, anyhow,
I'll kill you if you quote it!

(It is not the dream of any serious poet to be remembered only for a single four-line stanza written in a fleeting moment of levity. However, that was exactly the case for Gelett Burgess.) His moment of frivolity became an instant hit and was widely disseminated in print and on the airwaves. Approximately five years after releasing "The Purple Cow", he penned the above lament. It is now uncommon to find either verse printed without the second verse. To his dismay, Burgess became famous for two poems.)

241

THE POST THAT FITTED

Rudyard Kipling

Though tangled and twisted the course of true love,
This ditty explains,
No tangle's so tangled it cannot improve
If the Lover has brains.

Ere the steamer bore him Eastward,
        Sleary was engaged to marry
An attractive girl at Tunbridge,
        Whom he called "my little Carrie."
Sleary's pay was very modest,
        Sleary was the other way.
Who can cook a two-plate dinner
        On eight rupees a day?

Long he pondered o'er the question
        In his scantly furnished quarters—
Then proposed to Minnie Boffkin,
        Eldest of Judge Boffkin's daughters.
Certainly an impecunious Subaltern
        Was not a catch,
But the Boffkins knew that Minnie
        Mightn't make another match.

So they recognized the business and,
        To feed and clothe the bride,
Got him made a Something, Something
        Somewhere on on the Bombay side.
Anyhow, the billet carried pay
        Enough for him to marry—
As the artless Sleary put it:—
        "Just the thing for me and Carrie."

Did he, therefore, jilt Miss Boffkin—
        Impulse of a baser mind?
No! He started epileptic fits
        Of an appalling kind.
(Of his modus operandi
        Only this much I could gather:—
"Pear's shaving sticks will give you
        Little taste and lots of lather.")

242

Frequently in public places
  His affiction used to smite
Sleary with distressing vigour—
  Always in the Boffkins' sight.
Ere a week was over
  Minnie weepingly returned his ring,
Told him his "unhappy weakness"
  Stopped all thought of marrying.

Sleary bore the information
  With a chastened holy joy,—
Epileptic fits don't matter
  In Political employ,—
Wired three short words to Carrie—
  Took his ticket, packed his kit—
Bade farewell to Minnie Boffkin
  In one last, long, lingering fit.

Four weeks later, Carrie Sleary read—
  And laughed until she wept—
Mrs. Boffkin's warning letter
  On the "wretched epilept." . . .
Year by rear, in pious patience,
  Vengeful Mrs. Boffkin sits
Waiting for the Sleary babies
  To develop Sleary's fits.

THE POWER OF THE DOG

Rudyard Kipling

There is sorrow enough in the natural way
From men and women to fill our day;
And when we are certain of sorrow in store,
Why do we always arrange for more?
Brothers and Sisters, I bid you beware
Of giving your heart to a dog to tear.

Buy a pup and your money will buy
Love unflinching that cannot lie—
Perfect passion and worship fed
By a kick in the ribs or a pat on the head.
Nevertheless it is hardly fair
To risk you heart for a dog to tear.

When the fourteen years which Nature permits
Are closing in asthma or tumor or fits,
And the vet's unspoken prescription runs
To lethal chambers or loaded guns.
Then you will find—it's your own affair—
But . . . you've given your heart to a dog to tear.

When the body that lived at your single will,
With its whimper of welcome, is stilled (how still!)
When the spirit that answered your every mood
Is gone—wherever it goes—for good,
You will discover how much you care,
And will give your heart to a dog to tear.

We've sorrow enough in the natural way,
When it comes to burying Christian clay.
Our loves are not given, but only lent,
At compound interest of cent per cent.
Though it is not always the case, I believe,
That the longer we've kept 'em, the more do we grieve;

For, when debts are payable, right or wrong,
A short-time loan is as bad as a long—
So why in—Heaven (before we are there),
Should we give our hearts to a dog to tear?

THE PREACHER'S VACATION

Author Unknown

The old man went to meetin', for the day was bright and fair,
Though his limbs were very totterin' and 'twas hard to travel there;
But he hungered for the Gospel, so he trudged the weary way
On the road so rough and dusty, 'neath the summer's burning ray.

By and by he reached the building, to his soul a holy place;
Then he paused and wiped the sweat drops
                               Off his thin and wrinkled face.
But he looked around bewildered, for the old bell did not toll,
And the doors were shut and bolted, and he did not see a soul.

So he leaned upon his crutches, and he said, "What does it mean?"
And he looked this way and that till it seemed almost a dream;
He had walked the dusty highway, and he breathed a heavy sigh-
Just to go once more to meetin', ere the summons came to die.

But he saw a little notice tacked upon the meetin' door,
So he limped along to read it, and he read it o'er and o'er.
Then he wiped his dusty glasses, and he read it o'er again
Till his limbs began to tremble and his eyes began to pain.

As the old man read the notice, how it made his spirit burn!
"Pastor absent on vacation – church is closed till his return."
Then he staggered slowly backward, and he sat him down to think;
For his soul was stirred within him, till he thought his heart would sink.

So he mused along and wondered, to himself soliloquized —
"I have lived to almost eighty and was never so surprised
As I read that oddest notice, stickin' on the meetin' door,
'Pastor on vacation' – never heard the like before.

"Why, when I first jined the meetin' very many years ago,
Preachers traveled on the circuit in the heat and through the snow;
If they got their clothes and vittels ('twas but little cash they got),
They said nothin' 'bout vacation, but were happy in their lot.

Would the farmer leave his cattle or the shepherd leave his sheep?
Who would give them care and shelter or provide them food to eat?
So it strikes me very sing'lar when a man of holy hands
Thinks he needs to have vacation and forsakes his tender lambs.

Did St. Paul git such a notion? Did a Wesley or a Knox?
Did they in the heat of summer turn away their needy flocks?
Did they shut their meetin' house, just go and lounge about?
Why, they knew that if they did, Satan certainly would shout.

Do the taverns close their doors, just to take a little rest?
Why, 'twould be the height of nonsense,
                        For their trade would be distressed.
Did you ever know it happen or hear anybody tell,
Satan takin' a vacation, shuttin' up the doors of hell?

And shall preachers of the gospel pack their trunks and go away,
Leavin' saints and dyin' sinners git along as best they may?
Are the souls of saints and sinners valued less than settlin' beer
Or do preachers tire quicker than the rest of mortals here?

Why it is I cannot answer, but my feelings they are stirred;
Here I've dragged my totterin' footsteps for to hear the Gospel Word,
But the preacher is a travelin' and the meetin' house is closed;
I confess it's very tryin', hard, indeed, to keep composed.

Tell me, when I tread the valley and go up the shining height,
Will I hear no angels singin' – will I see no gleamin' light?
Will the golden harps be silent? Will I meet no welcome there?
Why, the thought is most distressin', would be more than I could bear.

Tell me, when I reach the city over on the other shore,
Will I find a little notice tacked upon the golden door,
Tellin' me 'mid dreadful silence, writ in words that cut and burn—
'The Lord is absent on vacation, heaven closed till his return'. "

THE RAVEN

Edgar Allan Poe

Once upon a midnight dreary, while I pondered, weak and weary,
Over many a quaint and curious volume of forgotten lore.
While I nodded, nearly napping, suddenly there came a tapping,
As of some one gently rapping, rapping at my chamber door.
" 'Tis some visitor," I muttered, "tapping at my chamber door—
   Only this, and nothing more."

Ah, distinctly I remember it was in the bleak December;
And each separate dying ember wrought its ghost upon the floor.
Eagerly I wished the morrow — vainly I had sought to borrow
From my books surcease of sorrow – sorrow for the lost Lenore —
For the rare and radiant maiden whom the angels name Lenore —
   Nameless here for evermore.

And the silken sad uncertain rustling of each purple curtain
Thrilled me — filled me with fantastic terrors never felt before;
So that now, to still the beating of my heart, I stood repeating
" 'Tis some visitor entreating entrance at my chamber door —
   This it is, and nothing more."

Presently my soul grew stronger; hesitating then no longer,
"Sir," said I, "or Madam, truly your forgiveness I implore;
But the fact is I was napping, and so gently you came rapping,
And so faintly you come tapping, tapping at my chamber door,
That I scarce was sure I heard you" — here I opened wide the door;—
   Darkness there and nothing more.

Deep into that darkness peering, long I stood there wondering, fearing,
Doubting, dreaming dreams no mortal ever dared to dream before;
But the silence was unbroken, and the darkness gave no token,
And the only word there spoken was the whispered word, "Lenore!"
This I whispered and an echo murmured back the word, "Lenore!"
   Merely this, and nothing more.

Back into the chamber turning, all my soul within me burning,
Soon I heard again a tapping somewhat louder than before.
"Surely," said I, "surely that is something at my window lattice;
Let me see, then, what thereat is, and this mystery explore —

Let my heart be still a moment and this mystery explore —
        "Tis the wind and nothing more!"
Open here I flung the shutter, when, with many a flirt and flutter,
In there stepped a stately Raven of the saintly days of yore;
Not the least obeisance made he; not a moment stopped or stayed he;
But, with mien of lord or lady, perched above my chamber door –
Perched upon a bust of Pallas just above my chamber door –
        Perched, and sat, and nothing more.

Then this ebony bird beguiling my sad fancy into smiling,
By the grave and stern decorum of the countenance it wore,
"Though thy crest be shorn and shaven, thou," I said, "art sure no craven,
Ghastly grim and ancient Raven wandering from the Nightly shore —
Tell me what thy lordly name is on the Night's Plutonian shore!"
        Quoth the Raven, "Nevermore."

Much I marveled this ungainly fowl to hear discourse so plainly,
Though its answer little meaning — little relevancy bore;
For we cannot help agreeing that no living human being
Ever yet was blessed with seeing bird above his chamber door –
Bird or beast upon the sculptured bust above his chamber door,
        With such name as "Nevermore."

But the Raven, sitting lonely on the placid bust, spoke only
That one word, as if his soul in that one word he did outpour.
Nothing farther then he uttered – not a feather then he fluttered —
Till I scarcely more than muttered, "Other friends have flown before —
On the morrow he will leave me, as my Hopes have flown before."
        Then the bird said, "Nevermore."

Startled at the stillness broken by reply so aptly spoken,
"Doubtless," said I, "what it utters is its only stock and store
Caught from some unhappy master whom unmerciful Disaster
Followed fast and followed faster till his songs one burden bore —
Till the dirges of his Hope that melancholy burden bore
        Of 'Never – nevermore.' "

But the raven still beguiling all my sad soul into smiling,
Straight I wheeled a cushioned seat in front of bird and bust and door;
Then upon the velvet sinking, I betook myself to linking
Fancy unto fancy, thinking what his ominous bird of yore —
What this grim, ungainly, ghastly, gaunt, and ominous bird of yore
        Meant in croaking "Nevermore."

This I sat engaged in guessing, but no syllable expressing
To the fowl whose fiery eyes now burned into my bosom's core;
This and more I sat divining, with my head at ease reclining
On the cushion's velvet lining that the lamplight gloated o'er,
But whose velvet violet lining with the lamplight gloating o'er,
        She shall press, ah, nevermore!

Then, methought, the air grew denser, perfumed from an unseen censer
Swung by angels whose faint foot-falls tinkled on the tufted floor.
"Wretch," I cried, "thy God hath lent thee – by these angels he hath sent thee
Respite – respite and nepenthe from thy memories of Lenore!
Quaff, oh quaff this kind nepenthe and forget this lost Lenore!"
        Quoth the Raven, "Nevermore."

"Prophet!" said I, "thing of evil! —prophet still, if bird or devil! —
Whether Tempter sent, or whether tempest tossed thee here ashore,
Desolate, yet all undaunted, on this desert land enchanted —
On this home by Horror haunted — tell me truly, I implore —
Is there – is there balm in Gilead? – tell me – tell me, I implore!"
        Quoth the Raven, "Nevermore."

"Prophet!" said I, "thing of evil — prophet still, if bird or devil!
By that Heaven that bends above us — by that God we both adore —
Tell this soul with sorrow laden if, within the distant Aidenn,
It shall clasp a sainted maiden whom the angels name Lenore –
Clasp a rare and radiant maiden whom the angels name Lenore."
        Quoth the Raven, "Nevermore."

"Be that word our sign of parting, bird or friend!" I shrieked, upstarting—
"Get thee back into the tempest and the Night's Plutonian shore!
Leave no black plume as a token of that lie thy soul hath spoken!
Leave my loneliness unbroken! – quit the bust above my door!
Take thy beak from out my heart, and take thy form from off my door!"
        Quoth the Raven, "Nevermore."

And the Raven, never flitting, still is sitting, still is sitting
On the pallid bust of Pallas just above my chamber door;
And his eyes have all the seeming of a demon's that is dreaming,
And the lamplight o'er him streaming throws his shadow on the floor;
And my soul from out that shadow that lies floating on the floor
        Shall be lifted – nevermore!

THE RIME OF THE ANCIENT MARINE

Samuel Taylor Coleridge

(Recited by Richard Burton)

PART I

An ancient Mariner meets three gallants bidden to a wedding feast and detaineth one.

It is an ancient Mariner
And he stoppeth one of three.
—"By thy long gray beard and glittering eye,
Now wherefore stopp'st thou me?

The Bridegroom's doors are opened wide,
And I am next of kin;
The guests are met, the feast is set:
May'st hear the merry din."

He holds him with his skinny hand,
"There was a ship," quoth he.
"Hold off! unhand me, graybeard loon!"
Eftsoons his hand dropped he.

The wedding guest is spellbound by the eye of the old seafaring man and constrained to hear his tale.

He holds him with his glittering eye—
The Wedding Guest stood still,
And listens like a three years' child:
The mariner hath his will.

The Wedding Guest sat on a stone:
He cannot choose but hear;
And thus spake on the ancient man,
The bright-eyed Mariner.

"The ship was cheered, the harbor cleared,
Merrily did we drop
Below the kirk, below the hill,
Below the lighthouse top.

The Mariner tells how the ship sailed southward with a good wind and fair weather, till it reached the line.

The Sun came up upon the left,
Out of the sea came he!
And he shone bright, and on the right
Went down into the sea.

250

Higher and higher every day,
Till over the mast at noon—"
The Wedding Guest here beat his breast,
For he heard the loud bassoon.

The wedding guest hearth the bridal music; but the mariner continueth his tale.

The bride hath placed into the hall,
Red as a rose is she;
Nodding their heads before her goes
The merry minstrelsy.

The Wedding Guest he beat his breast,
Yet he canot choose but hear;
And thus spake on that ancient man,
The bright-eyed Mariner.

The ship is driven by a storm toward the South Pole.

"And now the STORM-BLAST came and he
Was tyrannous and strong;
He struck with his o'ertaking wings,
And chased us south along.

With sloping masts and dipping prow,
As who pursued with yell and blow
Still treads the shadow of his foe,
And forward bends his head.
The ship drove fast, loud roared the blast,
And southward aye we fled.

And now there came both mist and snow,
And it grew wondrous cold:
And ice, mast-high, came floating by,
As green as emerald.

The land of ice and of fearful sounds where no living thing was to be seen.

And through the drifts the snowy clifts
Did send a dismal sheen:
Nor shapes of men nor beasts we ken—
The ice was all between.

The ice was here, the ice was there,
The ice was all around:
It cracked and growled, and roared and howled,
Like noises in a swound!

251

At length did cross an Albatross,
Through the fog it came;
As if it had a Christian soul,
We hailed it in God's name.

It ate the food it ne'er had eat,
And round and round it flew.
The ice did split with a thunder-fit;
The helmsman steered us through!

And a good South wind sprung up behind;
The Albatross did follow,
And every day, for food or play,
Came to the mariners' hollo!

In mist or cloud, on mast or shroud,
It perched for vespers nine;
Whiles all the night, through fog-smoke white,
Glimmered the white Moon-shine."

"God save thee, ancient Mariner!
From the fiends that plague thee thus!—
Why look'st thou so?"—With my crossbow
I shot the ALBATROSS.

PART II

The Sun now rose upon the right:
Out of the sea came he,
Still hid in mist, and on the left
Went down into the sea.

And the good south wind still blew behind,
But no sweet bird did follow,
Nor any day for food or play
Came to the mariner's hollo!

And I had done a hellish thing,
And it would work 'em woe:
For all averred, I had killed the bird
That made the breeze to blow.
Ah wretch! Said they, the bird to slay,
That made the breeze to blow!

252

But when the fog cleared off, they justifiy the same and thus make themselves accomplices in the crime.

Nor dim nor red, like God's own head
The glorious Sun uprist:
Then all averred, I had killed the bird
That brought the fog and mist.
"Twas right," said they, such birds to slay
That bring the fog and mist.

The fair breeze continues; the ship enters the Pacific Ocean and sails northward, even till it reaches the Line

The fair breeze blew, the white foam flew,
The furrow followed free;
We were the first that ever burst
Into that silent sea..

The ship hath been suddenly becalmed.

Down dropped the breeze, the sails dropped down.
'Twas sad as sad could be;
And we did speak only to break
The silence of the sea!

All in a hot and copper sky,
The bloody Sun, at noon,
Right up above the mist did stand,
No bigger than the Moon.

Day after day, day after day,
We stuck, nor breath nor motion;
As idle as a painted ship
Upon a painted ocean.

And the Albatross begins to be avenged.

Water, water, everywhere,
And all the boards did shrink;
Water, water, everywhere,
Nor any drop to drink.

The very deep did rot: O Christ!
That ever this should be!
Yea, slimy things did crawl with legs
Upon the slimy sea.

About, about, in reel and rout
The death-fires danced at night;
The water, like a witch's oils,
Burnt green, and blue and white.

A Spirit had followed them; one of the invisible inhabitants of this planet, neither departed souls nor angels; conceerning whom the

And some in dreams assured were
Of the Spirit that plagued us so;
Nine fathoms deep he had followed us
From the land of mist and snow .

learned Jew, Josephus, and the Platonic Constantin-opolitan, Michael Psellus, may be consulted. They are very numerous and there is no climate or element without one or more.

The shipmates, in their sore distress, would fain throw the whole guilt on the ancient Mariner: in sign whereof they hang the dead sea bird around his neck.

And every tongue, through utter drought,
Was withered at the root;
We could not speak, no more than if
We had been choked with soot.

Ah! well-a-day! what evil looks
Had I from old and young!
Instead of the cross, the Albatross
About my neck was hung.

PART III

There passed a weary time. Each throat
Was parched and glazed each eye.
A weary time! a weary time!
How glazed each weary eye,
When looking westward, I beheld
A something in the sky.

The ancient Mariner beholds a sign in the element afar off.

At first it seemed a little speck,
And then it seemed a mist;
It moved and moved and took at last
A certain shape, I wist.

A speck, a mist, a shape, I wist!
And still it neared and neared:
As if it dodged a water sprite,
It plunged and tacked and veered.

At its nearer approach, it seemeth him to be a ship; and at a clear ransom, he freeth his speech from the bonds of thirst.

With throats unslaked, with black lips baked,
We could not laugh nor wail;
Through utter drought all dumb we stood!
I bit my arm, I sucked the blood,
And cried, a sail! a sail!

A flash of joy.

With throats unslaked. With black lips baked,
Agape they heard me call:
Gramercy! they for joy did grin,
And all at once their breath drew in,
As they were drinking all.

And horror follows. For can it be a ship that comes onward without wind or tide?

See! see! (I cried) she tacks no more!
Hither to work us weal;
Without a breeze, without a tide,
She steadies with upright keel!

The Western wave was all aflame.
The day was well nigh done!
Almost upon the Western wave
Rested the broad bright Sun;
When that strange shape drove suddenly
Betwixt us and the Sun.

It seemeth him but the skeleton of a ship.

And straight the Sun was flecked with bars,
(Heaven's Mother send us grace!)
As if through a dungeon grate he peered
With broad and burning face.

And its ribs seem as bars on the face of the setting sun

Alas! (thought I, and my heart beat loud)
How fast she nears and nears!
Are those her sails that glance in the Sun,
Like restless gossameres?

The Specter-Woman and her Deathmate and no other on board the skeleton ship.

Are those her ribs through which the Sun
Did peer, as through a grate?
And is that Woman all her crew?
Is that a DEATH? And are there two?
Is DEATH that woman's mate?

Like vessel, like crew!

Her lips were red, her looks were free.
Her locks were yellow as gold:
Her skin was as white as leprosy,
The Nightmare LIFE-IN-DEATH was she,
Who thicks man's blood with cold.

Death and life-in Death have diced for the ship's crew and she (the latter) has won the ancient Mariner.

The naked hulk alongside came,
And the twain were casting dice;
"The game is done! I've won! I've won!"
Quoth she, and whistles thrice.

No twilight within the courts of the Sun.

The Sun's rim dips; the stars rush out:
At one stride comes the dark;
With far-heard whisper, o'er the sea,
Off shot the specter-bark.

We listened and looked sideways up!
Fear at my heart, as at a cup,
My lifeblood seemed to sip!
The stars were dim and thick the night,
The steersman's face by his lamp gleamed white;
From the sails the dew did drip—
Till clomb above the Eastern bar
The horned Moon, with one bright star
Within the nether tip.

One after one, by the star-dogged Moon,
Too quick for groan or sigh,
Each turned his face with ghastly pang,
And cursed me with his eye.

Four times fifty living men,
(And I heard nor sigh nor groan)
With heavy thump, a lifeless lump,
They dropped down one by one.

But Life-in-Death begins
her work on the ancient
Mariner.

The souls did from their bodies fly—
They fled to bliss or woe!
And every soul, it passed me by,
Like the whizz of my cross-bow!

PART 1V

The wedding guest feareth
that a Spirit is talking to
him.

"I fear thee, ancient Mariner!
I fear thy skinny hand!
And thou art long, and lank, and brown,
As is the ribbed sea-sand.

I fear thee and thy glittering eye,
And thy skinny hand, so brown."—
Fear not. fear not, thou Wedding Guest!
This body dropped not down.

But the ancient Mariner
assureth him of his bodily
life and proceedeth to re-
late his horrible penance.

Alone, alone, all, all alone,
Alone on a wide wide sea!
And never a saint took pity on
My soul in agony.

He despiseth the creatures of the calm

The many men, so beautiful,
And they all dead did lie:
And a thousand thousand slimy things
Lived on; and so did I.

And envieth that they should live and so many lie dead.

I looked upon the rotting sea,
And drew my eyes away;
I looked upon the rotting deck,
And there the dead men lay.

I looked to heaven, and tried to pray;
But or ever a prayer had gushed,
A wicked whisper came, and made
My heart as dry as dust.

I closed my lids, and kept them close,
And the balls like pulses beat,
For the sky and the sea, and the sea and the sky
Lay like a load on my weary eye,
And the dead were at my feet.

But the curse liveth on for him in the eye of the dead men.

The cold sweat melted from their limbs,
Nor rot nor reek did they:
The look with which they looked on me
Had never passed away.

An orphan's curse would drag to hell
A spirit from on high;
But oh! More horrible than that
Is the curse in a dead man's eye!
Seven days, seven nights, I saw that curse,
And and yet I could not die.

In his loneliness and fixedness position, he yearneth towards the journeying Moon and the stars that still sojourn, yet still move onward; and everywhere the blue sky belonges to them and is their appointed rest and their native country and their own natural homes, which they enter unannounced, as lords that are certainly expected and yet there is a silent joy at their arrival.

The moving Moon went up the sky
And nowhere did abide;
Softly she was going up
And a star or two beside—

Her beams bemocked the sultry main,
Like April hoar-frost spead;
But where the ship's huge shadow lay,
The charmed water burnt alway
A still and awful red.

257

Beyond the shadow of the ship,
I watched the water snakes:
They moved in tracks of shining white
And when they reared, the elfish light
Fell off in hoary flakes.

Within the shadow of the ship
I watched their rich attire:
Blue, glossy green, and velvet black,
They coiled and swam; and every track
Was a flash of golden fire.

O happy living things! No tongue
Their beauty might declare:
A spring of love gushed from my heart,
And I blessed them unaware:
Sure my kind saint took pity on me,
And I blessed them unaware.

The self-same moment I could pray;
And from my neck so free
The Albatross fell off, and sank
Like lead into the sea.

PART V

Oh sleep! it is a gentle thing,
Beloved from pole to pole!
To Mary Queen the praise be given!
She sent the gentle sleep from Heaven
That slid into my soul.

The silly buckets on the deck,
That had so long remained,
I dreamt that they were filled with dew;
And when I awoke, it rained.

My lips were wet, my throat was cold,
My garments all were dank;
Sure I had drunken in my dreams
And still my body drank.

I moved and could not feel my limbs;
I was so light—almost
I thought that I had died in sleep,
And was a blessed ghost.

He heareth sounds and seeth strange sights and commotions in the sky and in the element.

And soon I heard a roaring wind:
It did not come anear;
But with its sound it shook the sails,
That were so thin and sere.

The upper air burst into life!
And a hundred fire-flags sheen,
To and fro they were hurried about!
And to and fro, and in and out,
The wan stars danced between.

And the coming wind did roar more loud,
And the sails did sigh like sedge;
And the rain poured down from one black cloud;
The Moon was at its edge.

The thick black cloud was cleft, and still
The Moon was at its side:
Like waters shot from some high crag,
The lightning fell with never a jag,
A river steep and wide.

The bodies of the ship's crew are inspirited and the ship moves on;

The loud wind never reached the ship,
Yet now the ship moved on!
Beneath the lightning and the Moon
The dead men gave a groan.

They groaned, they stirred, they all uprose,
Nor spake, nor moved their eyes;
It had been strange, even in a dream,
To have seen those dead men rise.

The helmsman steered, the ship moved on;
Yet never a breeze up-blew;
The mariners all 'gan work the ropes,
Where they were wont to do;
They raised their limbs like lifeless tools—

We were a ghastly crew.
The body of my brother's son
Stood by me, knee to knee:
The body and I pulled at one rope,
But he said nought to me.

"I fear thee, ancient Mariner!"
Be calm, thou Wedding Guest!
'Twas not those souls that fled in pain,
Which to their corses came again,
But a troop of spirits blest:

For when it dawned—they dropped their arms,
And clustered round the mast;
Sweet sounds rose slowly through their mouths,
And from their bodies passed.

Around, around, flew each sweet sound,
Then darted to the Sun;
Slowly the sounds came back again,
Now mixed, now one by one.

Sometimes a-dropping from the sky
I heard the sky-lark sing;
Sometimes all little birds that are,
How they seemed to fill the sea and air
With their sweet jargoning!

And now 'twas like all instruments,
Now like a lonely flute;
And now it is an angel's song,
That makes the heavens be mute.

It ceased; yet still the sails made on
A pleasant noise till noon,
A noise like of a hidden brook
In the leafy month of June,
That to the sleeping woods all night
Singeth a quiet tune.

Til noon we quietly sailed on,
Yet never a breeze did breath:
Slowly and smoothly went the ship,
Moved onward from beneath.

Under the keel nine fathom deep,
From the land of mist and snow,
The spirit slid: and it was he
That made the ship to go.
The sails at noon left off their tune,
And the ship stood still also.

The Sun, right up above the mast,
Had fixed her to the ocean:
But in a minute she 'gan stir,
With a short uneasy motion—
Backwards and forwards half her length
With a short uneasy motion.

Then like a pawing horse let go,
She made a sudden bound:
It flung the blood into my head,
And I fell down in a swound.

How long in that same fit I lay,
I have not to declare;
But ere my living life returned,
I heard and in my soul discerned
Two voices in the air.

"Is it he?" quoth one, "Is this the man?
By him who died on cross,
With his cruel bow he laid full low
The harmless Albatross.

The spirit who bideth by himself
In the land of mist and snow,
He loved the bird that loved the man
Who shot him with his bow."

The other was a softer voice,
As soft as honey-dew:
Quoth he, "The man hath penance done,
And penance more will do."

PART VI

FIRST VOICE:

> "But tell me, tell me! Speak again,
> Thy soft response renewing—
> What makes that ship drive on so fast?
> What is the ocean doing?"

SECOND VOICE:

> "Still as a slave before his lord,
> The ocean hath no blast;
> His great bright eye most silently
> Up to the Moon is cast—
>
> If he may know which way to go;
> For she guides him smooth or grim.
> See, brother, see! How graciously
> She looketh down on him."

FIRST VOICE:

> "But why drives on that ship so fast,
> Without or wave or wind?"

The Mariner had been cast into a trance; for the angelic power caused the vessel to drive northward faster than human life could endure.

SECOND VOICE:

> "The air is cut away before,
> And closes from behind.
>
> Fly, brother, fly! more high, more high!
> Or we shall be belated:
> For slow and slow that ship will go,
> When the Mariner's trance is abated."

The supernatural motion is retarded. The Mariner awakes and his penance began anew.

I woke, and we were sailing on
As in a gentle weather:
'Twas night, calm night, the moon was high;
The dead men stood together.

All stood together on the deck,
For a charnel-dungeon fitter:
All fixed on me their stony eyes,
That in the Moon did glitter.

The pang, the curse, with which they died,
Had never passed away:
I could not draw my eyes from theirs,
Nor turn them up to pray.

And now this spell was snapped: once more
I viewed the ocean green,
And looked far forth, yet little saw
Of what had else been seen—

Like one, that on a lonesome road
Doth walk in fear and dread,
And having once turned round walks on,
And turns no more his head;
Because he knows, a frightful fiend
Doth close behind him tread.

Buat soon there breathed a wind on me,
Nor sound nor motion made:
Its path was not upon the sea,
In ripple or in shade.

It raised my hair, it fanned my cheek
Like a meadow-gale of spring—
It mingled strangely with my fears,
Yet it felt like a welcoming.

Swiftly, swiftly flew the ship,
Yet she sailed softly too:
Sweetly, sweetly blew the breeze—
On me alone it blew.

Oh! Dream of joy! Is this indeed
The lighthouse top I see?
Is this the hill? Is this the kirk?
Is this mine own countree?

We drifted o'er the harbor-bar,
And I with sobs did pray—
O let me be awake, my God!
Or let me sleep alway.

The harbor-bay was clear as glass,
So smoothly it was strewn!
And on the bay the moonlight lay,
And the shadow of the Moon.

The rock shone bright, the kirk no less,
That stands above the rock:
The moonlight steeped in silentness
The steady weathercock.

The angelic spirits leave the dead bodies.

And the bay was white with silent light,
Till rising from the same,
Full many shapes, that shadows were,
In crimson colors came.

And appear in their own forms of light.

A little distance from the prow
Those crimson shadows were:
I turned my eyes upon the deck—
Oh, Christ! What saw I there!

Each corse lay flat, lifeless and flat,
And, by the holy rood!
A man all light, a seraph-man,
On every corse there stood.

This seraph-band, each waved his hand:
It was a heavenly sight!
They stood as signals to the land,
Each one a lovely light;

This seraph-band, each waved his hand,
No voice did they impart—
No voice; but oh! the silence sank
Like music on my heart.

But soon I heard the dash of oars,
I heard the Pilot's cheer;
My head was turned perforce away
And I saw a boat appear.

The Pilot and the Pilot's boy,
I heard them coming fast:
Dear Lord in Heaven! it was a joy
The dead men could not blast.

I saw a third—I heard his voice:
It is the Hermit good!
He singeth loud his godly hymns
That he makes in the wood.
He'll shrieve my soul, he'll wash away
The Albatross's blood.

PART VII

The Hermit of the Wood

This Hermit good lives in that wood
Which slopes down to the sea.
How loudly his sweet voice he rears!
He loves to talk with mariners
That come from a far countree.

He kneels at morn, and noon, and eve—
He hath a cushion plump:
It is the moss that wholly hides
The rotted old oak stump.

Approacheth the ship
with wonder.

The skiff-boat neared: I heard them talk,
"Why, this is strange, I trow!
Where are those lights so many and fair,
That signal made but now?"

"Strange, by my faith!" the Hermit said—
"And they answered not our cheer!
The planks looked warped! and see those sails,
How thin they are and sere!
I never saw aught like to them,
Unless perchance it were

Brown skeletons of leaves that lag
My forest-brook along;
When the ivy tod is heavy with snow,
And the owlet whoops to the wolf below,
That eats the she-wolf's young."

"Dear Lord! it hath a fiendish look,"
The Pilot made reply,
"I am a-feared"—"Push on, push on!"
Said the Hermit cheerily.

265

The boat came closer to the ship,
But I nor spake nor stirred;
The boat came close beneath the ship,
And straight a sound was heard.

The ship suddenly sinketh.

Under the water it rumbled on,
Still louder and more dread:
It reached the ship, it split the bay;
The ship went down like lead.

The ancient Mariner is saved in the Pilot's boat.

Stunned by that loud and dreadful sound,
Which sky and ocean smote,
Like one that hath been seven days drowned
My body lay afloat;
But swift as dreams, myself I found
Within the Pilot's boat.

Upon the whirl, where sank the ship,
The boat spun round and round;
And all was still, save that the hill
Was telling of the sound.

I moved my lips—the Pilot shrieked
And fell down in a fit;
The holy Hermit raised his eyes,
And prayed where he did sit.

I took the oars: the Pilot's boy,
Who now doth crazy go,
Laughed loud and long, and all the while
His eyes went to and fro.
"Ha! Ha!" quoth he, "full plain I see,
The Devil knows how to row."

And now, all in my own countree,
I stood on the firm land!
The Hermit stepped forth from the boat,
And scarcely he could stand.

The ancient Mariner earnestly entreateth the Hermit to shrieve him; and the penance of life falls on him.

"O shrieve me, shrieve me, holy man!"
The Hermit crossed his brow.
"Say quick," quoth he, "I bid thee say—
What manner of man art thou?"

266

Forhwith this frame of mine was wrenched
With a woeful agony,
Which forced me to begin my tale;
And then it left me free.

And ever and anon
throughout his future life
an agony constraineth him
to travel from land to land;
Since than, at an uncertain hour,
That agony returns:
And till my ghastly tale is told,
This heart within me burns.

I pass, like night, from land to land;
I have strange power of speech;
That moment that his face I see,
I know the man that must hear me:
To him my tale I teach.

What loud uproar bursts from the door!
The wedding guests are there:
But in the garden—bower the bride
And bridesmaids singing are:
And hark the little vesper bell,
Which biddith me to prayer!

O Wedding Guest! This soul hath been
Alone on a wide sea:
So lonely 'twas, that God himself
Scarce seemed there to be.

O sweeter than the marriage feast,
'Tis sweeter far to me,
To walk together to the kirk
With a goodly company!

To walk together to the kirk,
And all together pray,
While each to his great Father bends,
Old men, and babes, and loving friends
And youths and maidens gay!

And to teach by his own example, love and reverence to all things that God made and loveth.

Farewell, farewell! But this I tell
To thee, thou Wedding Guest!
He prayeth well, who loveth well
Both man and bird and beast.

He prayeth best, who loveth best
All things both great and small;
For the dear God who loveth us,
He made and loveth all.

The Mariner, whose eye is bright,
Whose beard with age is hoar,
Is gone: and now the Wedding Guest
Turned from the bridegroom's door.

He went like one that hath been stunned,
And is of sense forlorn:
A sadder and a wiser man,
He rose the morrow morn.

THE RODEO CLOWN

James Ploss

I went to an indoor rodeo,
To see the heroes of my youth
Show off their skills and masculinity,
And learned the gosh-awful truth.

After paying my ten bucks admission,
I casually looked all around,
And I couldn't find one single sign,
There'd been a horse on that purified ground.

And an overpowering antiseptic odor,
Hung around in that air-conditioned space.
Then the truth, that same God-awful truth,
Hit me smack damn in my face!

My heroes, those cowboys appearing,
Were just actors and this just a show.
They were strange to the range and it really was plain,
They were cowboys for ribbons and gold.

My hero didn't sleep under starlight,
A sweaty saddle to pillow his head.
Why he spent each night in the wholesome delight,
Of an air-conditioned RV instead.

And there wasn't any waking at sunrise
For some coffee and bacon and beans.
No dressing in clothes that would strangle the nose,
My heroes wore dry-cleaned designer jeans.

Worse, they talked like us mere earthly mortals,
Instead of that slow Texas drawl.
And I sure was hard-pressed and mighty distressed,
Why I'd ever worshipped cowboys at all!

Then somewhere out behind the cowbarns,
With manure caked to his age-old boots,
I came upon a genuine old time cowboy,
Billy Bowlegs, the rodeo substitute.

He wasn't as tall or as handsome
As the stars of the pro-rodeo,
But when one hurt his backside or was too hungover to ride,
Well, "Billy Bowlegs" was cast in the show.

His Stetson was battered and sweatstained
And girdled by a real rattlesnake band.
And his face, it was wrinkled with miles of smiles
As he offered me his callused leather hand.

Billy's figure? He was jugeared and toothless
With tobacco stained whiskers and lean.
He was ugly to some, but to me he was one
Of the handsomest cowboys I'd seen.

He was something left over from history
And one look was all that it'd take,
That whatever it took from picture or book,
Billy Bowlegs was how cowboys were made.

But the odors that he radiated,
Well, he'd been arrested if smell was a crime.
So I'd just turn aside and the smell I'd abide
Just to be near that cowboy of mine.

And smell. . Oh, Lord did he smell!
Of manure and sweatstained leather;
Of sagebrush and out-in-the-open weather;
Of horse and cowboys working together,
To find a home in heaven or hell,
Oh, Lord, did Bowlegs smell!

As we sat side by side on the hay bales,
Billy longed for a good cigarette.
"I'd roll one for you if I'd the makin's for two,
One handed? You damn well can bet!"

From under the hay bales came a bottle
Of rotgut and we each took a try.
A few drinks more and we stopped keeping score;
We were riding our herd in the sky.

Billy Bowlegs and I branded dogies,
Sweated bullets 'neath the wide-open sky.
We were buddies, hard riding cowboys,
Then his bottle and our dreaming ran dry.

"Billy Bowlegs! You're on!" blared the P.A.,
And with apologies, my partner jumped down
From the hay bales on which we were riding,
To become Billy Bowlegs, the rodeo clown.

And I was out there with Billy, the cowboy,
With Billy Bowlegs, the last of his kind.
A genuine cowboy this world has passed by,
But he lives on in my heart and my mind.

And as soon as the last show was ended,
They deodorized the whole stupid place;
For a tractor pull scheduled that evening,
Another slap in Billy's weather stained face.

And after the last curtain descended,
I rushed backstage for a final bravo.
But ol' Billy had hitched up rode off in his pickup
Down the road only Billy's kind know.

But he was the only reason I went there,
And this is the gospel truth.
He alone in that Western twilight zone
Brought back the heroes of my youth.

My heroes have always been cowboys,
But none of these new ones were worth
The price of admission, to reach the decision,
Billy's the very last cowboy on earth.

And you'll know him if ever you see him,
Protecting stars of an indoor rodeo.
But, "Is it really Billy?" The question might seem silly,
Just, take a deep breath and you'll know.

'Cause smell? Oh Lord does he smell!
Of manure and sweatstained leather
Of sagebrush and out-in-the-open weather
Of horse and cowboys working together
To find a home in heaven or hell,
Oh, Lord, does Billy Bowlegs smell!

THE RUINED MAID

Thomas Hardy

"O 'Melia, my dear, this does everything crown!
 Who could have supposed I should meet you in Town"
And whence such fair garments, such propri-ety?"
"O didn't you know I'd been ruined?" said she.

"You left us in tatters, without shoes or socks,
Tired of digging potatoes, and spudding up docks;
And now you've gay bracelets and bright feathers three!"
"Yes: that's how we dress when we're ruined," said she.

"At home in the barton you said 'thee' and 'thou,'
But now I'm bewitched by your delicate cheek,
And your little gloves fit as on a la-dy!" –
"We never do work when we're ruined," said she.

"You used to call homelife a hag-ridden dream,
And you'd sigh, and you'd sock; but at present you seem
To know not of megrims or melancho-ly."
"True. One's pretty lively when ruined," said she.

"I wish I had feathers, a fine sweeping gown,
And a delicate face, and could strut about Town!"
 "My dear – a raw county girl, such as you be,
Cannot quite expect that. You ain't ruined," said she.

THE SAUSAGE COLORED DOG

Joseph J. McDonough

The rain was pouring down that day
As I arrived at work.
The lightning flashed; the thunder clashed;
The world seemed all berserk.
Wind whistled through the building's halls
As I made my way past art-hung walls.
Then, through a storm-streaked door I saw
A Sausage-Colored Dog.

He stood there looking in at me,
That Sausage-Colored Dog.
His brown and darkly-speckled fur
All dripping in the fog.
His eyes looked out so sorrowfully
As though accusing me:
"Please let me in!" he seemed to plea,
That Sausage-Colored Dog.

My company is rich and strong
With corporate power to spare.
But, for a Sausage-Colored Dog,
There's no room anywhere.
The executive suite's replete with men
Concerned with the quarterly dividend.
Earnings, profits, ten times ten,
But not a Sausage-Colored Dog.

This dog no assets has, nor will.
This dog from who knows where?
He buys no stocks or couponed bonds
Nor has a market share.
He probably sneaked out that day,
A harmless jaunt across the way,
But, alas, got lost — got lost at play,
That Sausage-Colored Dog.

And there but for the grace of God
Goes someone you might know,
Another time might we not find
The indifference that we sow.
For there but for the grace of God
We all shall lose our way
And once outside will we abide
That Sausage-Colored Dog?

I turned the dog away that day,
That Sausage-Colored Dog.
I thought I could escape the eyes
And lose him in the fog.
But every night this dog I see.
In piercing shrieks I hear his plea.
"Cannot you invest one moment for me,
A Sausage-Colored Dog?"

THE SEA-WIFE

Rudyard Kipling

There dwells a wife by the Northern gate,
And a wealthy wife is she;
She breeds a breed of roving men
And casts them over sea.

And some are drowned in deep water
And some in sight o' shore,
And word goes back to the weary wife
And ever she sends more.

For since that wife had gate or gear
Or hearth or garth or field,
She willed her sons to the white harvest
And that a bitter yield.

She wills her sons to the wet ploughing
To ride the horse of tree,
And syne her sons come back again
Far-spent from out the sea.

The good wife's sons come home again
With little into their hands,
But the lore of men that have dealt with men
In the new and naked lands.

But the faith of men that has brothered men
By more than easy breath,
And the eyes of men that have read with men
In the open books of Death.

Rich are they, rich in wonders seen,
But poor in the goods of men;
So what they have got by the skin of their teeth,
They sell for their teeth again.

And whether they lose to the naked life
Or win to their hearts' desire,
They tell it all to the weary wife
That nods beside the fire.

Her hearth is wide to every wind
That makes the white ash spin.
And tide and tide and 'tween the tides
Her sons go out and in.

(Out with great mirth that do desire
Hazard of trackless ways—
In with content to wait their watch
And warm before the blaze).

And some return by failing light
And some in waking dream,
For she hears the heels of the dripping ghosts
That ride the rough roof-beam.

Home, they come home from all the ports,
The living and the dead;
The good wife's sons come home again
For her blessing on their head!

THE SHOOTING OF DAN McGREW

Robert Service

A bunch of the boys were whooping it up
In the Malamute saloon;
The kid that handles the music-box
Was hitting a jag-time tune;
Back of the bar, in a solo game,
Sat Dangerous Dan McGrew,
And watching his luck was his light-o'-love,
The lady that's known as Lou.

When out of the night, which was fifty below,
And into the din and the glare,
There stumbled a miner fresh from the creeks,
Dog-dirty and loaded for bear.
He looked like a man with a foot in the grave
And scarcely the strength of a louse,
Yet he tilted a poke of dust on the bar,
And he called for drinks for the house.
There was none could place the stranger's face,
Though we searched ourselves for a clue;
But we drank his health, and the last to drink
Was Dangerous Dan McGrew.

There's men that somehow just grip your eyes,
And hold them hard like a spell;
And such was he, and he looked to me
Like a man who had lived in hell
With a face most hair and the dreary stare
Of a dog whose day is done,
As he watered the green stuff in his glass,
And the drops fell one by one.
Then I got to figgering who he was,
And wondering what he'd do,
And I turned my head – and there watching him
Was the lady that's known as Lou.

His eyes went rubbering round the room
And he seemed in a kind of daze,
Till at last that old piano fell
In the way of his wandering gaze.

277

The ragtime kid was having a drink;
There was no one else on the stool,
So the stranger stumbles across the room
And flops down there like a fool.
In a buckskin shirt that was glazed with dirt
He sat, and I saw him sway;
Then he clutched the keys with his talon hands
—My God, but that man could play!

Were you ever out in the Great Alone,
When the moon was awful clear,
And the icy mountains hemmed you in
With a silence you most could hear;
With only the howl of a timber wolf,
And you camped there in the cold,
A half-dead thing in a stark, dead world,
Clean mad for the muck called gold;
While high overhead, green, yellow and red,
The North Lights swept in bars? –
Then you've a hunch what the music meant . . .
Hunger and night and the stars.

And hunger not of the belly kind
That's banished with bacon and beans,
But the gnawing hunger of lonely men
For a home and all that it means;
For a fireside far from the cares that are,
Four walls and roof above;
'But oh! So cramful of cozy joy,
And crowned with a woman's love –
A woman dearer than all the world,
And true as Heaven is true . . .
(God! How ghastly she looks through her rouge –
The lady that's known as Lou.)

Then on a sudden the music changed
So soft that you scarce could hear,
But you felt that your life had been looted clean
Of all that it once held dear,
That someone had stolen the woman you loved;
That her love was a devil's lie,
That your guts were gone, and the best for you
Was to crawl away and die.

"'Twas the crowning cry of a heart's despair,
And it thrilled you through and through —
"I guess Ill make it a spread misere,"
Said Dangerous Dan McGrew.

The music almost died away . . .
Then it burst like a pent-up flood;
And it seemed to say, "Repay, repay,"
And my eyes were blind with blood.
The thought came back of an ancient wrong,
And it stung like a frozen lash.
And the lust awoke to kill, to kill . . .
Then the music stopped with a crash;
And the stranger turned, and his eyes they burned
In a most peculiar way.

In a buckskin shirt that was glazed with dirt
He sat, and I saw him sway.
Then his lips went in in a kind of grin,
And he spoke, and his voice was calm.
And "Boys," says he, "you don't know me,
And none of you care a damn;
But I want to state, and my words are straight,
And I'll bet my poke they're true
That one of you is a hound of hell . . .
And that one is Dan McGrew."

Then I ducked my head, and the lights went out,
And two guns blazed in the dark,
And a woman screamed, and the lights went up,
And two men lay stiff and stark.
Pitched on his head and pumped full of lead
Was Dangerous Dan McGrew,
While the man for the creeks lay clutched to the breast
Of the lady that's known as Lou.

These are the simple facts of the case,
And I guess I ought to know.
They say that the stranger was crazed with "hooch,"
And I'm not denying it's so.
I'm not so wise as the lawyer guys,
But strictly between us two –
The woman that kissed him – and pinched his poke –
Was the lady that's known as Lou.

THE TONE OF YOUR VOICE

Author Unknown

Now, it ain't so much the words you say,
As the manner in which you say it.
It's not so much the language you use,
As the tone in which you convey it.

"Come here!" I said,
And the child cowered and wept.
"Come here," I said, with love and a smile,
And straight to my lap he crept.

You see, words may be mild and fair,
But the tone may pierce like a dart.
Words may be soft as the summer air,
But it's the tone that breaks the heart.

For the words that come from within the mind,
Grow by study and art,
But a terrible tone from the inner self
Reveals the state of your heart.

So whether you know it or know it not,
Whether you mean it or even care,
Gentleness, kindness, love and hate,
Envy, and anger are there.

So, if you'd hurt and quarrels avoid,
And in peace and love rejoice,
Keep anger not only out of your words,
But, keep it out of your voice.

THE VILLAGE BLACKSMITH

Henry Wadsworth Longfellow

Under a spreading chestnut tree
    The village smithy stands;
The smith a mighty man is he,
    With large and sinewy hands;
And the muscles of his brawny arms
    Are strong as iron bands.
His hair is crisp and black and long;
    His face is like the tan,
His brow is wet with honest sweat,
    He earns whate'er he can,
And looks the whole world in the face,
    For he owes not any man.

Week in, week out, from morn till night,
    You can hear his bellows blow,
You can hear him swing his heavy sledge
    With measured beat and slow;
Like a sexton ringing the village bell,
    When the evening sun is low.
And children coming home from school
    Look in at the open door—
They love to see the flaming forge
    And hear the bellows roar,
And catch the sparks that fly like chaff
    From a threshing floor.

He goes on Sunday to the church
    And sits amongst his boys,
He hears the parson pray and preach;
    He hears his daughter's voice
Singing in the village choir,
    And it makes his heart rejoice.
It sounds to him like her mother's voice
    Singing in paradise;
He needs must think of her once more,
    How in the grave she lies,
And with his hard rough hand
    He wipes a tear from out his eyes.

Toiling, rejoicing, sorrowing,
    Onward through life he goes,
Each morning sees some task begin,
    Each evening sees its close;
Something attempted, something done,
    Has earned a night's repose.
Thanks, thanks to thee, my worthy friend,
    For the lesson thou hast taught,
Thus at the flaming forge of life,
    Our fortunes must be wrought;
Thus, on its sounding anvil shaped
    Each burning deed – each thought.

WHAT TO DO WITH A WATERMELON

Author Unknown

When you thump it with your fingers
    And it gives a heavy sound,
Like summer rain a-fallin'
    On the dry an' dusty ground,
Jes' get your Barlow ready
    An' prepare to make a swipe,
And carve it straight an' steady,
    Till it opens red an' ripe!

Then fold your Barlow careful,
    An' take your melon flat;
Put one-half on this side o' you
    The other half on that;
Then, take the biggest in your lap
    An' rear the heart out, so!
An' smack your lips, an' praise the Lord
    From whom all blessin's flow!

(Note: A Barlow was probably a well known pocket knife.)

282

THE WALRUS AND THE CARPENTER

Lewis Carroll

The sun was shining on the sea,
Shining with all his might:
He did his very best to make
The billows smooth and bright
And this was odd, because it was
The middle of the night.

The moon was shining sulkily,
Because she thought the sun
Had got no business to be there
After the day was done—
"It's very rude of him," she said,
"To come and spoil the fun!"

The sea was wet as wet could be,
The sands were dry as dry.
You could not see a cloud because
No cloud was in the sky:
No birds were flying overhead—
There were no birds to fly.

The Walrus and the Carpenter
Were walking close at hand:
They wept like anything to see
Such quantities of sand:
"If this were only cleared away,"
They said, "It would be grand!"

"If seven maids with seven mops
Swept it for half a year,
Do you suppose," the Walrus said,
"That they could get it clear?"
"I doubt it," said the Carpenter,
And shed bitter tear.

"O Oysters, come and walk with us!"
  The Walrus did beseech.
"A pleasant walk, a pleasant talk,
  Along the briny beach:
We cannot do with more than four,
  To give a hand to each."

The eldest Oyster looked at him
  But never a word he said:
The eldest Oyster winked his eye
  And shook his heavy head—
Meaning to say he did not choose
  To leave his oyster-bed.

But four young Oysters hurried up,
  All eager for the treat.
Their coats were brushed, their faces washed,
  Their shoes were clean and neat—
And this was odd, because, you know,
  They haven't any feet.

Four other Oysters followed them,
  And yet another four;
And thick and fast they came at last,
  And more and more and more—
All hopping through the frothy waves
  And scrambling to the shore.

The Walrus and the Carpenter
  Walked on a mile or so,
And then they rested on a rock
  Conveniently low.
And all the little Oysters stood
  And waited in a row.

"The time has come," the Walrus said,
  "To talk of many things:
Of shoes—and ships—and sealing wax—
  Of cabbages—and kings—
And why the sea is boiling hot—
  And whether pigs have wings."

"But wait a bit," the Oysters cried,
    "Before we have our chat;
For some of us are out of breath,
    And all of us are fat!"
"No hurry!" said the Carpenter.
    They thanked him much for that.

"A loaf of bread," the Walrus said,
    "Is what we chiefly need:
Pepper and vinegar besides
    Are very good indeed—
Now, if you're ready, Oysters dear,
    We can begin to feed."

"But not on us!" the Oysters cried,
    Turning a little blue.
"After such kindness, that would be
    A dismal thing to do!"
"The night is fine," the Walrus said,
    "Do you admire the view?

"It was so kind of you to come!
    And you are very nice!"
The Carpenter said nothing but,
    "Cut us another slice.
I wish you were not quite so deaf—
    I've had to ask you twice!"

"It seems a shame," the Walrus said,
    "To play them such a trick,
After we've brought them out so far,
    And made them trot so quick!"
The Carpenter said nothing but,
    "The butter's spread too thick!"

"I weep for you," the Walrus said:
    "I deeply sympathize."
With sobs and tears he sorted out
    Those of the largest size,
Holding his pocket-handkerchief
    Before his streaming eyes.

"O Oysters," said the Carpenter,
    "You've had a pleasant run!
Shall we be trotting home again?"
    But answer came from none—
And this was scarcely odd, because
    They'd eaten every one.

THEY WERE MIXED

Author Unknown

I studied my tables over and over,
    And backward and forward, too;
But I couldn't remember six times nine,
    And I didn't know what to do.
Till sister told me to play with my doll
    And not to bother my head,
"If you call her 'Fifty-four' for awhile
    You'd learn it by heart," she said.

So I took my favorite, Mary Ann
    (Though I thought 'twas a dreadful shame
To give such a perfectly lovely doll
    Such a perfectly horrid name),
And I called her my dear little "Fifty-four"
    A hundred times, till I knew
The answer of six times nine as well
    As the answer of two times two.

Next day Elizabeth Wigglesworth,
    Who always acts so proud,
Said "Six times nine is fifty-two,"
    And I burst out laughing aloud.
But I wished I hadn't when teacher said,
    "Now, Dorothy, tell everyone if you can.
For I thought of my doll and—sakes alive!
    I answered, "Mary Ann!"

THE WOMAN'S RESOLUTION

Edward L. Wier

You could crawl across the desert on your hands and knees
Or run to me in tears while being stung by bees.
Sail across the ocean like some love-crazed maniac
And although I would feel pity, I would not take you back!

Leave your friends and family. Ignore your shrink's advice
Trudge through mud and rain and wind and fire, flood and ice.
Beg and plead and kiss my feet with a bloody solemn pact,
And although I would be sorry, I would not take you back!

Give me all your credit cards and fill my bank accounts.
Pile up your worldy goods in wonderful amounts.
Sell your condo, loose some weight and live in some old shack
And although I would be touched, I would not take you back!

Give up coffee, beer and smoke and cook my favorite meal.
Plunge me into seas of pleasure 'til I begin to squeal.
Wash the car and change the oil; clean till you turn black,
And although I'd be appreciative, I would not take you back!

Take me to your private park and say the perfect thing.
Tell me I'm the only one as you begin to sing.
Tie a big, red ribbon around my nice new Cadillac,
And although I would think twice, I would not take you back!

Line up all the Playboy pets and tell me I look better.
Send me gifts and poetry and every day a letter.
Give me flowers, jewels and clothes in a vicious love attack,
And although I would be flattered, I would not take you back!

Bolster up my ego and praise me to the hilt.
Have my portrait painted and knit me my own quilt.
Have the world's best sculptor render me in wax,
And although I would be honored, I would not take you back!

Stare at me for hours with your face all drenched in love.
At Christmas you could give me rings and a dozen turtledoves.
Treat me with all the courtesies, honor, care, and tact,
And although I would be humbled, I would not take you back!

You could love me like no other has ever loved before.
Honor, treasure, cherish me, and all my ways adore.
Juggle, joke, and make me laugh, become an acrobat,
And though I would be much amused, I would not take you back!

Put me on a rustic farm and stock it full of horses.
Get your Ph.D. and take self-improvement courses.
Win the Nobel Prize and then become a diplomat,
And although I would be very proud, I would not take you back!

Write for me a symphony of matchless sound and beauty.
Kneel before my awestruck ears and swear it was your duty.
Protect me and defend me from every harmful act,
And although I'm sure I'd feel more secure,
I would not take you back!

Plant a garden with my name in growing calligraphy.
Devote your life to work and write my own biography.
Journey back to fill in the slack, (and rearrange some facts,)
And although I'd really be amazed, I would not take you back!

Hire maids and butlers to pamper, await, and serve.
Get me plastic surgery to immortalize my curves.
Buy me famous paintings, both classic and abstract,
And although I would be grateful, I would not take you back!

Spend each waking moment with only me on your mind.
Take charge of my crazy, reckless life just like a knight divine.
Wine me, dine me, hunt and find me; Give me what I lack!
And although I would cherish you, I would not take you back!

You could sacrifice your very soul, so I could go to Heaven.
Forgive me for my previous sins (of seventy times seven.)
Suffer for my children and teach them how to act,
And although I would be indebted, I would not take you back!

Love me more in one moment than in all the other's years.
Sail me into pure delight on your sea of salty tears.
And although it will do nothing to draw my sweet heart nigh,
Don't let this note discourage you. Please feel free to try!

THE WORLDLY WAY

Monroe H. Rosenfeld

"Come back, my child," said the father fond
      To his boy who had gone astray.
Out in the bitter world of sin—
      Out in the sorrowed way;
"Thou hast erred, my child, yet what of that?
      And frailty's name is mine,
Thy path of sin is naught to me,
      For repentance is divine!"

And so it chanced that the lad returned
      One night, when the low'ring day
Of life had cast its dark'ning gloom
      And lured him from his way;
And wine and song and kindly hands,
      Like the dream of the prodigal son,
Were lent in humble, sweet embrace,
      To welcome the erring one!

A maiden fair in tattered gown,
      Aweary and sad at heart,
Passed out in the rabble of the street
      With penance for a part.
Hers was the fate of passion's love,
      And she a thing of scorn.
"Thou hast erred and sinned," cried the bitter world,
      " 'Twere better to be unborn!"

"Thou art not my child!" the father said,
      As he closed the mansion door—
"Passion and sin go hand in hand,
      Seek thou another shore!"
And the girl went forth forever, aye,
      A penitent child of shame—
One of the millions wandering on
      For woe and death to claim.

Ah! This was many years ago,
      When life was a youthful dream,
And yesterday I saw two graves,
      In a churchyard near a stream.
The glittering waters rippled soft,
      Their cadence for a song—
Of the sinner and sinned who buried lay,
      Apart from the madding throng.

The same sweet carol of the birds
      Overhead that sang their strain,
The same sweet zephyrs lingering by
      Made dirges for the twain.
One forgiven! The other spurned!
      Both in the depths of clay,
Yet each again to rise despite
      The cross of the worldy way!

TO A LITTLE PAL

Emily Hopkins Drake

We've lived together, you and I, old fellow,
Friends, tried and true, for ten long happy years;
And when I smiled, your stubby tail wagged gladly,
And when I wept, you licked away my tears.

But, all too soon, our comradeship was ended;
The shears of Fate, relentlessly unkind,
Snipped the frail thread that bound our lives together,
And you went on, while I remained behind.

I miss you, boy, — Your gay, loud-spoken greeting,
Your small feet pattering about the place!
And, ah! The pathos of that empty window
Where I could always find your watching face!

When life's short, hectic journey here is over,
And I fare forth alone; and in the dark,
Be at my journey's end, dear Pal, to greet me!
I'll know it's home, if I but hear you bark!

THE YARN

OF THE NANCY BELL

Sir William Schwenck Gilbert

'Twas on the shores that round our coast
    From Deal to Ramsgate span,
Where I found alone on a piece of stone
    An elderly naval man.

His hair was weedy and his beard was long,
    And weedy and long was he;
And I heard this wight on the shore recite
    In a singular minor key:

"Oh, I am the cook and a captain bold,
    And the mate of the Nancy brig
And a bo'sun tight and a midshipmite,
    And the crew of the captain's gig!"

And he shook his fists, and he tore his hair,
    Till I really felt afraid;
For I couldn't help thinking
        The man had been drinking,
    And so I simply said:

"Oh, elderly man, it's little I know
    Of the duties of men of the sea,
And I'll eat my hand if I understand
    How you can possibly be

At once a cook and a captain bold
        And the mate of the Nancy brig
And a bo'sun tight and a midshipmite
    And the crew of the captain's gig."

Then he gave a hitch to his trowsers, he did,
    Which is a trick all seamen larn,
And having got rid of a thumpin' quid,
    He spun this mournful yarn:

"Twas in the good ship Nancy Bell
      That we sailed to the Indian sea,
And there on a reef we come to grief
      Which has often occurred to me.

And pretty nigh all o' the crew was drowned,
      (There was seventy-seven o'soul),
But only ten of the Nancy's men
      Said, "Here" to the muster-roll.

There was me and the cook and the captain bold
      And the mate of the Nancy brig
And the bo'sun tight and a midshipmite
      And the crew of the captain's gig.

For a month we'd neither vittles nor drink
      Till a-hungry we did feel,
So we drawd a lot, and accordin' shot
      The captain for our first meal.

The next lot fell to the Nancy's mate,
      And a delicate dish he made;
Then our appetite with the midshipmite
      We seven survivors stayed.

And then we murdered the bo'sun tight,
      And he much resembled pig;
Then we wittled free, did the cook and me,
      On the crew of the captain's gig.

Then only the cook and me was left,
      And the delicate question, 'Which
Of us two goes to the kettle?' arose,
      And we argued it out as sich:

For I loved that cook as a brother, I did,
      And the cook he worshiped me;
But we'd both be blowed if we'd either be stowed
      In the other chap's hold, you see.

"I'll be eat if you dines off me," says Tom,
        "Yes that," says I, "you'll be.
I'm boiled if I die, my friend," quoth I,
        And, "Exactly so," quoth he.

Says he, "Dear James, to murder me
        Were a foolish thing to do,
For don't you see that you can't cook me,
        While I can—and will cook you?"

So he boils some water and takes the salt
        And the pepper in portions true,
And some chopped shallot (which he never forgot),
        And some sage and parsley, too.

"Come here," says he, with a proper pride,
        Which his smiling features did tell,
" 'Twill soothing be if I let you see
        How extremely nice you'll smell."

And he stirred it round and round and round
        And he sniffed at the foaming froth—
When I ups with his heels, and smothers his squeals
        In the scum of the boiling broth.

And I eat that cook in a week or less,
        And—as eating I be,
The last of his chops, why, I almost drops
        For a vessel in sight I see.

And I never grieve and I never smile
        And I never larf nor play,
But I sit and croak, and a single joke
        I have—which is to say:

"Oh, I am a cook, and a captain bold,
        And the mate of the Nancy Brig,
And a bo'sun tight, and a midshipmite,
        And the crew of the captain's gig."

TO ALTHEA, FROM PRISON

Richard Lovelace

When Love with unconfined wings
    Hovers within my gates,
And my divine Althea brings
    To whisper at the grates;
When I lie tangled in her hair
    And fetter'd to her eye,
The birds that wanton in the air
    Know no such liberty.

When flowing cups run swiftly round
    With no allaying Thames,
Our careless heads with roses bound,
    Our hearts with loyal flames;
When thirsty grief in wine we steep,
    When healths and draughts go free—
Fishes that tipple in the deep
    Know no such liberty.

When, like committed linnets, I
    With shriller throat shall sing
The sweetness, mercy, majesty,
    And glories of my king;
When I shall voice aloud how good
    He is, how great should be,
Enlarged winds, that curl the flood
    Know no such liberty.

Stone walls do not a prison make,
    Nor iron bars a cage;
Minds innocent and quiet take
    That for an hermitage;
If I have freedom in my love
    And in my soul am free,
Angels alone, that soar above,
    Enjoy such liberty.

THE YOUNG BRITISH SOLDIER

Rudyard Kipling

(Recited by Jennie O'Neill Potter)

When the 'arf-made recruity goes out to the East
'E acts like a babe an' 'e drinks like a beast,
An' 'e wonders because 'e is frequent deceased
Ere 'e's fit for to serve as a soldier.
      Serve, serve, serve as a soldier,
      Serve, serve, serve as a soldier,
      Serve, serve, serve as a soldier,
      So-oldier hof the Queen.

Now all you recruities what's drafted to-day,
You shut up your rag-box an' 'ark to my lay,
An' I'll sing you a soldier as far as I may:
A soldier what's fit for a soldier.
      Fit, fit, fit for a soldier . . .

First, mind you steer clear o' the grog-sellers' huts,
For they sell you Fixed Bay'nets that rots out our guts—
Ay, drink that 'ud eat the live steel from your butts—
An' it's bad for the young British soldier.
      Bad, bad, bad for the soldier . . .

When the cholera comes—as it will past a doubt—
Keep out of the wet and don't go on the shout,
For the sickness comes in as the liquor dies out,
An' it crumples the young British soldier.
      Crump, crumm- crumples the soldier . . .

But the worst o' your foes is the sun over'ead:
You must wear your 'elmet for all that is said:
If 'e finds you uncovered 'e'll knock you down dead,
An you'll die like a fool of a soldier.
      Fool, fool, fool of a soldier . . .

If you're cast for fatigue by a sergeant unkind,
Don't grouse like a woman nor crack on nor blind;
Be handy and civil, and then you will find
That it's beer for the young British soldier.
      Beer, beer, beer for the soldier . . .

Now, if you must marry, take care she is old—
A troop-sergeant's widow's the nicest I'm told,
For beauty won't help if your vittles is cold,
An' love ain't enough for a soldier,
        'Nough, 'nough, 'nough for a soldier . . .

If the wife should go wrong with a comrade be loth
To shoot when you catch 'em—you'll swing, on my oath!—
Make 'im take 'er and keep 'er; that's hell for them both,
And you're shut o' the curse of a soldier.
        Curse, curse, curse of a soldier . . .

When first under fire an' you're wishful to duck
Don't look or take 'eed at the man that is struck.
Be thankful you're livin' an' trust to your luck
An' march to your front like a soldier.
        Front, front, front like a soldier . . .

When 'arf of your bullets fly wide in the ditch,
Don't call your Martini a cross-eyed old bitch;
She's human as you are—you treat her as sich,
An' she'll fight for the young British soldier.
        Fight, fight, fight for the soldier . . .

When shakin' their bustles like ladies so fine,
The guns o' the enemy wheel into line,
Shoot low at the limbers and don't mind the shine,
For noise never startles the soldier.
        Start-, start-, startles the soldier . . .

If your officer's dead and the sergeants look white,
Remember it's ruin to run from a fight:
So take open order, lie down, and sit tight,
An wait for supports like a soldier.
        Wait, wait, wait like a soldier . . .

When you're wounded an' left on Afghanistan's plains,
An the women come out to cut up what remains,
Just roll to your rifle an' blow out your brains
An' go to your Gawd like a soldier.
        Go, go, go like a soldier,
        Go, go, go like a soldier,
        Go, go, go like a soldier,
        So-ldier of the Queen!

TROUBLE IN THE AMEN "CORNER"

Thomas Chalmers Harbaugh

'Twas a stylish congregation, that of Theophrastus Brown,
And its organ was the finest and the biggest in the town;
And chorus — all the papers favorably commented on it;
For 'twas said each female member had a forty dollar bonnet.

Now in the "amen corner" of the church sat Brother Eyer,
Who persisted every Sabbath day in singing with the choir.
He was poor, but genteel looking and his heart as snow was white;
And his face beamed with sweetness when he sung with all his
might.

His voice was cracked and broken; age had touched his vocal cords.
And nearly every Sunday he would mispronounce the words
Of the hymns, and 'twas no wonder; he was old and nearly blind,
And the choir rattling onward always left him far behind.

The chorus stormed and blustered, Brother Eyer sang too slow,
And then he used the tunes in vogue a hundred years ago.
At last the storm cloud burst and the church was told in fine
That the brother must stop singing or the choir would resign.

Then the pastor called together in the lecture room one day
Seven influential members, who subscribe more than they pay,
And having asked God's guidance in a printed prayer or two
They put their heads together to determine what to do.

They debated, thought, suggested, till at last "dear Brother York,"
Who last winter made a million on a sudden rise in pork,
Rose and moved that a committee wait at once on brother Eyer
And proceed to rake him lively "for disturbin' of the choir."

Said he: "In that 'ere organ I've invested quite a pile,
And we'll sell it if we cannot worship in the latest style.
Our Philadelphy tenor tells me 'tis the hardest thing
For to make God understand him when the brother tries to sing.

"We've got the biggest organ, the best-dressed choir in town,
We pay the steepest sal'ry to our pastor, Brother Brown;
But if we must humor ignorance because it's blind and old —
If the choir's to be pestered, I will seek another fold."

297

Of course the motion carried, and one day a coach-and-four
With the latest style of driver rattled up to Eyer's door.
And the sleek, well-dressed committee,
                    Brothers Sharkey, York and Lamb,
As they crossed the humble portal took good care to miss the jamb.

They found the choir's great trouble sitting in his old armchair,
And the summer's golden sunbeams lay upon his thin white hair.
He was singing "Rock of Ages" in a voice both cracked and low,
But the angels understood him; 'twas all he cared to know,

Said York: "We're here, dear brother, with the vestry's approbation,
To discuss a little matter that affects the congregation."
"And the choir, too," said Sharkey, giving Brother York a nudge.
"And the choir, too," he echoed, with the graveness of a judge.

"It was the understanding when we bargained for the chorus,
That it was to relieve us, that is, do the singing for us.
If we rupture the agreement, it is very plain, dear brother,
It will leave our congregation and be gobbled by another.

"We don't want any singing except that what we've bought!
The latest tunes are all the rage; the old ones stand for naught;
And so we have decided – are you listening, Brother Eyer?—
That you'll have to stop your singin', for it flurrytates the choir."

The old man slowly raised his head, a sign that he did hear,
And on his cheeks the trio caught the glitter of a tear.
His feeble hands pushed back the locks white as the silky snow
As he answered the committee in a voice both sweet and low:

 "I've sung the Psalms of David for nearly eighty years;
They've been my staff and comfort and calmed life's many fears.
I'm sorry I disturb the choir, perhaps I'm doing wrong;
But when my heart is filled with praise I can't keep back a song.

I wonder if beyond the tide that's breaking at my feet,
In the far-off heavenly temple, where the Master I shall greet —
Yes, I wonder when I try to sing the songs of God up higher
If the angel band will chide me for disturbing Heaven's choir?"

A silence filled the little room; the old man bowed his head.
The carriage rattled on again, but Brother Eyer was dead!
Yes, dead! His hand has raised the veil; the future hangs before us,
And the Master dear had called him to the everlasting chorus.

The choir missed him for a while, but he was soon forgot!
A few churchgoers watched the door; the old man entered not.
Far away, his voice no longer cracks, he sings his heart's desires,
Where there are no church committees and no fashionable choirs!

WHEN I WAS ONE-AND-TWENTY

Alfred Edward Housman

When I was one-and-twenty
I heard a wise man say,
"Give crowns and pounds and guineas
But not your heart away;
Give pearls away and rubies
But keep your fancy free."
But I was one-and-twenty,
No use to talk to me.

When I was one-and-twenty
I heard him say again,
"The heart out of the bosom
Was never given in vain;
'Tis paid with sighs a plenty
And sold for endless rue."
And I am two-and-twenty,
And oh, 'tis true, 'tis true.

VIOLETS

Herbert H. Taylor

In a garden filled with posies
    Where the beauty of the roses
Overshadowed all the flowers
    When the summer sun had set,
Nearly hidden by the nettles
    And the weeds around its petals,
Unassuming and neglected, grew a modest violet.

There were heliotropes admired
    For their fragrance sweet — and yet,
All the beauty of the posies,
    All the grandeur of the roses,
Were rejected by the one who plucked the modest violet.

And when twilight softly closes
    Over nature's fairest roses,
Mid the perfume of the posies
    Come a host of sad regrets.
Though we gaze in admiration
    On the beautiful carnation,
There's a most pathetic story in a bunch of violets.

There's a garden filled with pleasures
    Where we find the sweetest treasures,
And we strew them idly
    O'er a pathway filled with vain regrets.
But we still revere the roses
    And the aftermath discloses
That the flowers that we plucked were just the modest violets.

For the lilies white are fairer,
    And the roses sweet are rarer;
And they share in all the sunshine of our lives.
    But don't forget
That the beauty of a flower
    Is not measured in an hour,
And the perfume lasts the longer on the little violet.

TRILBY

Herbert H. Taylor

Trilby was my companion
    She shared my joys and tears,
Tried and true and faithful
    For ever so many years.

She was tender and kind and gentle
    And followed wherever I led,
And I loved—as a man loves his sweetheart
    Every hair in that little dog's head.

Her instinct was more than human,
    Her affection almost divine;
And she trembled with joy when I petted
    This little Scotch Collie of mine.

Her beautiful hair was glossy
    And black as a raven's crown,
And over her eyes—that looked so wise—
    Were two little spots of brown.

And when one day she left me
    With a sad farewell in her eyes,
I knew what it is men suffer
    When the nearest and dearest dies.

And I crept downstairs in the morning
    Just at the break of day,
And called her my little sweetheart
    And kissed her—and went away.

And I thought of the Christian teaching
    That God has the power to save
The sinner whose sins are blackest,
    But a dog's life ends in the grave.

But I knew as she lay before me
    There in the early dawn,
That that which I loved was missing,
    That which loved me was gone.

For a labor of love was ended
        In a look which the brown eyes cast,
And a great big soul went—somewhere—
        When a little dog breathed her last.

WAITING AT THE FERRY

David Lee Wharton

On the banks of that lonely river
        Where the Stygian waters roll,
All patiently through the weary years
        Waiteth a little dog soul.

O, long are the years and weary
        Since the little dog stepped ashore,
But halted, humbly there to wait
        By the stream he will cross no more.

To the water's edge he hurries
        When Charon's barque draws near,
For "When HE comes," the little dog thinks,
        "He must find me watching here."

With faith undimmed, heart unafraid,
        He waits on that lonely strand
For the smile of an unforgotten face,
        For the touch of his master's hand.

While the far-away master never dreams
        That where Stygian waters brim,
Unheeding the pearly gates flung wide
        His little dog waits for him.

VANITY, VANITY

Nancy Rustici

Ceceile was the bride of Armand Colbert
In the Brittany village of Berne.
And happy they wed and happy they died,
But between was the lesson she learned.

Armand would sing in the fields as he plowed
Of his love for the woman, his wife.
"Oh, lovely Ceceile, my beauty Ceceile,
For her smile I would give up my life."

Now Ceceile knew full well that he felt her a queen
And gave thanks for the day they were wed.
But a diet of praise was too much for her blood,
And his compliments went to her head.

She scorned the poor kitchen, the pots and the pans,
And cracks in the rough tiled floor.
And she asked herself, "Why should I tie myself here,
When the whole world is mine to explore?

Such beauty as mine merits pheasants and wine,
Furs, and jewelry fit for a belle.
So to Paris I'll travel, and find me a lord
Who'll be wealthy and handsome as well!"

So she took off her apron and scrubbed her brown face,
Preening proudly in front of the mirror.
Then dressed in her bonnet, she fled out the door
Before her poor Armand could hear her.

To Paris she came then, by wagon and train,
And sat down in a sidewalk cafe
Quite certain that fate would cooperate
And send a young blueblood her way.

But all day she sat by the hot dusty street,
And though dozens of men passed her by;
Not one of them so much as gave her a smile,
Nor for that matter, gave her an eye.

At the end of the day, with a tear-splattered cheek,
She got back on the Brittany train.
And the long way back home, she puzzled the reason
She'd fallen from pride to such pain.

From her black crocheted purse, she took out a glass
To study the face she knew well.
The eyes, Armand told her, were brighter than jewels;
And her smiling lips cast a sweet spell.

But how was it he never mentioned the mole
That sat by the side of her nose?
And the freckles that dappled her fat double chin?
Or the bushy brows, what about those?

The hair was not "silken," but more like a mop.
And the blackened teeth were a disgrace.
She looked long and hard, for a long, long while;
And at length, she leaned back in her place.

"Oh, God," she prayed, "Don't let him see me like this.
Keep his eyes ever blinded by love.
And let me be thankful the rest of my life
For my husband, our home, and his love."

WHISPERING BILL

Author Unknown

(Recited by Jennie O'Neill Potter)

So you're takin' the census, mister?
   There's three of us livin' still,
My wife, and I, an' our only son
   That folks call Whisperin' Bill.
But, Bill couldn't tell ye his name, Sir
   An' so it's hardly worth givin';
For you see a bullet killed his mind
   An' left his body livin'.

Set down for a minute, Mister.
   Ye see Bill was only fifteen.
At the time of war, an' as likely a boy
   As ever this world has seen.
An' what with the news o' battles lost,
   The speeches an' all the noise,
I guess every farm in the neighborhood
   Lost a part of its crop o' boys.

"Twas harvest time when Bill left home;
   Every stalk in the fields of rye
Seemed to stand tiptoe to see him off
   An' wave him a fond good-bye;
His sweetheart was here with some other girls,
   The sassy little miss!
An' pretending she wanted to whisper'n his ear,
   She gave him a rousin' kiss.

Oh, he was a han'some feller,
   An' tender an' brave an' smart,
An' tho' he was bigger than I was,
   The boy had a woman's heart.
I couldn't control my feelin's,
   But I tried with all my might,
An his mother an' me stood a-cryin
   Till Bill was out o' sight.

305

His mother she often told him
      When she knew he was goin' away,
That God would take care o' him, maybe,
      If he didn't forgit to pray;
An' on the bloodiest battlefields
      When bullets whizzed in the air,
An Bill was a-fightin' desperate,
      He used to whisper a prayer.

Oh, his comrades has often told me
      That Bill never flinched a bit,
When every second a gap in the ranks
      Told where a ball had hit.
An' one night when the field was covered
      With the awful harvest of war,
They found my boy 'mongst the martyrs
      O' the cause he was fightin' for.

His fingers were clutched in the dewy grass.
      . . Oh, no, Sir, he wasn't dead,
But he lay sort o' helpless an' crazy
      With a rifle ball in his head.
An' if Bill had really died that night,
      I'd give all I got worth givin';
For you see the bullet had killed his mind
      An' left his body livin'.

An officer wrote and told us how
      The boy had been hit in the fight.
But he said that the doctors reckoned
      They could bring him around all right.
An' then we heard from a neighbor,
      Disabled at Malvern Hill,
That he thought in a course of a week or so
      He'd be comin' home with Bill.

We was that anxious t' see him
      We'd set up an talk o' nights.
Till the break o' day had dimmed the stars,
      An' put out the northern lights.
We waited and watched for a month or more,
      An' the summer was nearly past
When a letter came one day that said
      They'd started fer home at last.

I'll never fergit the day Bill came,
      'Twas harvest time again;
An' the air blown over the yellow fields
      Was sweet with the scent o' the grain.
The dooryard was full o' the neighbors
      Who had come to share our joy,
An' all of us sent up a mighty cheer
      At the sight o' that soldier boy.

An' all of a sudden somebody said:
      "My God! Don't the boy know his mother?"
An' Bill stood a-whisperin', fearful like,
      An' starin' from one to another.
"Don't be afraid, Bill," said he to himself,
      As he stood in his coat o' blue,
"Why, God'll take care o' you, Bill;
      God'll take care o' you."

He seemed to be loadin' an' firin' a gun,
      An' to act like a man who hears
The awful roar o' the battlefield
      A soundin' in his ears.
I saw that the bullet had touched his brain
      An' somehow made it blind
With the picture o' war before his eyes
      An' the fear o' death in his mind.

I grasped his hand, an' says I to Bill,
      "Don't ye remember me?
I'm yer father – Don't ye know me?
      How frightened ye seem to be!
But the boy kep' a whisperin' to himself
      As if t'was all he knew.
"God'll take care o' you, Bill;
      "God'll take care o' you."

He's never known us since that day,
      Nor his sweetheart, an' never will.
Father an' mother an' sweetheart
      Are all the same to Bill.
An' many's the time his mother
      Sets up the whole night through
An' smoothes his head, and says,
      "Yes, Bill, God'll take care o' you."

Unfortunit? Yes, but we can't complain.
It's a livin' death more sad
When the body clings to a life o' shame
An' a soul has gone to the bad.
An' Bill is out o' the reach o' harm
An' danger of every kind;
We only take care of his body,
But, God takes care o' his mind.

WITHOUT A DOG

Douglas Malloch

A man may have his share of gold,
Though hard to get and hard to hold,
May even have a little fame
Although they soon forget your name.
May even have a little bliss,
The rapture of a faithless kiss,
And yet, the while the world you jog,
Life isn't much without a dog.

Life gives him friends a-plenty,
Friends as many as the coins he spends,
Yet, when he has a trail to go
Up hill, down dale, through rain or snow,
One, only one, will rise and leave
The good red fire, grieve when you grieve
Go where you go, the peak, the bog –
Life isn't much without a dog.

Unless a man can say, "Come, Jack,
Come Sport or Scotty," life will lack.
The only love man ever knew
That would not vanish like the dew.
To ev'ry man must come a day
When he must walk some hurt away,
And in that hour of doubt, of fog,
Life isn't much without a dog.

WHO SHARED HER VIEW

Douglas Kruger

When aged sun and weary hills
Agreed upon a truce,
Passed a silent walker by
Where lived a young recluse.

Halfway up the sloping hills,
A house alone, unoccupied,
But for one form, which, in one room,
Secluded there did hide.

And from the windows of that place,
She looked upon a road,
A solitary winding thing,
To where she feared to know.

And from the house and from the road,
God placed each flower and tree,
Was plain to view, which sadly few,
Had ever stopped to see.

Sadly few – but for this one,
This stranger passing by,
Who paused in awe at what two saw
As daylight gently died.

From the solitude of her phantom cell,
She watched the world outside
When from her vantage point she caught
His form, she sought to hide.

But something here would not permit
The girl to hide and so
She slowly raised her anxious eyes
To this stranger down below.

Of years this man would have been the same,
The age of a love betrayed,
And her mind recalled with bitter gall,
The love for which she strayed.

And then as one they looked upon
A scene no man could tender,
A mighty portrait of the close of day,
That only God could render.

Both stood fast and gazed thereon,
Those fleeting moments few.
But aside the curse, he was the first
Who'd ever shared her view.

And though he could not hope to know,
He stood there with a friend.
For 'twas as close as she could go,
To cringe there and pretend.

Till daylight faded, interest ebbed,
And passed the passerby.
Again alone the young recluse
Could not but sit and cry.

She daily by her window sat,
Upon the hour she waited,
But time upon time he was not there
When daylight's glow abated.

For full six days thus faithfully
At dusk she did the same,
And nearly lost all hope, but then,
The seventh day, he came.

He came and stood and watched the sight
The colors clear and true,
And once again, though not aware,
He briefly shared her view.

Until once more the day was past
'Til passed the passerby,
And once again the young recluse,
In heartbreak, knelt to cry.

That day each week 'round five of hour,
She'd seek a long closed chest,
And from within to show to him,
An unworn wedding dress.

And girlish to the window frame,
She'd go for to beguile;
And though he saw, not once he saw,
The bride with the haunting smile.

With each new week his eyes she'd seek
Until one day he turned
To barely sight the bride in white,
Whose image in him burned.

Thus she may have carried on
Never to love relent,
And all the years and all the tears
Would pass but for one event.

It was a day that some would say
The devil spawned the course.
The air was still and they felt the chill,
A feel of dreadful force.

She seated at her windowsill,
He on the road below,
When lightning rent the pictured sky,
And rain in torrents flowed.

The vision in white was blurred from sight,
And the stranger turned to flee.
But, alas to late, the earth gave way,
And she saw her dreams take leave.

For as he reeled and turned about,
The earth began to shake
And violently and viciously,
And ruthlessly to quake.

And when at last the terror past
From her window up on high,
The maiden searched the landscape
Searching for the passerby.

And her eyes beheld what her heart forbid,
A crumpled, awkward sight,
The body of her visioned friend,
Her seeming lifeless knight.

She ran. She fled the prison home
Of selfish pity born.
She ran to kneel and clasp her hands
In prayer for the lifeless form.

Then with the strength unknown to her,
She grasped the life she found
And lifted it without a thought,
To seek his needs in town.

Up hill and down this simple soul
Pursued her heart's own need
And cried petitions to Heaven's ears,
A prayer for God to heed.

Aloud she begged the storm soaked sky,
And yet her words were few,
A wept petition for the life,
Of he who shared her view.

To claim is fair, the Lord was there,
Who else could guide their way
To the village's only doctor
On that dark and stormy day?

And arms of kindness held her now,
Sweet people kept her warm,
And spoke to her and offered her,
Warm shelter from the storm.

And all the time she could but shake;
        She could but gasp and cry.
And in-between each weeping breath,
        Was heard, "Don't let him die."

Whispered through her tear stained hands:
        "Please don't let him die."

*   *   *

When age'd sun and weary hills
        Agree upon a truce,
Way up a hill you'll see a house
        Where lived a young recluse.

And from that place, a short way down,
        You'll look upon a road,
        A solitary winding thing,
        Just down from that abode.

When the bright sun shines on the green, green grass,
        When the sky's a blanket of blue,
You'll see two figures, hand in hand,
        Sharing that lovely view.

WIT'S END

Linda Robertson

When your babies are hurt and cryin',
And you feel like cryin' too.
When your husband's wanting dinner,
And you're really feeling blue.

When your head is pounding like your heart,
And your legs feel just like lead;
When you've burned your fingers on the stove,
And you wish that you were dead.

When your best friend calls to tell you
That she's got a brand new beau,
And that you should be so happy for her—
'Cause the guy is rollin' in dough!

When you just sit down for coffee,
And you've finally calmed down;
You hear a scream out in the yard,
And your kid is on the ground.

When you have a minute to yourself,
And everything is well;
You can actually hear the silence —
Oh, no! The front doorbell!

When everything's topsy-turvy;
Your vacation's been postponed;
When your baby's diaper rash is back
And they're cutting off your phone.

When you've worked all day at cleaning house,
And your company doesn't show.
When the kids want to have a picnic,
But there's no way you can go;

When all is lost and your sanity's gone,
Your energy 's flown away;
Just give yourself a little shove —
Tomorrow's another day!

#

Young E. Allison

Fifteen Men on the Dead Man's Chest—
  Yo-ho-ho and a bottle of rum!
Drink and the devil had done for the rest—
  Yo-ho-ho and a bottle of rum!
The mate was fixed by the bos'n's pike,
The bos'n brained with a marlinspike,
And Cookey's throat was marked belike
  It had been gripped
   By fingers ten;
  And there they lay,
   All good dead men,
Like break-o'day in a boozing-ken—
  Yo-ho-ho and a bottle of rum!

Fifteen men of a whole ship's list—
  Yo-ho-ho and a bottle of rum!
Dead and bedamned and the rest gone whist!—
  Yo-ho-ho and a bottle of rum!
The skipper lay with his nob in gore
Where the scullion's ax his cheek had shore—
And the scullion he was stabbed times four.
  And there they lay,
   And the soggy skies
  Dripped all day long
   In upstaring eyes--
At murk sunset and at foul sunrise—
Yo-ho-ho and a bottle of rum!

Fifteen men of 'em stiff and stark—
  Yo-ho-ho and a bottle of rum!
Ten of the crew had the Murder mark—
  Yo-ho-ho and a botttle of rum!
'Twas a cutlass swipe, or an ounce of lead,
Or a yawing hole in a battered head—
And the scuppers glut with a rotting red.
  And there they lay—
   Aye, damn my eyes!—
  All lookouts clapped
   On Paradise—
All souls bound just contrariwise—
  Yo-ho-ho and a bottle of rum!

Finteen men of 'em good and true--
      Yo-ho-ho and a bottle of rum!
Every man jack could ha' sailed with Old Pew--
      Yo-ho-ho and a bottle of rum!
There was chest on chest full of Spanish gold,
With a ton of plate in the middle hold,
And the cabins riot of stuff untold.
      And they lay there,
        That had took the plum,
      With sightless glare
        And their eyes struck dumb,
While we shared all by the rule of thumb--
      Yo-ho-ho and a bottle of rum!

More was seen through the sternlight screen--
      Yo-ho-ho- and a bottle of rum!
Chartings ondoubt where a woman had been!-
      Yo-ho-ho and a bottle of rum!
A flimsy shift on a bunker cot,
With a thin dirk slot through the bosom spot
And the lace stiff-dry in a purplish blot.
      Or was she wench . . .
        Or some shuddering maid . . . ?
      That dared the knife--
        And that took the blade!
By God! she was stuff for a plucky jade--
      Yo-ho-ho and a bottle of rum!

Fifteen men on the Dead Man's Chest--
      Yo-ho-ho and a bottle of rum!
Drink and the devil had done for the rest--
      Yo-ho-ho and a bottle of rum!
We wrapped 'em all in a mains'l tight,
With twice ten turns of a hawser's bight,
And we heaved 'em over and out of sight--
      With a yo-heave-ho!
        And a fare-you-well!
      And a sullen plunge
        In the sullen swell,
Ten fathoms deep on the road to hell!
      Yo--ho-ho and a bottle of rum!

CHRISTMAS TAILS

Robert X. Leeds

(Recited by Orson Welles)

Christmas was coming and all o'er the earth
Children welcomed the season of joy and of mirth.
They chattered and frolicked in the new-fallen snow,
Counted hours and minutes and the seconds to go.

For the story was known by all girls and boys
Of jolly old Santa, his candy and toys
Of eight tiny reindeer who guided his sleigh
Of his wonderful journey on that wondrous day.

That there wouldn't be Christmas, no child even dreamed.
But that was exactly the case, or so it then seemed.
For the worst of the worries, that fiercest of fears —
Santa wouldn't be coming for the first time in years.

For up at the North Pole the toys sat on shelves.
No order to pack them had come for the elves.
No hustle, no bustle, no signs of the season.
For Santa had told them, "I'm afraid there's no reason!"

"It's a virus, you see. All the reindeer are ill.
They're confined to their beds taking syrups and pills.
It doesn't look good. Indeed what can I do?
You can't move a sleigh when you've no one to pull."

Santa slunk in his chair, his dog Snuggles at his feet.
Mrs. Claus shook her head and was heard to repeat,
"You can't travel hither and yonder and fro.
You can't deliver gifts — without leaving the North Pole."

"Why, there are millions of children depending on me.
There are millions of hearts and there are bushels of glee.
There are dreams to be reckoned with and doubts to make bright.
I must. . . yes, I must take my sleigh out tonight!"

Santa stroked Snuggles' head. Then he stroked his own beard.
Mrs. Claus watched the clock as the time to leave neared.
But, try as they might, no answer they found.
While the hands on the clock spun around and around,

Six o'clock, seven o'clock, eight o'clock, nine —
The silence was frightening, but not a soul gave a sign
That doubts that he'd make it were constantly growing —
If Santa didn't leave soon, it'd be too late for going!

He was so deep in his thoughts with his eyes closed so tight,
Santa didn't see Snuggles go out in the night.
Nor was Santa aware when old Snuggles returned,
Till he felt a cold nose and knew his dog was concerned.

Santa opened his eyes, sat up straight in his chair,
And smiled as he saw his loyal friend there.
For there on the floor with the most wonderful grin,
Was Snuggles, his dog, and Santa knew where he'd been.

He was dressed in a harness that belonged to a deer,
And as he tugged at poor Santa, his intentions were clear.
"Oh, Snuggles, faithful Snuggles," Santa laughed till he shook,
"Would you pull my sleigh over mountain and brook?"

"Would you brave the long night and the bitter cold blasts?
Could you fight those fierce snowstorms? How long could you last?
My reindeer are hardy; they're trained in my ways.
They're big and they're young; they were made to pull sleighs."

"If you were strong as your faith and as big as your heart,
If your effort matched your devotion, maybe then we could start.
But you're small and you're old and though brimming with love,
A dog pulling my sleigh? I'm afraid it's unheard of."

"Says who?" came a challenge. Mrs. Claus was the one.
"I think Snuggles is right . . . Perhaps it could be done.
Dogs might be the answer if you think back aways,
Before they were pets, dogs used to pull sleighs!"

Consider this world when first it was made,
Why dogs served their masters and helped in their trades.
They guarded their lodgings and they guided their ways;
And here at the North Pole, they even pulled sleighs!"

A bright spark was kindled deep within Santa's eyes.
His heart started thumping; his mouth opened in surprise.
"That's it!" Santa shouted, "You've shown me a way.
We'll do it with dogs. Why, they'll pull my sleigh."

"Quickly, gather my elves and spread the good news.
Load all of the toys, for we've no time to lose.
I'll need special dogs from all parts of the world.
Ones that know each country, each boy and each girl."

"But, where will you find them?" Mrs. Claus paused to say.
"It's late in the hour. It's late in the day.
Your needs are too special, your time much too fleeting,
To gather precisely the dogs you'll be needing."

"But I know of a place — It's a hotel for pets,
For horses and birds, for dogs and for cats.
The innkeeper's kindly and I know if I ask,
He'll loan me the dogs that I need for this task."

And so Santa journeyed uphill and down,
To a small rural village called Prairie View Town.
With Snuggles beside him, he read signs aloud,
"Slow — Animals Play Here — No People Allowed."

The hotel was quiet although carols were heard,
And the desk clerk awakened when Santa appeared.
"I've a problem," sighed Santa, "of gigantic proportions.
Please listen while I tell you without any distortions."

Santa told of his plight, from beginning to end,
While the desk clerk stood listening to his bearded old friend.
"We've never missed Christmas; not ever, you know."
The clerk's eyes became misty. A tear suddenly showed.

Yes, the innkeeper listened and when Santa was through,
Said, "Santa, stop worrying; here is what we'll do!
You've no time for training or making a list, Sir.
You've got to have dogs that know right where the kids are."

"Dogs from the cities and dogs from the farms,
Dogs from apartments and dogs from the barns,
Poodles and pointers, retrievers and hounds . . .
Dogs who'll find children, wherever they're found!"

"I've got them all here – in two's and in three's.
Why, we'll form a dog team of superlative breeds."
He spoke into the intercom saying, "All dogs pay attention!
Our friend Santa has a problem that I'd like to mention.

"Now I know the sleigh's heavy and the trip will be long;
But there's a task for each one of us, the weak and the strong.
If we all pull together, just do our fair share,
We'll prove on this Christmas just how much we care."

"You all know the hazards," the innkeeper said.
"And I won't think any less if some stay in your beds.
But for those with the spirit and those so inclined,
Come at once to the lobby and form in a line."

Well, you couldn't imagine, unless you were near,
The response for ol' Santa was immediately clear.
They came down the corridors in a pack wall-to-wall,
Filling the lobby, spilling out of the halls.

They jumped over tables. They ran under chairs.
They stumbled and tumbled, but they didn't care.
Yipping and yelping, still onward they came,
Sheepdogs and spaniels, retrievers and Danes.

Till, lo and behold, to Santa's surprise,
Every dog in the hotel was in front of his eyes.
And the process of choosing only one from each breed
Was carried to completion with the greatest of speed.

A Norwegian elkhound. An Italian greyhound.
Some red dogs, some black dogs, some white and some brown.
Twenty-six different terriers formed in a row,
With ten different spaniels, their eyes all aglow.

A beagle named Snoopy and a bulldog named Jed,
A boxer named Gretchen and a basset named Fred.
An Akita, a collie (named Lassie of course),
And Brandy, the Saint Bernard, she was big as a horse.

A kelpie, a keeshond and a dachshund, so small,
Then Brutus, the pug — He made the dachshund look tall—
From Northland and Southland, from East and from West,
Each dog was selected for the night's grueling test.

From deserts and mountains, where'er they were bred,
Each breed had a place before that wonderful sled.
When the innkeeper had chosen, and they stood head-by-head,
He called a white poodle, a standard named Fred.

"Now, Fred, You're in charge of this wondrous lot.
You'll seek out each child, each toddler and tot!
You'll ne'er miss a dwelling on land or at sea,
If a child abides there, then that's where you'll be."

Santa turned to the Innkeeper, "Now, one favor I lack.
I would have you board Snuggles until I get back.
With pedigree hounds I'm afraid we would find
He'd be too out of place with the pureblooded kind.

"His color's a rainbow. His ears reach the ground.
He lacks the fine points of the registered hound.
With a nose too far forward, a tail too far behind,
He just wouldn't fit in with the pedigree kind."

Snuggles crouched to the floor; all his glee disappeared.
He turned to the wall feigning not to have heard.
But the innkeeper noticed when the dog turned his head
There were tears in his eyes – So he turned and he said:

"Friend Santa –" the innkeeper asked, quite forlorn –
"Did any of these dogs ask where you were born?
Before volunteering, did they measure your nose?
Check out your height or the cut of your clothes?"

It suddenly struck Santa. His mouth opened wide.
His hands clasped his head. His heart tingled inside.
"Forgive me, poor Snuggles, what I said was misleading,
No friendship that matters is a result of the breeding!

Why, who still seeks your hand when there's no food that day?
When fortune has fled, who still wants to stay?
When success is elusive, when life's promises fail,
Who remains at your side, no matter the trail?

Who sees man as a king, though a pauper he be?
Who never deserts him though his other friends flee?
Courage, compassion, — love that's not learned,
Measure for measure deserve being returned.

Man pays tribute to friends in many fine ways,
A statue, a plaque, a flowery phrase.
But his honors and compliments certainly pale,
With the tribute expressed by a hound's wagging tail.

Why, it isn't the color of the hair or the eyes;
It's things that you *don't* see. It's the greatness *inside*!
In all of life's blessings no greater I've found,
Than the blessings exchanged in the eyes of my hound."

Santa knelt to the floor and he stroked Snuggles' head.
Then lifted him gently and gently he said,
"Innkeeper, cancel that room for my friend won't be staying.
We're together, you see, and together we'll go sleighing!"

Then he led them all outside and bade them be quick,
To follow him northward for the start of their trip.
Such a barking and howling arose as they left,
That the citizens of Prairie View arose from their beds.

They ran to their windows and peered at the skies,
Not believing the sight that they saw with their eyes:
A bearded old man with a dog at his right
Leading dozens of dogs away in the night?

"An impossible sight," the mayor exclaimed.
"All the pudding I ate," one councilman blamed.
And still to this day the townsfolk deny,
That they saw on that night what they saw in the sky.

While back at the North Pole when Santa descended,
He found the sleigh loaded, the harnesses mended.
He called for attention and the dogs gathered 'round,
Except Burgy, the schnauzer, always acting the clown.

Each dog take your place at the front of the sled,
To guide us in front will be the poodle named Fred.
And the shepherd, of course, will go at Fred's side."
(For a shepherd, you know, makes a wonderful guide.)

Santa placed all the dogs in two rows by their kind,
The big ones in front and the small ones behind.
And a hassle arose when a dachshund kept charging
To the front of the line where he persisted in arguing:

"See the size of my nose? It's an absolute fact,
I could sniff better in front than I could in the back!"
But Santa assured him that while he was right,
Santa needed him most where his crew was so slight.

"The Chihuahua, the papillon, and the pekingnese, too,
I don't think they'd make it if they didn't have you!"
"Quite right!" said the dachshund, "An obvious fact.
I should not desert my small friends in the back."

The argument settled, Santa took up the reins
And bade them all listen while he carefully explained,
"Lift your eyes to the heavens, fill your hearts with a dream,
No child without Christmas! Now, onward my team!"

Five score and eighteen dogs eager to trudge
Grunted and strained, but the sleigh would not budge
First one, then another with all of his might
Failed in his efforts to bring them to flight.

Then the word went out to the forest nearby,
That a friend could be helped, if enough friends would try.
A bird told the owl and the owl told the hare,
Who told the whole story to the great white bear.

A meeting was called and all the animals came
And the great bear addressed them and carefully explained,
He told them about Christmas and its clarion call,
For peace in the land and good will for all.

"But, why should we help/" said raccoon from his tree.
"When I need help, man never helps me.
Why all of us know they're supposed to be brothers.
Why should we help those who won't help each other?"

"That's exactly the point," said the great white bear.
"Man needs to be reminded about this world we share.
Perhaps if we aid them and help free Santa's sleigh,
They'll think also of us on each Christmas day."

All the animals discussed it and in the end all agreed,
That love was like a flower and every kindness a seed.
Then they all marched together toward the site of the sleigh,
Singing aloud as they went on their way.

They joined with the others, using every device,
To free Santa's sleigh from the grip of the ice.
With their shoulders to the sleigh and their backs to the wind,
They never gave up and they didn't give in.

In that small North Pole town, where few people abide,
In their own special way, each living thing tried.
But, all of their efforts, though nobly inspired,
Failed to achieve the dream they desired.

Then, over the racket of barking and howls,
The flailing of legs and the flapping of jowls,
Came a shrill squeaky order from Brutus, the pug,
"When I count to three, then everyone tug!"

324

"Yip," squeaked little Brutus." (That's one, don't you know?)
"Yip, Yip, was the next count. All tensed in the snow.
"Yip, Yip, Yip," hardly sounded when the reins were stretched tight,
And all of the dogs pulled with all of their might.

First the creaking and squeaking of wood runners on snow,
Then a sigh of relief as they started to go,
Faster and farther the sleigh soon was moving.
The rhythm of bells kept their teamwork improving.

Then they looked to the heavens, filled their hearts with a dream.
And they all lifted skyward like a heavenly scene.
But the most amazing feeling came when each of the dogs found,
He could pull in the air like he could on the ground.

Upward and onward at a furious pace.
'Twas half past the evening, 'Twas late in the race.
Up to the North Star, then south to the bay.
Then they followed the trail of the bright Milky Way.

'Twas a tiring task, climbing chimneys all night,
But, soon Snuggles joined in, much to Santa's delight.
And together they placed every candy and toy.
Together two friends shared a new Christmas joy.

Never passing, but stopping at each little town,
A merry old man and his faithful old hound.
They stopped at every dwelling where a child was sniffed.
The better the child, the better the gift.

To Scotland and Ireland, England and Wales,
Then on to the continent the lot of them sailed.
From Greenland and Iceland, through the cold Arctic sleet,
To the tip of the Cape and the African heat.

Westward to Russia, that mighty expanse,
Not missing one child, not even by chance.
Then down through the Orient to the middle of the East
Where they placed with each present a large wish for peace.

To the highest of mountains, then the valleys below,
They soared and they dived leaving gifts to behold.
To the thousands of islands that dot all the seas,
Not one child was missed and Santa was pleased.

Then quick to the Americas, the North and the South,
Where the last gift was placed and time finally ran out.
So they scurried on, hurried on, back to the Pole,
Where they drifted on down to land back in the snow.

There was joy and camaraderie from the spirit of "well done!"
They had challenged the challenge, and by doing, had done.
And Santa admitted (and Snuggles did too,)
If you have friends you can trust, there's no task you can't do.

"Now back to the pet hotel, 'tis a quarter past dawn,
When your families come calling, you mustn't be gone!"
Up over the landscape, 'twas easier now,
Then down to the hotel in Prairie View Town.

They arrived as they'd left, with a thunderous noise
That awakened some townsfolk, some girls and some boys.
And the sight the folks saw on that clear Christmas Day,
Led to closing of blinds and the pulling of shades.

"It just couldn't happen, not here in my town,"
The mayor exclaimed with smirk 'neath his frown.
The Council discussed it and then voted all,
What they saw couldn't have happened, so it didn't happen at all!

While back at the pet hotel, each dog went to his bed.
Where he noticed an object hanging over his head.
'Twas a tri-colored stocking filled to the brim
With milk bones and chewies and a note just for him.

"To friends who have taught me,
I will never forget!
Merry Christmas!
Merry Christmas!
Your faithful friend, St. Nick."

ACKNOWLEDGMENTS

A special thanks is due to the following contemporary poets for the privilege of introducing their poems in this special collection:

Faith Frances Berlin for *Mr. McJones, Quiet! . . Please* and *The Dancer.*
Jerry Betts for *Ballad of Christmas Present.*
Sonja Christina for *The Maid.*
Royal L. Craig for *The Homecoming.*
Bill Foster for *General Delivery, Alaska, My Malamute Dog, The Fastest Goat Alive,* and *The Great Provider.*
Rosalie Kramer for *Never Spend the Principal.*
Douglas Kruger for *Who Shared Her View.*
Michele S. Kurlander for *The Defective Mirror* and *The Politician.*
John Large for *Malice Aforethought.*
Bo Tandy Magruder for *That Cocker Spaniel Mutt.*
Joseph J. McDonough for *The Sausage Colored Dog.*
James Ploss for *The Ballad Of Me and Sourdough Dan* and *The Rodeo Clown.*
Linda Robertson for *A Gift And A Present* and *A Little Angel.*

The task of researching the copyrights for the included poems was immeasurably facilitated by the generous assistance of the following individuals and publishers:

Carol Christiansen, Permissions Manager of Random House, Inc. and Bantam Doubleday Dell publishing companies for her assistance and direction to obtain permission for printing the following poems: *An Old Sweetheart of Mine* by James Whitcomb Riley, *Casey's Revenge* by James Wilson, *Casey-Twenty Years Later* by S. P. McDonald, *Sleepin' At the Foot 'O the Bed* by Luther Patrick, *The Legend of the Organ Grinder* by Julia C. R. Dorr, *The Preacher's Mistake* by William Croswell Doane, and *The Purple Cow* by Gelett Burgess. These poems are only a few of the over 575 poems collected by Hazel Felleman and published by Doubleday in the book, *The Best Loved Poems of the American People.* The following poems, by Rudyard Kipling, are from the book, Rudyard Kipling Complete Verse, published by Anchor Books – Doubleday: *Gunga Din, The Betrothed, The Female of the Species, The Last of the Light Brigade, The Post That Fitted, The Power of the Dog, The Sea-*

Wife, and The Young British Soldier. No permission was expressed or implied for any copyrighted material not under their auspices.

A special acknowledgment is in order to Marsha Kramer of the National Anti-Vivisection Society for permission to reprint many of the poems included in their publication, *The Dog's Scrapbook.* These poems include *An Outcast Even In Hell* by Harry S. Grannatt, *Buying Loyalty* by Anne Cambell, *Dog,* by Nick Kenny, *Dog's For Disposal* by Margaret M. Mackay, *He's Just A Dog* by Joseph M. Anderson, *Just Dogs* by Charlotte Becker, *Little Lost Pup* by Arthur Guiterman, *Lonely* by – Walker, reprinted from the London Opinion, *Mr. Bones* by Dixie Wilson, *My Dog* and *The Little Dog Angel* by Burr McIntosh, *Outside Are Dogs* by Bertha A. Ellis, *Pals* by Charles F. Doran, *Pals* by Mae Norton Morris, *Paw Marks* by W. J. Hickmott, Jr., *Rags* by Edmund Vance Cooke*, The Dog That Went To Church* by Hilda Van Stockum, *The New Dog* by L. B. Malleson, *The Road To Vagabondia* by Dana Burnet, *To A Little Pal* by Emily Hopkins Drake, *Turn About* by W. Williams, *Waiting At The Ferry* by David Lee Wharton and *Without A Dog* by Douglas Malloch.

INDEX OF POETS

INDEX OF POETS

INDEX OF POETS

28
24 DAYS